A Cinema of Nonfiction

A Cinema of Nonfiction

William Guynn

Rutherford ● Madison ● Teaneck
Fairleigh Dickinson University Press
London and Toronto: Associated University Presses

Associated University Presses
440 Forsgate Drive
Cranbury, NJ 08512

Associated University Presses
25 Sicilian Avenue
London WC1A 2QH, England

Associated University Presses
P.O. Box 488, Port Credit
Mississauga, Ontario
Canada L5G 4M2

The paper used in this publication meets the requirements
of the American National Standard for Permanence of Paper
for Printed Library Materials Z39.48-1984.

Library of Congress Cataloging-in-Publication Data

Guynn, William.
  A cinema of nonfiction / William Guynn.
    p. cm.
  Bibliography: p.
  Filmography: p.
  Index.
  ISBN 0-8386-3340-4 (alk. paper)
  1. Documentary films—History and criticism. 2. Historical films—
  History and criticism. 3. Film criticism. I. Title.
  PN1995.9.D6G89 1990
  791.43'53—dc19   88-45736
                                                                CIP

For Stefanie

Contents

Acknowledgments

I am grateful to The Central Office of Information, United Kingdom for permission to use frame enlargements taken from Humphrey Jennings's *Listen to Britain*.

I would like to express my appreciation to Richard Karas, Dean of Administrative Services, and Don Cabrall, Media Services, both of Sonoma State University, California, for the support they gave to producing frame enlargements from *Listen to Britain*.

Chapter 5, "The Nonfiction Film and Its Spectator," was originally accepted for publication by Mouton de Gruyter as part of a volume entitled *The Semiotic Bridge: Trends from California.* Scheduled publication date: July 1989.

I would like to acknowledge the permission granted me by Macmillan Press, Ltd., London and Basingstoke to use extracts from Christian Metz's *Psychoanalysis and the Cinema* (U.S.A. title: *The Imaginary Signifier*).

A Cinema of Nonfiction

Documentary Film Theory and the Tradition of Historic Discourse

Documentary film—the designation already situates its object in a cultural field. The sort of films in question belong to the class of social discourses—juridical or historical—that seek to account for actual occurrences in the phenomenal world. They take as their reference events that are perceptible, have been observed, and can be specifically located in time and space. Documentary films are constituted of documents, in the sense by which this word obtains in the human sciences: faithful representations (here, filmed rather than written) of events that exist outside the consciousness of the documentarist. Furthermore, the designation nonfiction film (which in most critical practice is synonymous with documentary) suggests that a polarity exists. The nonfiction film is to be distinguished by that to which it stands in opposition: it excludes in its very definition all elements that evoke those fields of imaginary reference we call fictional. Thus documentary film aligns itself with the historical sciences in their presumed antagonism to the literature of imagination, for which the classic narrative film stands as the counterpart in cinema.

As Hayden White points out in his work on the historical imagination, the scientism of historical discourse is of relatively recent date.[1] Historiography established its current orthodoxy in the nineteenth century. Eschewing poetics in the name of truth, historiography established its scientific method on the strict recitation of facts in the order of their occurrence, in the conviction that truth would emerge from this "faithful" representation of phenomenal reality. Historians scrupulously abandoned as fictive techniques the devices and figures of classical rhetoric, which the art of history had long shared with the literature of imagination. They sought instead a language without artifice—a transparent medium of representation by means of which historic discourse could transform the phenomenal into the verbal without loss or distortion. The discourse of historiography is founded, as Roland Barthes suggests, on a reduction of the tripartite nature of the linguistic sign: the referent is set apart from discourse—it is external and causal; the signified is eclipsed behind the referent, conflated with it. Thus the historiographer does not produce history as meaning; he or she does not speak, except under the dictation of external events. According to this model of historic discourse, the signifier directly expresses the real, despite what modern linguistics has established concerning the nature of all signification: "It turns out that the only feature which distinguishes historical discourse from other kinds is a paradox: the 'fact' can only exist linguistically, as a term in a discourse, yet we behave as if it were a simple reproduction of something on another plane of existence altogether, some extra-structural 'reality.' "[2]

The invention of photography and a fortiori of cinematography bears witness to the taste western civilization has for the (seeming) real, its predilection for documentary evidence, unsullied by human subjectivity. The putative transparency of the cinematographic image has the distinct advantage of effacing, more than could ever be possible in a written text, what André Bazin recognizes as the "creative intervention of man."[3] Cinema offers what seems the perfect medium for historic discourse. It eliminates the verbal transcriptions of events—the articulations of language that acknowledge the subject of discourse. Cinema produces an image whose power of analogy is prodigious and capable of mimicking the chronology of real events by representing the movement of persons and objects through time. Documentary cinema would appear to respond to the conception of historicity evoked by Thiers: "To be simply true, to be what things are, neither more, nor less, nor otherwise, nor other."[4] How much closer can one get to the thing itself than the cinematographic effigy? Indeed, one has the impression in documentary cinema that the events are figuring themselves forward, that they are "speaking" on their own behalf.

This conception of a spontaneous historic discourse rests on certain presuppositions. It assumes the latent existence in reality of historical facts. It is on this already constituted material that the historian performs his work of interpretation. Further, it assumes that historic narratives are unlike other discourses in that they do not invent but rather discover their discursive order, which already exists in something like a state of nature within the events themselves. Among other critics of classic historiography, Lévi-Strauss has called into question the reputed nature of the historical fact:

> As historical knowledge is claimed to be privileged, I feel entitled (as I would not otherwise feel) to make the point that there is a twofold antimony in the very notion of an historical fact. For, *ex hypothesis,* a historical fact is what really took place, but where did anything take place? Each episode in a revolution or a war resolves itself into a multitude of individual psychic movements. Each of these movements is the translation of unconscious development, and these resolve themselves into cerebral, hormonal or nervous phenomena, which themselves have reference to the physical or chemical orders. Consequently, historical facts are no more *given* than any other. It is the historian, or the agent of history, who constitutes them by abstraction and as though under the threat of infinite regress.[5]

On the subject of interpretation and writing, Lévi-Strauss quite as categorically denies that there is a natural order to the most "faithful" discourse:

> What is true of the constitution of facts is no less so of their selection. From this point of view, the historian and the agent of history choose, sever and carve them up, for a truly total history would confront them with chaos. . . . In so far as history aspires to meaning, it is doomed to select regions, periods, groups of men and individuals in these groups and to make them stand out, as discontinuous figures, against a continuity barely good enough to be used as a backdrop. A truly total history would cancel itself out—its product would be nought.[6]

In order to distinguish history from fiction, there remains the question of reference: history refers to a reality that presumably has existence outside of language, while fiction—to simplify the formulation—creates a discursive universe that is largely imaginary. One could hardly disagree in principle, but, as Lévi-Strauss's propositions suggest, the question is quite imponderable and closed off from textual analysis. How could analysis distinguish, for example, the part played by fiction and that played by nonfiction in Robert Flaherty's films of *mise en scène documentaire,* or identify the "twisted facts" that masquerade as truth in *Mondo Cane?* There is nothing within discourse, written or filmic, which bears infallible witness to the "truth" or "falsehood" of a field of reference. We accept "truth" on faith or judge it according to signs of truth we find in the text, but these signs can be—and in certain realist texts both fictional and documentary often are—simulated.

If we accept that historical science attempts to evoke in its narration a sequence of events that has been the object of observation in the interest of an historical consciousness of these events, whereas fiction takes as its object events that may be either "historic" or invented but whose narration is intended to activate the reader's imaginary, how can the discourses of history and fiction as narrative be distinguished?

In *Tropics of Discourse,* Hayden White hypothesizes that all narratives, fictional or historiographical, are constituted on the basis of forms—"pregeneric plot structures" or *mythoi*—which are the shared knowledge of a cultural group.[7] These "stories of a particular kind" operate according to distinct literary conventions and are limited in number to the "modes of emplotment which the myths of Western literary tradition sanction as appropriate ways of endowing human processes with meaning."[8] To tell a story about historical events, which have no meaning in themselves, whence their inherent strangeness, is to inscribe the unfamiliar within a familiar form:

> In the process of studying a given complex of events, [the historian] begins to perceive the *possible* story form that such events *may* figure. In his narrative account of how this set of events took the shape which he perceives to inhere within it, he emplots his account as a story of a particular kind. The reader, in the process of following the historian's account of those events, gradually comes to realize that the story he is reading is of one kind rather than another: romance, tragedy, comedy, satire, epic, or what have you. And when he has perceived the class or type to which the story that he is reading belongs, he experiences the effect of having the events in the story explained to him. He has at this point not only successfully *followed* the story; he has grasped the point of it, *understood* it as well.[9]

Hayden White's analysis of historiographic discourse suggests that the strategies by which historians or novelists make sense of the world, whether it is conceived as real or imaginary, belong first of all to the literary craft, to the art of fiction-making, and it is not surprising that these familiar narrative forms are to be found in all storytelling arts. Are we not justified in suspecting that within cinema the discourses of fiction and nonfiction share many basic signifying structures? Is it not quite possible that in cinema as well as in literary narrative, the theory of nonfiction erects barriers of myth against fiction in order to posit a difference of nature between the discourses of truth and of the imaginary? If, as Roland Barthes suggests, myth transforms history into nature (so as to make itself

16

unassailable), the mythologist attempts to reverse this movement: he or she examines the history of discursive forms in order to determine if there is a basis in reality—the reality of semiological systems—for the designation nonfiction. For the documentary film, the work of demystification consists in analyzing the documentary text as a signifying practice in the light of what we know about codic systems in the fiction film. In the production of a text, does the documentarist make choices from within the same paradigms as the feature filmmaker? Is the documentary text organized according to the codes that govern the unfolding of the fictional text?

This is the kind of inquiry that Hayden White has conducted with regard to historical and fictional discourses, in which he discerns the functioning of the same poetic operations. In historiography, the narrative is constructed through the work of abstraction (i.e., exclusion—not all the "facts" offered by archival material are chosen) and by arrangement (i.e., the establishment of a chronology of represented events that implies at the same time a chain of cause and effect). There are in essence two moments at which the historical agency prepares the historic discourse: in the "past," the moment of the chronicled event; in the "present," the discourse of the historian who selects and orders the "facts," i.e., places them on the syntagmatic chain of discourse. Documentary footage, like the historical chronicle, has the status of archival material—the equivalent of the kinds of "facts" gathered by the historian. But the documentarist's relation to the production of the text is different. The historian's intervention is posterior to the data, which is already constituted; the documentarist intervenes at both moments in the constitution of the historic discourse. He does not simply rework (except in the case of the compilation film) the material that history presents him, he doesn't only give a discursive form to the "documents," emplotting them, to use Hayden White's phrase. Rather he shapes the material of which the documents are constituted. As theorists of cinema maintain (putting aside the most extreme positions articulated by the exponents of *montage*), the discursive act in cinema is not restricted to a single moment (the *monteurs* would say editing) but is the process of production, which includes all stages from scenario to the final mixing of optical and acoustic tracks. The "facts" are far from apodictically provided; the documentarist—or rather the plurality of artists and technicians who produce the film—exclude and order, and form the discourse in a continuous succession of operations.

It is only possible to understand the theory of documentary film by reference to a certain moment in western civilization in which

17

the opposition between truth and error, history and fiction has established itself in archetypal fashion and has moreover produced distinct institutional forms. Our civilization has acquired a taste for the attestably "real," for the "document," for what Roland Barthes has called secularized relics: "the present sign of a dead thing."[10] This generalized social inclination, whose manifestations include the realist novel, historical exhibitions, and the development of photography, is highly paradoxical, most markedly in the literary arts. The nineteenth century produced a theory of "true" historical discourse based on the *récit* (the written or oral recitation of an event), but the origins of the *récit* are to be found in the long tradition of myths, epic poetry, romances, and novels. Similarly, documentary theory, which proposes a new discursive form based on the new technology of cinema, confronts the historic predominance of the fiction film, whose kinship, both formal and social, with theatrical and literary traditions was recognized early. It is precisely against fiction and its traditions that documentary theory has been constituted. Like the literary theory of nineteenth-century historiography, documentary seeks to overcome its paradoxical situation by covering over the traces of its relation to the dominant form of cinema. This is the reason why documentary theory is seldom analytical and almost always polemical.

The critical literature on the nonfiction film is extensive and unusually fervent. Each new "school" of documentary filmmaking and many individual documentarists have felt called upon to make a theoretical apology for documentary film practice. Although it is not possible to undertake an exhaustive review of this critical literature, I would like to present briefly several major bodies of writing on documentary in order to situate the critical inquiry I propose to pursue in the following chapters. The theoretical works I have chosen may appear to be quite disparate, emerging as they do from different historical periods and from very distinct social tendencies: the critical writings produced by the British documentary movement (1930 to 1945); the nonfiction theory of Soviet filmmaker Dziga Vertov; the writings of postwar realist André Bazin; the critical literature on ethnographic methodology in film. However, as I will attempt to show, theoretical tendencies in documentary are surprisingly homogeneous and take up many of the theses that sustain classical historiography. Documentary theory concerns itself, almost obsessively, with three major themes:

1. The question of lineage. Documentary is seen as the natural progeny of cinema, whose vocation is to rid the medium of extra-

cinematic accretions imposed by the literary and theatrical arts: *mise en scène* and *montage*.

2. The question of institution. Documentary places itself in opposition to the fiction film as an institution and proposes a critique of its conditions of finance, production, and distribution. Thus documentary distinguishes itself not only in its specific "content," its forms and methodologies, but also by the place it assumes as a social formation.

3. The question of the real. Documentary asserts the "realism" of its discourse as against the imaginary world of fiction. The documentary film manifests the inherent relationship between cinematographic technology and the real; it assumes its "natural" function in relation to its "natural" object.

British Documentary Film

The British documentary movement, under the tutelage of John Grierson, elaborated in the 1930s what became at least until the postwar period the dominant conception of documentary film.[11] Inspired by Eisenstein's example, Grierson dreamed of "putting the working class on the screen," a task that required new institutional forms and new sources of money: "And, of course, the great event in the history of documentary was that we didn't go to Hollywood for money. We went to government for money and thereby tied documentary, the use of realistic cinema, to purposes."[12] Purposes meant public utility. Grierson's movement found an institutional base by affiliating itself with government service, at first with the Empire Marketing Board and its program of "national projection" focused on the colonial territories, and subsequently with the public relations department of the General Post Office. Thus initially at least, the British documentary movement attempted to establish an alternative, self-perpetuating film institution, deliberately removed from the private sector and situated within the state apparatus, where along with other social programs it constituted part of capitalist overhead.

Embracing the Hegelian notion of the state as the neutral arbiter of class conflict, the left-leaning British documentarists nonetheless found themselves on the "razor's edge": stability and funding could be maintained only through a precarious balance of forces. On the one hand, as Stewart Legg observed, "documentary has always flourished in times of trouble,"[13] and the British movement was significant insofar as it addressed the social problems of depression

Britain. The British documentarists were strongly motivated and defended the integrity of their political and artistic practices. The movement on the other hand was dependent on Grierson's "sponsorship formula" and the good graces of the government bureaucracy. As Paul Rotha commented, "Now Grierson, as head of the EMB and GPO film units, was in a very handcuffed situation. After all, he was using government money, and obviously he could not make films which would in any way express a, shall we say, socially progressive outlook."[14] Thus Grierson, a bureaucrat of genius, arbitrated between the political and artistic aspirations of his filmmakers and the political and artistic constraints imposed by government service. Institutional equilibrium was delicate, to say the least.

Such a radical shift in institutional forms involved the transformation of the modes of finance, production, and distribution established by the commercial film industry, and it redefined the place ascribed to the spectator within the circuit of this economy. It was not that theatrical distribution was rejected—the first films produced for the Empire Marketing Board were sold to the giant exhibition network of Gaumont British. However, documentary's place was marginal within cinematic programs of the day: documentary films preceded the real spectacle and they constituted, along with the cartoon or the newsreel, a part of the wait for the feature film. Realizing that theatrical distribution was difficult and that documentary films were not really addressed to the pleasure-seeking spectator, Grierson came to his historic pronouncement: there are more seats available outside the movie theater than within it. Distribution should be sought, he argued, within other institutional settings—schools, factories, trade unions, hospitals, films societies, and so forth—where documentaries could address the needs and concerns of an interested public.

According to this model of production and consumption, the product, the film, is no longer financed and distributed according to the conditions of the marketplace; the spectator does not pay to see the film, returning profit to the commercial enterprise, from which capital the industry produces more products (and profits). Thus the pleasure the spectator seeks in the movie theater is no longer such a crucial link in the circuit of finance and production. This disjunction between what has been called the libidinal and political aspects of the economy of cinema poses the problem of motivation. In the absence of the filmic pleasure that the fiction film exists to produce, why does the spectator go to see a documentary? In dislocating certain features of cinema's economic system, documentary is responsible for its own instability as an institution.

The conception of documentary film practice advocated by the British movement is summed up in Grierson's formulation: "the creative treatment of actuality." Frequently cited in anthologies and critical studies, this consecrated definition of classic documentary is more complex than it would first appear. Both John Grierson and Paul Rotha, the major theoreticians of the movement, sought to identify the distinctive features of documentary in a double movement of opposition: 1) The documentary was to be distinguished from the fiction film because it concerned itself with "actuality," and referred to an observable world, not an imaginary one. 2) It was to be distinguished from simple "films of fact"; documentary film was "creative," not simply reproductive, in its interpretation of the real.

In the view of the British theorists, documentary film constitutes a legitimate form of discourse, the natural product of cinematographic technology. The feature film, on the other hand, diverts cinema from its true purpose and links it with the archaic fiction of the nineteenth-century theater and novel. Documentarists find in early film history the signs of a natural impulse and an ultimate purpose which belong to the filmic apparatus itself and determine what can and should be expressed in the new medium. This determinism is grounded in a widely shared notion about cinematic origins, in particular in the mythic figures of Louis Lumière and Georges Méliès, who embody for the British documentarists the essential opposition between the discourses of fiction and nonfiction. To Méliès they ascribe the role of the progenitor of the fiction film, or the "theatrical" film as it was designated, which they stigmatize as mere reproduction of theatrical performance: "The storyfilm has *followed* closely in the theatrical tradition for its subject matter; converting, as time went on, stage forms into film forms, stage acting into film acting, according to the exacting demands of the reproducing camera and microphone."[15] In this view, the fiction film represents a transference to the screen of theatrical codes that, while they accommodate themselves to the new medium, remain fundamentally unchanged. In Lumière, on the other hand, the documentarists see the first practitioner—and in his films the first texts—of a natural cinematographic "language." The Cinematographe appears as the culminating moment in a technological evolution whose original impulse can be found in the photographic experiments of scientists like Marey and Muybridge.

Lumière's portable apparatus moves out into the world to encounter its natural object—the real. Grierson speaks in quite mythic terms of this "natural" genesis of cinema:

> When Lumière turned his first historic strip of film, he did so with the fine careless rapture which attends the amateur effort today. The new moving camera was still, for him, a camera and an instrument to focus on life about him. He shot his own workmen filing out of the factory and this first film was a "documentary." He went on as naturally to shoot the Lumière family, child complete. The cinema, it seemed for a moment, was about to fulfill its natural destiny of discovering mankind. It had everything for the task. It could get about, it could view with a new intimacy; and what more natural than that the recording of the real world should become its principal inspiration?[16]

According to the British theorists, then, the distinctive feature of documentary film is, to use Grierson's phrase, the "treatment of actuality," the "reality" of the objective world that the Cinematographe was predestined to explore. The argument concerning the properties inherent in cinematographic technology turns on the mobility of the camera and the realism of the image it produces. In the fiction film, the paraphernalia of theatrical illusionism—sets, costumes, actors, the profilmic materials in general—are brought before the imprisoned camera for the purpose of creating spectacle. With documentary, cinematographic technology—the mobile machine of analogical reproduction—seeks its natural object by its movement into "reality."

In a manner that anticipates the realist theory of the postwar period, the British documentarists endeavored to distinguish nonfiction as discourse from the narrative arts of theater and novel. They did not exclude narrative: documentary films could in fact tell stories. But like the historiographer, the documentarist did not invent the actors, their actions, and the articulated sequence of events; rather, he or she discovered the elements of a story in latent form within the real. The narrative act consisted in transforming the latent story into its manifest form in filmic discourse. Thus, plot, character, and setting were not contrived in the manner of the theatrical film; they emerged fully formed from the real. In documentary, the character is the shadow of the individual, the story mimics the unfolding of real events, *mise en scène* is indistinguishable from historic contingency: "We believe that the original (or native) actor, and the original (or native) scene are better guides to a screen interpretation of the modern world. . . . We believe that the materials and the stories thus taken from the raw can be finer (more real in the philosophic sense) than the acted article."[17]

The British conception of documentary owes much to Robert Flaherty—significantly the postwar realists will turn again to his example—whom Grierson in his "First Principles of Documentary" designates as the creator of documentary methodology. It was Flaherty who reconciled the apparently conflicting roles of the documentarist: he is at once the discreet observer who respects the integrity of the real and the narrator who arranges and orders his story: "[Documentary] must master its material on the spot, and come in intimacy to ordering it. Flaherty digs himself in for a year, or two maybe. He lives with his people till the story is told 'out of himself.'"[18] Thus the documentarist becomes an instrument of a discourse that does no more than refer to meanings and structures already inherent within the real.

In a second phase of their apology, the British documentarists strive to distinguish the documentary film from other "films of fact," which share the common feature of being constructed of "natural materials." What these theorists call descriptive factual films fall into two genres: the newsreel and the "interest" film (short subjects in commercial distribution in film programs of the period). The newsreel, they assert, simply exploits the camera's "reproductive capacities" but does not represent a working of the material on the level of the image. True documentary film is not simply descriptive; it is analytical: "It is important to make the primary distinction between a method which describes only the surface values of a subject, and the method which more explosively reveals the reality of it. You photograph the natural life, but you also, by your juxtaposition of detail, create an interpretation of it."[19] The "interest" film, on the other hand, is not documentary because in this genre it is the spoken commentary that takes charge of the text, and the image serves as a simple illustration of the dominant discourse. Documentary, Grierson argues, is a film of fact constructed according to codes that belong specifically to cinema, in particular, those that govern the articulation of the image track. It is by means of the documentarist's intervention that "natural materials" take on their cinematographic form. While rejecting the artifice of studio shooting, professional actors, and contrived scripts, Grierson acknowledges implicitly a kinship of structure between fiction and documentary. The material may be "raw and unrehearsed," the shooting "purely impulsive," the finished film must give that sense of motivated sequence and narrative movement we have come to expect

from the fiction film. In criticizing the "interest film," it is precisely
the lack of theatrical structure that Grierson finds unforgiveable:
"These films, of course, would not like to be called lecture films,
but this, for their disguises, is what they are. They do not dramatize, they do not even dramatize an episode. . . . Their silent form is
cut to the commentary, and shots are arranged arbitrarily to point
the gags or conclusions."[20]

Dziga Vertov

In his conception of cinema, Dziga Vertov shares many principles with the major theorists of documentary. His theoretical
position begins with a critique of dominant cinema, radical in its
questioning of the signifiying structures of the classic narrative film.
It is against the fiction film that "true," essential cinema with its
new forms and new institutional structures must be constructed.
Vertov places his faith in what he believes are the basic instrumental features of the camera that prescribe specific features of cinematic discourse. Cinematographic technology with its capacity to
seize fragments from the real has an intrinsic vocation—it can lay
bare social reality. As we will see, however, Vertov's theory cannot
be confined within the tradition of realist discourses in which
meaning and reference are confused. Vertov does not conceive of
film as a transparent medium of representation which offers the
viewer unmediated access to an already formed world. He asserts,
rather, that the coherence of any discourse is the work of an agency,
here not the bourgeois filmmaker as individual but a collectivity of
filmworkers who create in the progressive stages of production a
representation of the visible world.

From the first manifesto of 1919, it was evident that Vertov
intended to carry the idea of socialist revolution into the sphere of
cinematic practice. Political and social revolution could not leave
intact the forms of bourgeois culture; for the revolutionary filmmaker, political praxis consisted in the elaboration of new forms.
Cinema—a cinema of nonfiction—was to have a privileged and
instrumental role in the struggle against bourgeois tendencies and
in the construction of a socialist society. The Soviet cinema under
state sponsorship was capable, he argued, of establishing new institutional forms and of repudiating the model of cinema ex-
emplified by the American and German film industries. Vertov
called for the expulsion from cinema of all incursions of bourgeois
culture, so that cinema's essential quality could be rediscovered:

"We are cleansing our cinema of what has infiltrated it, music, literature, and theater, we are looking for a proper rhythm, a rhythm which has not been pilfered from elsewhere and which we find in the movement of things."[21] Vertov's theoretical position is radically antitheatrical and antiliterary: it calls for abandoning *mise en scène,* scenarios, studios, sets, actors, costumes—all the props of psychologized representation. Although film historian Georges Sadoul links Vertov's critique of narrative cinema to the imitative mediocrity of films in distribution in the Soviet Union immediately after the civil war, Vertov's position against narrativity is fully ideological: against the romantic bourgeois lies that sustain all fiction, the commited filmmaker builds a revolutionary cinema of nonfiction.

The idealism that can be seen in aspects of Vertov's theory of nonfiction, in particular in his belief in the camera as an objective instrument of investigation, can be traced to his early involvement in the Futurist movement. The Futurists advocated a new art based on the complete obliteration of the past. Futurist veneration of the machine—a mythopoeic gesture toward new technology—which Vertov shared was ultimately grounded in late nineteenth-century scientism and the experimental use of the Cinematograph for the analysis of visible phenomena in movement. Camera perception, Vertov argues, has an instrumental advantage over human perception because it can decompose movement into its constituent units:

The cine-eye lives and evolves in time and in space, it perceives and it fixes its impressions not in the human manner, but in a completely different way. The position of our body at the moment of observation, the number of moments we perceive of a visual phenomenon in a second are not at all obligatory for the camera, which perceives all the better because it is more perfect.[22]

Vertov's notion of "cine-perception," an opening out on the world, claims, in a manner that recalls realist theory, that cinema has an essential function: the exploration of the "real." The filming strategy he called "life caught unawares" (with clear reference to Lumière's *"nature prise sur le vif"*) reflects certain practices of the avant-garde of that period: assemblage of found objects, photomontage, integration of "real" objects into the plastic arts of representation. However, this strategy clearly emanates from Vertov's belief in the objectivity of the cinematographic apparatus, which promises to produce under specific conditions of shooting "factual" images stripped of all fictionality.

"Life caught unawares" is a method for disrupting and unmasking *mise en scène*. It aims to exclude the codes of theatrical staging—of costume, lighting, acting, and so forth—and forestall the practice of manipulating the profilmic materials—everything placed in front of the camera to be shot—in conformity with an already-written scenario. It also seeks to suppress the *mise en scène* of social attitudes, which the filmed subjects assume in the presence of the camera, in order to "capture" them in their real social relationships:

> Every instant of life filmed without staging, every separate shot preserving in itself "Life-As-It-Is," whether filmed by a hidden camera or by surprise, or any other similar shooting technique, appear on the screen in the form of "film-fact." A dog running along a street is to be perceived as a fact only when we do not force him to run and do not read what is written on his collar. An Eskimo remains an Eskimo on the screen even if it is not written on his head that he is Nanook.[23]

Vertov asks the questions that would preoccupy not only the new documentary filmmakers of the 1960s, but for scientific reasons those that would occupy the makers of the ethnographic film: what constitutes an authentic document of observed social life? Is the only pure document one that represents the filmed subjects absorbed in social practices and hence "undisturbed": ritual, work, political action? What is the effect of the filmmaker/observer and of the film equipment on the facts observed? Georges Sadoul recognizes in the principles of "life caught unawares" a second documentary methodolgy, which he opposes to Flaherty's work in *mise en scène documentaire*—the "slight narrative," the "natural" actor, the "fictionalization" of certain episodes. Vertov's strategy of film shooting is to interrogate reality and his object is the recording of "life-facts." He is above all concerned with the "truthfulness" of the image, its authenticity: "The 'Film-Eye' offers the opportunity of making the visible—clear, the concealed—public, the acted—nonacted, and the false—true."[24] Like the historical "facts," which the historiographer regards as irrefragable—as objects, not products—the footage produced by the strategies of the kino-eye has the same status as the irreducible document.

As a programmatic part of "life caught unawares," Vertov sought to integrate film work, as a type of work among others, into the daily life of society. The notion of the artist-worker occupied a central place in constructivist ideology, which aimed to destroy the sanctification of the arts under bourgeois domination and return them to a useful role in the daily life of the masses. For Vertov, it was at once a question of cinema's situation within society (the relation of the cinema as a social praxis to social life in general) and a political program that was directed at the transformation of social relations and the divisions of labor in cinema: the abdication of the filmmaker as priest, the effacing of distinctions between the elite technicians and the filmed subjects, between "actor," audience, and filmmaker: "This change from authorship of one man or a group of people to mass authorship and production will lead, in our minds, to a quickening in the downfall of bourgeois artistic cinematography and its attributes: the actor making faces, the story book scenario, the expensive toy—the sets and the priest director."[25]

In effect Vertov proposed a theoretical model for an institution of cinema in which not only would the techniques of the theatrical film be abandoned and the hierarchies of labor in production be overturned, but the relationship between "creator" and consumer, viewer and text, and consequently the viewing situation itself would be transformed. Vertov's conception of film work as a political praxis whose forms must be subjected to political analysis led him to a reformulation of a theory of *montage* in terms of all the phases of production. In the capitalist institution of cinema, Vertov argued, the technique of production with its finely articulated division of labor serves not simply to coordinate the work of technicians but in fact to subordinate all work to the "master" of the artistic operation. In the period of the Kinoks, the team of young film workers he began to gather around him, Vertov conceived of *montage* in a global fashion as the "organization of the visible world."[26] It is the entire process by which the film is constructed, from the point of the first "observations" to the final reorganization of the filmic material on the editing bench. In the successive stages of production, Vertov repudiated all hierarchical relations: the film was to become the collective product of the team of film workers. In practice, the vast organization of the Kinoks never came to fruition and the alternative cinematic institution that it might have constituted remained theoretical.

The methodological assumptions of "life caught unawares" cannot be abstracted from Vertov's global theory of cinema. (Such an abstraction was in fact made by the apologists of *cinéma vérité* in the 1960s as they appropriated those aspects of Vertov's theory that appeared to have anticipated and justified historically their conception of cinema.) Unlike the postwar realists, Vertov did not assume the natural coherence of the visible world, nor did he believe in the native power of the camera to uncover the "truth"

27

immanent in reality. The "organization of the visible world"—that crucial discursive moment—was for Vertov the essential creative act in which the filmmaker intervened to give order and meaning to recorded phenomena taken from the real. He reworked in terms of cinema a notion that had wide currency in avant-garde circles: that a work of art could be constructed of objects (in this case, pieces of film) which preexist the creative intervention. His early experiments in phonographic *montage* of recorded sound and his compilation film, *Anniversary of the Revolution* (1919), were manifestations of this conception of artistic work.

In contrast with the realists, who prescribe the effacement of "technique" before the apparent coherence of the "real," Vertov conceives of the film as an imaginary construct. While the fiction film produces through the cinematic apparatus and the codes of narrative continuity the illusion of an organic unity of space and time in the consciousness of the spectator, Vertov seeks to assert the discursive power of the medium through the visible work of *montage:* "I force the spectator to see, in the way I find most advantageous, such and such a visual phenomenon. The eye is subjected to the will of the camera, which directs it toward the consecutive movements of the action."[27] The spectator undergoes the perpetual dislocation of unitary space/time that the Italian poet Marinetti seemed to be calling for in his "Futurist Cinema": "[Cinema] must become antigraceful, deforming, impressionistic, synthetic, dynamic, freewording."[28] Vertov's cinema points at the reality of the signifier by unexpected framings, angles, ruptures of continuity, superimpositions, visual jokes; it reveals the imaginary character of cinematic space/time and the collusion by means of which filmmaker and spectator work to produce the diegesis:

I am the Kino-Eye. I am a builder.

I have placed *you,* created by me, into the most extraordinary room, which did not exist before this moment, and which was created by me.

This room has twelve walls, taken by me from different parts of the world.

While combining among themselves the shots of walls and details,

I succeeded in arranging them in the order you like, and I succeeded in constructing with precision, on the intervals,

a kino-sentence which is nothing other than this room.[29]

It is clear in this passage that what Vertov proposed was not the expulsion of diegesis from cinema but an uncovering of the mechanisms by which a diegesis is constructed. His films seek to bring about simultaneously the production of a text and the analysis of the operations by means of which the text is produced. In his theory of "intervals" Vertov suggests how the film can be coherent and at the same time point to its own fragmentation. If *montage* is the joining together of pieces of film in order to create a filmic space/time, it is also the juncture itself in its negativity, in its denial of coherence. This insistence on the textuality of the film distinguishes Vertov's theoretical position from those held by the major voices of the documentary tradition.

André Bazin and Realist Theory

The work of André Bazin does not present a specific theory of documentary film. It is, however, the fullest expression of the realist aesthetic as it was formulated in the postwar period. Thus we take Bazin as exemplary, the most perceptive and rigorous theoretician of cinematic realism,[30] to which postwar movements—new documentary in particular—owe their theoretical substance. Bazin's reflections on documentary not only assert the privileged relationship between cinematographic technology and the real, but also specify the methodology, the *mise en scène*, by means of which a realist discourse can be constituted.

The central intention of Bazin's ontological historical theory is to set cinema apart from all other *langages* and to place it at the culmination of one of the universal tendencies of representational art: to provide an imitation of the real. Bazin sees a natural predisposition toward realism in cinema's capacity to produce the approximation of an illusion of reality (what he calls the myth of total cinema).[31] Cinema's realist vocation is founded on an ontology of the photographic image, which Bazin conceives as only partially representational. The photograph is not framed in the same way as the painting; it is not autonomous, integral in itself, a cohesive unit of meaning. It is not only iconic (by virtue of its resemblance to the visible), it is indexical; it participates in the "reality" for which it is at the same time a substitute: "The aesthetic world of the painter is of a different kind from that of the world around him. Its boundaries enclose a substantially and essentially different microcosm. The photograph as such and the object in itself share a common being, after the fashion of a fingerprint."[32] For Bazin, representational art is thus distinguished by its otherness in relation to what it represents; it has status as symbol, it is of the order of language. The

29

photographic image, on the other hand, retains an existential relationship to the referent and thus constitutes the ultimate historic document—unmediated, transparent, objective. It is like the slough of the world that Bazin describes in his analysis of films of reportage: "We live more and more in a world divested by cinema. A world which tends to slough off its own image. Scarcely formed, the skin of History comes off in film."[33]

In "Ontology of the Photographic Image," Bazin links photographic reproduction to the historical desire for duplication. It is, he argues, one of the fundamental impulses in the genesis of art to seek the salvation of being through appearance. The desire to duplicate is likened to the embalming of the dead. The choice of metaphor is significant in that it reveals Bazin's tendency to consider the photographic image not as sign, but as fetish: the photograph is like the mummy, the relic, the souvenir. In the process of fetishization, the desire for possession of the real becomes sublimated and displaced; the photographic image can be "possessed," as the "real" object cannot: "The photograph allows us . . . to admire in reproduction something our eyes alone could not have taught us to love."[34]

This possession depends on the perceived nature of the object. By describing the photographic image as a fetish, Bazin sets cinema apart from representation: cinematic *découpage* in the material sense (the framing of the image) is distinct from *découpage* considered as the act of representation. In "Diderot, Brecht, Eisenstein," Roland Barthes argues that representation is fetish not at the level of composition, but at the level of ideal meaning. In the arts of representation, the artist chooses to show us a moment that is complete, perfect, pregnant with the "historical meaning of the represented action." The *tableau* (the cut-out piece) is intellectual, constructed, organized. Presenting itself as significant and signifying, it demands a reading: "The *tableau* (pictorial, theatrical, literary) is a pure cut-out segment with clearly defined edges, irreversible and incorruptible; everything that surrounds it is banished into nothingness, remains unnamed, while everything that it admits within its field is promoted into essence, into light, into view."[35] For Bazin, however, the cinematographic image is fetish at the level of composition: it has been cut out of the "real" but cannot transcend the phenomenal, of which it remains an existential part. "Reality" floats at the edges of the frame, its presence constantly invoked. Since the photographic image cannot be fully appropriated nor become fully signifying, it retains a quasi-mystic relation to the real. The photo-fetish is the substitute that gives us something like

30

an unsymbolized access to the world of reference. Bazin's cinema seems to respond to Thiers' dream of historic discourse, already cited: "To be simply true, to be what things are, neither more nor less, nor otherwise, nor other."

Cinema's historic originality, Bazin argues, is technological. The camera, the "photographic eye," possesses "essential objectivity" precisely because it obstructs the process of mediation by means of which human beings represent the world: "For the first time, between the originating object and its reproduction there intervenes only the instrumentality of a nonliving agent. For the first time an image of the world is formed automatically, without the creative intervention of man."[36] For Bazin, then, the impression of reality in cinema is founded on the isomorphism of the retinal and filmic images and on a simple substitution: the camera eye takes the place of the human eye in the interest of a true vision of the real. The assumption is that, setting aside certain necessities of representation—selection, framing, chromatic distortions—the filmic image presents us with a radiation of the objective world. As Serge Daney asserts, "Cinema postulated that from the 'real' to the visual and from the visual to its filmed reproduction a same truth was infinitely reflected, without distortion or loss."[37]

Bazin's realist theory is thus predicated on the conception of a "natural" state of the image (before it has been subjected to plastic manipulation) and a "natural" *mise en scène* (depth of field); and "naturalism" is defined as the approximation of the conditions of normal vision: "Depth of focus brings the spectator into a relation with the image closer to that which he enjoys with reality. Therefore, it is correct to say that, independently of the contents of the image, its structure is more realistic."[38] It is pertinent here to recall the precepts of classic historiography, since, for Bazin, a realist discourse is founded on the supposition that a "faithful" recitation of the visible facts will permit the emergence of the truth lying latent in all reality. The cinematographic agency does not constitute the filmic fact; rather, according to Bazin's strategy, it effaces the visibility of its intervention in order to diminish the difference between reality and representation.

Bazin endows cinematic technique with a "natural" history in which he discerns the emergence of the "natural" figures of cinematographic language. His theory raises to the level of principle the descriptive language of a certain realist technique and reduces the history of cinema to a selectively constructed line of descent in which it is simply a question of distinguishing the milestones of true cinema from the diversions and detours. Bazin discerns in the

31

history of cinema a current of realist *mise en scène* that rejects the "violence" done to the image by Expressionism and the violation of the unity of space and event perpetrated by the practitioners of *montage*. This realist heritage—borne by Stroheim, Murnau, Flaherty—can be distinguished by its "Jansenism," its restraint, its rigorous submission to reality: "But these examples suffice to reveal, at the very heart of the silent film, a cinematographic art the very opposite of that which has been identified as *'cinéma par excellence,'* a language the semantic and syntactical unit of which is in no sense the Shot; in which the image is evaluated not according to what it adds to reality but what it reveals of it."[39]

In Bazin's view, *montage* is a necessary evil. In the films of the great realist directors, editing simply reflects the impossibility of seeing everything, of recording everything: "In their films, montage plays no part, unless it be the negative one of inevitable elimination where reality superabounds."[40] Bazin demands preservation of the unity of space in its integrality and decries the example of the Soviet *monteurs*. The first principle of realist *mise en scène* is the respect for the immanent ambiguity of the real. He proposes as exemplary the sequence in which Flaherty's Nanook hunts the seal: "It is inconceivable that the famous sealhunt scene in *Nanook* should not show us hunter, hole and seal all in the same shot. It is simply a question of respect for the spatial unity of an event at the moment when to split it up would change it from something real into something imaginary."[41] In this same segment, the unity of time, which disjunctive *montage* can only represent, is reproduced by the strict coincidence between the time of the diegesis and the time of the narration: "What matters to Flaherty, confronted with Nanook hunting the seal, is the relation between Nanook and the animal; the actual length of the waiting period. Montage could suggest the time involved. Flaherty however confines himself to showing the actual waiting period; the length of the hunt is the very substance of the image, its true object."[42] The ideal of this conception of *mise en scène* would be the radical suppression of all marks of enunciation, the denial of the material conditions of representation, the mythic shot that would envelope reality: "One could easily imagine as a matter of fact [*à la limite*] a film by Stroheim composed of a single shot as long-lasting and as close-up as you like."[43]

At all levels of his theory, Bazin has insisted on the repression of the discursive intervention of the filmmaker-subject in favor of a subjectless discourse, emanating from reality for which the filmmaker has become pure instrumentality. In historical narration, which recounts what is presumed to have actually happened, "concrete reality," as Roland Barthes suggests, becomes the "sufficient justification of discourse."[44] The realist film—and *a fortiori* the documentary film—receives its sufficient justification from its direct relation to the world of reference: "All this shows that 'reality' is deemed entirely self-sufficient, that it is strong enough to deny any idea of 'function,' that its enunciation has no need to be integrated into a structure, and that the 'having existed there' quality of things is a sufficient principle of language activity."[45]

As a discourse, the documentary film would seem to stand at the extreme of realism. In principle, all elements that appear in documentary are credited by the referent alone; all else is relegated to the dubious status of "reconstitution" or "fictionalization." For Bazin, the role of the filmmaker is to direct his look in the manner of an interrogator at reality and to discern the structures that are immanent there, and this methodology recalls the historiographer's notion of writing: "The composition of [Murnau's] image is in no sense pictorial. It adds nothing to the reality, it does not deform it, it forces it to reveal its structural depth, to bring out the preexisting relations which become constitutive of the drama."[46] Hence the ideal of discursive recitation is the submission to the "event," to its historicity. In *Kon-Tiki* (1951), Bazin sees the virtue of the physical constraints placed on the camera—its inability to frame adequately, to move, its failure to record completely: "*Kon-Tiki* is admirable and overwhelming. Why? Because its filming is absolutely identified with the action it recounts so imperfectly; because it is itself only an aspect of the adventure."[47] Bazin's position, taken at its most extreme moment, would establish realist discourse on its abolition as discourse. The camera pursues its mythic task as the unbridled instrument of referentiality. Thus liberated from the strictures of the historically constituted forms of discourse, it accepts only the constraints imposed by the real.

This is the myth of pure cinema, the moral and ideological underpinning of realist theory. But then, if the realist text remains unwritten, if there are no structural imperatives, what becomes of structure and constraints? Where does the "vertigo of notation" end? No one perceived this contradiction of the realist position better than Bazin:

Every form of aesthetic must necessarily choose between what is worth preserving and what should be discarded, and what should not even be considered. But when this aesthetic aims in essence at creating the illusion of reality, as does the cinema, this choice sets up a fundamental

33

contradiction which is at once unacceptable and necessary: necessary because art can only exist when such a choice is made. Without it, supposing total cinema was here and now technically possible, we would go back purely to reality. Unacceptable because it would be done definitely at the expense of that reality which the cinema proposes to restore integrally.[48]

Theory of the Ethnographic Film

For ethnographer-filmmakers, cinema constitutes a technique of observation and description, an often essential part of ethnographic investigation. Cinematographic technology is capable under the control of scientific methodology of producing what many practitioners consider an infallible image of social and cultural phenomena. Until the 1950s, however, most ethnographers regarded cinema with suspicion. As Margaret Mead points out, resistance to use of "new technologies" in the field can in part be explained by anthropology's historical development. Pioneer anthropologists directed their field work toward nearly abandoned social practices, for which the informants' memory provided the only material—and this material was exclusively verbal. Moreover, a general intellectual conservatism, as Mead suggests, meant a belief in the preeminence of the written work in all phases of ethnographic study, including observation, and a distrust for new, and costly, technologies.

Ethnographers' antagonism to cinema was not without its historic motivations. Dominant cinema had never shown any inclination to respect the scientific intention of ethnographic film practices. Despite the unanticipated (and isolated) commercial success of Robert Flaherty's *Nanook,* films with ethnographic subjects never occupied anything but a very marginal place in dominant production, and in film programs of the 1930s, ethnographic footage was exploited for the exoticism of setting, costume, and human behavior. As Jean Rouch notes, the admirable documentation produced by Marcel Griaule (*Au pays des Dogons,* 1935; *Sous le masque noir,* 1938) and by Patrick O'Reilly (*Bougainville,* 1931) was subjected to "wild, insensitive editing, oriental music, commentary in the style of a sportscast."[49]

As Christian Metz observes, cinema became so quickly and so irremediably, a "machine for telling stories," coalescing so perfectly with fiction and the traditions of the literature of imagination, that other evolutionary paths, in particular scientific ones, seem arrested in their development. It is significant that although historians situate ethnographic cinema's origins at the origins of cinema itself (it was one of Marey's associates who helped Félix-Louis Regnault, the first "practitioner" of the ethnographic cinema, to film a Wolof woman making pots at the Exposition Ethnographique de l'Afrique Occidentale in 1895), the ethnographic film can claim no elaborated theory or methodology nor a consistent history of any sort until after World War II. In "History of the Ethnographic Film," Emilie de Brigand can assert that the "ethnographic film became an institutionalized scientific field, with recognized specialists and a body of criticism, only during the 1950s."[50]

In order to sanction the use of cinematographic technology within a scientific practice, ethnographic theory was careful to separate the techniques and practices that belong to the fiction film from those appropriate to ethnographic modes of investigation. Scientific intentionality and objectivity of observation could be maintained only by setting the technology firmly within the scientific institution where film practice and filmed material could be subjected to the established methodologies of data collection and analysis. According to classic ethnographic methodology, this meant the subordination of cinematic observation to direct observation by the ethnographer, following the consecrated practice of the discipline. In this perspective, the filmic image constitutes an illustration of a social process that has already been observed, analyzed, and described. Thus, its place assigned in advance, the image was inserted within a scientific discourse where its function was simply to exemplify. The notion that ethnographic film could exist as a discourse of images, consumed under conditions like those of the movie theater, was inadmissible.

The pivotal work in the formation of a liberal ethnographic methodology is the field research carried out by Bateson and Mead in Bali and New Guinea from 1936 to 1938, which served to legitimate photographic and cinematic technologies as tools of investigation. Bateson and Mead's field strategy stood in rigorous opposition to methods of commercial film production. As Bateson makes clear, the techniques of montage and *mise en scène,* even as practiced within the nonfiction film, are thoroughly alien to scientific purposes. In *Balinese Character,* he distinguishes ethnographic field methodology from the manipulation and distortion he saw as characteristic of documentary film practice: "We tried to use the still and the moving picture camera to get a record of Balinese behavior, and this is a very different matter from the preparation of a "documentary" film or photographs. We tried to shoot what happened normally and spontaneously, rather than to decide upon the norms and then get the Balinese to go through these behaviors in suitable lighting."[51]

Mead argues that for ethnographers, photographic and cinematic technology is particularly instrumental in the early stages of research that precede conceptualization. Filmed records provide "hard data," precisely because of the photographic image's relatively low schematization of visual traits. In Mead's estimation, it is relatively unaffected by the selection inherent in any conceptualization and thus relatively free of distortions due to the ethnographer's cultural bias: "The shift in scale was directed primarily at recording the types of non-verbal behavior for which there existed neither vocabulary nor conceptualized methods of observation, in which the observation has to precede the codification."[52]

According to Bateson and Mead, then, the major function of the ethnographic film is to describe social phenomena that escape the ethnographer's direct observation and that elude the conceptualization inherent in language. This progressive outlook, now widely shared by visual anthropologists, holds that cinematic technology can be utilized as a scientific instrument—a corrective to the ethnographer's cultural bias and individual subjectivity. Cinematography provides a form of observation that seems to exist in a privileged relation to the real, outside the constraints of written or oral language. The discourses of science and aesthetic realism are strangely harmonious: ethnographers reiterate in another register the position held by theorists of cinematic realism. With Bazin, they assert that the camera is capable of rendering an unmediated image of reality: "Only the impassive lens, stripping its object of all those ways of seeing it, those piled-up preconceptions, that spiritual dust and grime with which my eyes have covered it, is able to present it in all its virginal purity to my attention and consequently to my love."[53] If Bazin's moral language is replaced by the vocabulary of ethnographic intentionality, this formulation accurately represents the dominant view. The most enlightened ethnographic observers are necessarily blinded by their own culture. As the anthropologist John Collier states, "We learn to see only what we pragmatically need to see. . . . And when we do see critically it is often with the aid of some technology."[54] Formulating the problem in terms reminiscent of Bazin, Collier asserts the "objectivity" of "mechanical" reproduction within the limits of a necessary human selectivity (camera angle, distance, lens):

The camera is another instrumental extension of our senses but one that is highly unspecialized and can record on the lowest possible scale of abstraction. The camera by its optical character has whole vision. No matter how select a unit we might wish to photograph, the camera instrument faithfully records this specialized part, and all the other associated parts within focus and scope of its lens.[55]

It is sufficient therefore, argues Mead in concert with Bazin, to renounce the fragmentation of *montage* and to embrace depth of field and the long take in order to produce a rigorously scientific (realistic for Bazin) document:

At the present time, films that are acclaimed as great artistic endeavors get their effect by rapid shifts of the camera and kaleidoscopic types of cutting. When filming is done only to produce a currently fashionable film, we lack the long sequences from one point of view that alone provide us with the unedited stretches of instrumental observation on which scientific work must be based.[56]

The dominant theory of visual anthropology is homologous in many of its features with Bazinian realism. It asserts that filmic representation must conform to the spatial proportions of normal vision (distortions are to be noted in order to guarantee the scientific character of observation). "Imaginary space," the creation of *montage,* is perceived as "dangerous" to the authenticity of the document and as a concession to "aestheticism." The film *Dead Birds* (1963), for example, has been criticized for its *montage* of a "battle" involving the interpolation of footage taken from several separate incidents. The ethnographic ideal is the respect of "real time," the preservation of "actual sequences." Ethnographic film demands maximal contextualization (ethnographic holism corresponds to Bazin's prescriptions regarding deep focus), and the framing of "whole bodies," in opposition to the excessive use of "fragmentary" close-ups. The purpose of such methodological principles is to preserve in the ethnographic document what Bazin called the "immanent ambiguity of reality," to reduce the subjectivity inherent in any conceptualization, to reveal more reality. As Bazin sought to leave the final stages of "editing" to the spectator, the ethnographer seeks to produce an ambiguous document that remains open to many kinds of conceptualization.

These principles are based on an unproblematic view of the cinematographic apparatus, according to which technique in the instrumental sense is a neutral product of science. The complex machinery of cinematic representation does not in itself constitute an intervention (one wonders at the ethnographers' failure to examine such a cultural artifact). Further, ethnographic theory works on the assumption (which is also Bazin's) that there are specific methods that can reduce the difference between representation and reality. It is assumed that such methods tend to suppress mediation and that the footage produced under the guidance of correct methodological principles constitutes "hard" data, precisely because the codes of *montage* have been supplanted by a "neutral" *mise en scène*. For an example of the utter positivism of such a stance, one need only consult the "synoptic attribute dimension grid," produced by K. G. Heider, who charts in unproblematic fashion the defining features of "ethnographicness" in cinema.[57]

It is significant that realist theory should find its near mirror image in classic ethnographic theory, which proposes to efface the marks of the ethnographer's intervention. To the extent that realist theory informs the production of ethnographic films, it serves to enhance the real-effect and privileges the diegetic instance (over the analytic one). It is doubtless for this reason that ethnographic film as organized discourse intended for projection remains controversial in ethnographic theory. The traditional view is that the filmed material has status only as raw data, that it must be subjected to analysis, and that it cannot constitute the means of transmission of ethnographic analysis: "In this phase [of synthesis] photographic evidence must, of course, be abstracted in the same way as all other data, verbalized, translated into statistics."[58] This is both the recognition of the image's incapacity in itself for presenting a logical system and the repudiation of the cinematic apparatus. There are ethnographers who deny the validity of any film text in ethnography and seek a return to primitive forms of cinematic research that have their original example in the decompositional analyses of Marey. Certain contemporary ethnographers insist on the disruption of the cinema effect: "When . . . [shots] are used as filmed documents in the social sciences, continuous projection in a dark room leads to artistic cinema with themes that may be more or less ethnographic. In contrast with this, discontinuous projection of a film might aid scientific research and allow for the criticism of sources which are in filmed documents."[59]

The conservative position seems to reduce the filmed record to the status of documentation, collected according to a rigorous methodology and maintained in its primitive state of fragmentation. But, as I argued in the case of historiography, pure documentation does not exist: a written or filmed record is a product of a complex sequence of mediations that are the very conditions of its existence. There is no "natural" state of the image, and arguments for the pure indexicality of the photographic image are far less admissible in ethnography than in the aesthetics of cinematic realism.

The early 1960s saw the advent of technology—lightweight, noiseless cameras using sensitive film stock and linked to portable sound equipment—which permitted the simultaneous recording in the field of both image and sound. This revolution in technique would have decisive implications for ethnographic methodology. It permitted for the first time the filming of long continuous shots in synchronous sound, mimicking the uninterrupted flow of human activities and social processes. Second, it increased the ethnographic film's power of documentation to include noise, music, and, most importantly, the human voice. Finally, this rich track of "real" sound could substitute for the commentator, whose voice in classic ethnographic film functioned to weave together the fragments of the image. We must also recognize that the addition of the full complement of diegetic sound (including the "living speech" characteristic of *cinéma direct*), the suppression of the ethnographic commentary, and the practice of shooting in continuity serve to intensify ethnographic cinema's real-effect and to bring it closer in a quite material way to the signifying structures of the fiction film.

It is easy to understand how this technology, which seemed to offer direct and authentic contact with the social processes under study, could hold the promise of a new discursive practice in ethnography. As Claudine de France demonstrates in her excellent work entitled *Cinéma et anthropologie*, this new methodology seeks to liberate ethnographic film from the tyranny of written discourse.[60] By choosing to film "in continuity" the unfolding of specific social practices, the ethnographer defers the moment of observation and analysis. Thus the film survives as a holistic document in which the uninterrupted temporal chain links together actions and pauses, foreground and background, retaining all the "imperceptible and discreet" acts that analysis would strip away as contingent and extraneous. In general, then, spatial-temporal articulation tends to merge and unify what analysis tends to cut and separate. From the new methodological perspective, the most valuable document is not one that is subjected to the control of ethnographic observation in the field, and the inevitable domination of the scientific discourse. Rather, according to this model, ethnographic and cinematographic realism are much closer than classic theory would admit:

Films guided by respect for spatial and temporal articulations obey . . . [a notion of] *découpage* which is more specifically cinematographic,

39

and tolerant, as we have seen, of clutter. The moving image is in effect capable of offering, for deferred observation, material to which new *découpages* can be applied thanks to repeated viewings and dialogue with the persons who have been filmed.[61]

Cinematographic and ethnographic, fiction and nonfiction—the classic lines of demarcation separating the human sciences from the realm of the imaginary seem in more recent work in visual anthropology far from unerringly stable. In the postwar period it is Jean Rouch, ethnographer-filmmaker and director of the liberal Comité International du Film Ethnographique et Sociologique, who is largely responsible for rethinking the assumptions of traditional ethnographic methodology. His reflections on subjectivity in ethnographic discourse, embodied in the extraordinary evolution of his film practice, mark a turning point in the history of film in the social sciences.

Like classic historiography, traditional theory in ethnography had argued for the maximal effacement of the scientific presence in the field of observation. To this end, ethnographic practice has elaborated typologies of sociality in order to judge the level of distortion of behavior ("camera consciousness") and to work out strategies of observation. Edgar Morin in his preface to Luc de Heusch's *The Cinema and Social Science,* for example, gauges the level of distortion according to "ritual," "intensive," "technical," and "intimate" types of sociality.[62] In the evolution of his ethnographic film practice, Jean Rouch came to reject this methodological approach to cinematorgraphic observation and, indeed, the very notion of observation, which he regards as inescapably ethnocentric. Far from espousing the effacement of the ethnographic presence, he argues that ethnographic film is inevitably the product of *mise en scène* and that ethnographers must recognize and embrace this reality of their film practice. Rouch criticizes the notion, common to naive realism and traditional ethnography, that there is such a thing as a transparent image of a positive (knowable) world. He refuses as a matter of political principle the "voyeurism" of the ethnographer who asserts the dominion of "scientific" discourse over the modes of thought of another culture: "When you indulge in such an exercise, you end up very often with a feeling of disgust, the very fruit of that intellectual imperialism which comes from the fact that we can only see others with our own eyes and with our own concepts."[63]

For Rouch it is a methodological and moral principle that all ethnographic film practice must be intersubjective. It is the ethnographer's task to break down the barriers separating the subject who studies and the subject who is studied. Rouch's strategy is to acknowledge filmmaking as a fiction-making activity and to engage all participants in the creative labor of production. Cinema is, of its very nature, spectacle; consequently, the most immediate and "truthful" subject for the ethnographic film is its own *mise en scène*. There remains, nonetheless, at the source of Rouch's methodology a positive notion of cinematic realism. The cinema-eye (the concept of a mobile, discerning conjunction of camera and human eye that Rouch attributes to Vertov) "captures," if not the truth of the real, then a psychological truth that emerges from the practice of the *cinéma de contact*.

Theories of nonfiction in film are quite diverse, for every theory of documentary bears the marks of the specific historical moment in which it was generated. I have attempted to recognize here that diversity and the ideological and aesthetic dimensions that characterize each critical position. At the same time, however, I wanted to demonstrate the currents of commonality running through every argument that holds that documentary filmmaking is a separate and inviolable form of discourse. The essential opposition between the documentary and the fiction film is part, I contend, of the convention that, since the emergence of modern historical consciousness, has posited an absolute distinction between the representation of "fact" and the representation of the "imaginable." What is necessarily part of every theory of documentary is the assertion of its difference from fiction. Documentary theory is distinguished first by the belief, held by all the theoreticians here studied, in a kind of teleology of cinematic technology: the apparatus itself determines its social function and its natural object. Second, documentary is distinguished by its content—it produces images of facts, not of fancy—and by the "natural" order of its discourse. It does not imagine its chronology or invent the causality of events; rather, it is reality that dictates the textual ordering, however that reality, phenomenal, psychological or social, may be conceived. It is also true of all theories of documentary that prescribe a specific film practice that they seek a social expression of their difference in the form of an oppositional institution.

Thus documentarists deny their intervention in the constitution of the material, which, they assert, is provided for them. Moreover, they deny responsibility for arranging the filmed facts; rather, filmmakers discover the latent causal successivity of events, which, they assume, exists immanently within the real. We need to dis-

41

tinguish of course between the position of a Vertov, who acknowledges the documentarist's intervention at a specific stage of the artistic operation (editing), and the position of Bazin, who can only admit intervention in the mode of self-abnegation—the negation of signification as an ordered human activity. Vertov accepts the text as figure (a symbolic structure that stands as the image of an event), whereas Bazin can only accept the text as fetish, as a quasi-magical evocation.

I will argue that the result of the cinematic operation taken in its broadest sense and in all its phases—from the constitution of cinema as technique of production, to the shooting of footage, to its editing and mixing, to its ultimate projection and consumption under the conditions imposed by the cinematic institution—is a distortion of the field of reality that the documentary film claims to represent to the spectator. There is no such thing as unmediated representation, and this applies to all levels and all units of discourse. All theories of documentary seek to repress the conceptual apparatus that necessarily functions in the constitution of films of "fact" and to leave unacknowledged the poetic act of sense-making without which the film would not be discourse. As Hayden White suggests, it is necessary to question the traditional divisions according to which discursive practices have been classified in order to discover whether they are based, in fact, on the same or similar cultural forms: "Contemporary critical theory permits us to believe more confidently than ever before that 'poetizing' is not an activity that hovers over, transcends, or otherwise remains alienated from life or reality, but represents a mode of praxis which serves as the immediate base of all cultural activity . . . even of science itself."[64]

In this inquiry, I will attempt to uncover the work of representation by means of which documentary film evokes those fields of reference we call the real. My initial hypothesis will be that in their "poetic" functioning there is an intimate kinship between the practice of documentary and fiction filmmaking. With this hypothesis, I do not mean to deny that the documentary film produces a specific effect, or that this effect is based in a certain working of the documentary text; nor do I mean to deny the specific kind of belief that the documentary film engenders in the spectator. Documentary as textual system, the nonfiction-effect, and the regime of spectatorial belief it invokes will be the subjects of the following chapters.

42

2

Order and Sequence in Documentary Film

Cinema and narrative—the historic marriage of a technique of representation and the storyteller's craft was perhaps unforeseen, but it quickly became, as Christian Metz observes, "a historical and social fact, a fact of civilization."[1] The creators of the new cinematographic "language"—Georges Méliès, Edwin S. Porter, G. A. Smith and James Williamson, D. W. Griffith, among others— were interested above all in film's potential as a medium for telling stories. It was in fact in the process of working out specific problems of narration that they invented many of cinema's basic signifying structures: "Men of denotation rather than connotation, they wanted above all to tell a story; they were not content unless they could subject the continuous, analogical material of photographic duplication to the *articulations*—however rudimentary—of a narrative discourse."[2]

Recent work in early film history has served to describe what Metz calls "this very broad historical and social collusion of cinema and narrative."[3] John L. Fell argues, for example, that emerging narrative film not only borrowed its substance from theatrical and literary melodrama, it brought to fruition a number of technical and formal features that had already made their appearance on the Victorian stage. According to this view, mobile sets, fast scenic transitions, and multiple staging of presumably simultaneous events anticipated cinema's moving camera, cutting, and the strategy of parallel editing that underlies the "last-minute rescue."[4] In the view of Noel Burch, the pioneers of the so-called primitive period worked to narrativize the filmic signifier at two distinct levels. First, through composition, lighting, and "dissection" of the visual scene, they produced shots that, rather than recreating the full expanse of theatrical space, centered on discrete moments of the action, offering the spectator pieces of visual information ready-made to take their place in the narrative sequence. Second, they endeavored to integrate these fragmentary shots into discursive units through the elaboration of editing patterns that produced those relationships of time and space characteristic of linear narrative.[5]

In this specific historical development, documentary film and other presumably nonnarrative genres played decidedly marginal roles. Documentarists may refer to the reproductive capacities of the new technology and speak of the emergence of a "natural" cinematographic discourse based on images taken from life, but in the formative years the new dramaturgy of film looked back, rather, to the fictions of nineteenth-century melodrama. It was the desire to tell such unnatural stories that inspired the pioneers to fashion the shot and to organize shots into narrative sequences. Moreover, the feature film quickly mobilized a complex and aggressive industry of production, distribution, and exploitation, imposing itself as the dominant cinematic institution. By the 1920s, the fiction film industry was a major force in the capitalist marketplace worldwide, whereas other cinematic forms including documentary were quite unable to assert their economic and social autonomy. With a few brilliant exceptions, e.g., Flaherty's *Nanook* (1922), Cooper and Schoedsack's *Grass* (1925), whose popular success gave hope for the new genre, documentary film has always struggled to eke out its uncertain existence on the margins of other institutions, both private and public. In the classic period roughly from 1935 to 1955, documentary films in commercial distribution played an ancillary role in film programs: they constituted, along with the cartoon and the news, part of the wait for the feature film.

Against the force of history that would seem to privilege the discourse of fiction, documentarists have held their ground. For them, fiction is an invasion of cinema that calls for the most rigorous aesthetic and ideological opposition. Derived from already-existing forms of theater and novel, the fiction film denatures cinema, forcing it to speak a language which is not its own. Documentary, on the other hand, following the proclivities of the medium, elaborates discursive forms that are inherent in cinema itself. This controversy, which poses fiction against nonfiction, leads us to examine several crucial questions. Does documentary film possess its own system of signifying structures? Or does it depend on those forms elaborated historically at the behest of narrative? Does nonnarrative film share the basic figures of fictional discourse: the codes of composition, of order and sequence, of relationships be-

44

tween sound and image, and so forth? Is there a reality to the designation "nonfiction" in film or is documentary continually reclaimed by fiction which imposes its specific formal hegemony? The answers to these questions lie in the documentary text itself.

In Metz's view, it is improbable that nonnarrative genres possess any kind of real formal autonomy: "It is by no means certain that an independent semiotics of the various nonnarrative genres is possible other than in the form of a series of discontinuous remarks on the points of difference between these films and 'ordinary' films."[6] It is precisely this assertion that our inquiry is designed to put to the test. Where should this investigation begin? With what films and with what codes?

The Question of Codes

It is widely recognized by film historians, such as André Malraux, Béla Belázs, Edgar Morin, and Jean Mitry, that the codes of *montage* are at the very center of the historical development of cinema as a specific discursive form. The individual shots are fashioned—composed and lit—according to the place they will occupy on the syntagmatic chain. It is this placing in sequence that must occupy the filmmaker at every stage of the process of production. *Montage* is the essential discursive act: "Cinema begins with the sequence of images; it is above all by the ordering of these images that cinema can organize itself into a discourse; it is the order of successions which institutes a language where the isolated image offered essentially only its mute analogy with a fragment of the real."[7]

I would begin this investigation by considering whether the codes of *montage* that order the unfolding of the story in the classic fiction film also order the sequencing of images in documentary film. For this initial step, I have chosen one such code: the Large Syntagmatic Category of the Image-Track described by Christian Metz.[8] The Large Syntagmatic unit corresponds to what is often popularly called the "sequence," an autonomous segment that groups together a number of shots intended to be read in their continuity. The Large Syntagmatic is a code among other codes of sequence, but it occupies a special place. As Raymond Bellour notes in his article, "To Analyze, To Segment," it is this code that most demonstrably fuses the syntagmatic chain of images and the sequentiality that is narrative: "For if the Large Syntagmatic is not more or less than a code among codes which are juxtaposed to it

45

and run through it, it envelops the other codes; and in a literal sense, this code is superior to them: forcibly, as the consequence and condition of the fiction."9

In his description of the Large Syntagmatic category, Metz distinguishes the following types of autonomous segments:

—the autonomous shot: a single shot constitutes a primary unit of the plot, either as a complete episode (the shot-sequence) or as an interpolation within another syntagmatic unit (the insert).

—the parallel syntagma: two or more series of motifs are interwoven in a pattern of alternation (A/B/A1/B1 and so forth); the motifs have no specific relationship in space and time, but set up a symbolic opposition (for example, in Shub's *Fall of the Romanov Dynasty* (1927), shots of peasant labor juxtaposed to those showing the leisurely life of landowners).

—the bracket syntagma: brief scenes lacking in syntagmatic development are linked by montage (and often by optical punctuation such as the dissolve); the scenes represent "typical samples of a same order of reality," without suggesting any chronological relationship. (For example, in Van Dyke and Stiener's *The City* the series of "scenes" of city life which, taken together, constitute an evocation of urban alienation.) The bracket syntagma is distinguished from the parallel syntagma by the absence of alternation.

—the descriptive syntagma: any sequence of shots which serves to describe a locale rather than relate an action. (Quite often the first sequence of the classic narrative film is descriptive and establishes the setting within which events will unfold.) The motifs of successive shots are understood to be occurring simultaneously in a coherent diegetic space; the motifs' consecutiveness does not refer to any progression in the plot.

—the alternate syntagma: two or more series of motifs are interwoven in a pattern of alternation which represents various foci of the action understood to be occurring simultaneously (for example, in the often cited Griffith's "last-minute rescue," shots of the imperiled heroine alternated with shots of the hero speeding to her deliverance).

—the scene: a succession of shots which represent a continuous temporal progression as in the theatrical scene. The signifier is fragmented (broken into shots, according to the techniques of analytic editing), but the signified (the event represented) is understood as unfolding "without flaws."

—the episodic sequence: brief scenes lacking in syntagmatic development are linked by montage (and often by dissolves, as in the "lightning
mixes" Welles developed for *Citizen Kane*); the scenes, which are
understood as occurring in a chronological progression, function as
condensed "abridgements" of much more extensive actions.

—the ordinary sequence: a succession of shots which represent a
complex, discontinuous, but unified temporal progression. As in the
scene, the signifier is fragmentary, but shot changes in this type of
sequence allow us to skip over presumably unimportant moments of the
action.[10]

The Question of the Films

The methodology I propose to follow makes a rather large assumption about the historical, social and cultural homogeneity of
the classic documentary film. It supposes as a point of departure
that the classification "documentary film" corresponds to a "natural reality," i.e., that the documentary as it is described in the
critical literature constitutes a textual-systemic unit. On reflection,
it is easy to point to several reasons for arguing that documentary
does not resemble those coherent bodies of films commonly called
genres. Unlike most genres, the documentary, defined in its most
inclusive sense, is not the product of a particular historical period.
Rather, as its historians assert, the origins of the documentary
coincide with those of cinema itself (Lumière launched the documentary spirit), and documentary film is considered to have had a
continuous existence at least since the early films of Flaherty and
Vertov. Moreover, documentary has never achieved (or, better, has
achieved only for brief periods of time) status as an institution
(unlike other genres especially in Hollywood). It has never had any
prescribed structures of production, or any secure circuit of finance
and distribution, or any consistent public. Even in those privileged
historic moments when documentary seems to have found its niche,
it has always been marginal, most often serving as the propagandistic arm of other institutional formations in government or the
private sector.

In undertaking a synchronic study of a group of films so apparently diverse and with so vast a history, there is a decided risk. It is
not at all likely that the classic documentary film has the coherence
of a genre. Is it possible to say, for example, that Flaherty's idyllic
Moana and Cavalcanti's abstract *Rien que les heures*, both released

47

in 1927, belong to a single genre? It is rather quite probable that documentary can itself be decomposed into genres whose defining features shift and change in relation to other genres of film in specific periods. The history of film genres has not yet been written, and the film analyst must be content to probe questions of genre in a rudimentary manner. What I propose is a preliminary inquiry to test the reality of a long-established, but largely unexamined distinction in cinema between fiction and nonfiction. My methodological approach will be to grant a tentative coherence to the classification "documentary film." As Metz notes, "it is not really a question of asserting that a cinematic genre is a vast single film, but rather of seeing what one comes up with if one decides to treat it as such."[11]

On this basis I have chosen a presumably coherent group of films to analyze from the point of view of a single code—the Large Syntagmatic Category of the Image-Track. In choosing the films, I applied certain criteria. First, the films represent, inadequately of course, the history of the documentary film from 1922 to 1960, i.e., from its first texts until documentary was profoundly altered by innovations in technique and methods of production—the invention of light-weight, portable cameras and sound equipment that made possible the documentary movements variously named *cinéma vérité*, direct cinema, and new documentary. Second, the films to be considered are major works of documentary and some are major works of identifiable schools or movements (e.g., the British documentary). Third, the films are diverse in structure. On simple viewing, some seem to conform to the narrative ordering of the fiction film; others appear to exhibit a different principle of order. Paradoxically, in constituting this "vast collective text which crosses over several interfilmic boundaries" (Metz's definition of the term *group* of films), I was concerned to make my corpus as heterogeneous as possible.

The following is that corpus, arranged chronologically according to the date of production:

Nanook of the North, Robert Flaherty, 1922/1949, 55 minutes.
Fall of the Romanov Dynasty, Esther Shub, 1927, 75 minutes.
Rien que les heures, Alberto Cavalcanti, 1927, 45 minutes.
Land Without Bread, Luis Buñuel, 1932, 27 minutes.
Night Mail, Basil Wright and Henry Watt, 1935, 30 minutes.
The River, Pare Lorentz, 1937, 32 minutes.
The City, Ralph Stiener and Willard Van Dyke, 1939, 43 minutes.
Listen to Britain, Humphrey Jennings, 1942, 19 minutes.

The Battle of Britain, Frank Capra (producer), 1943, 55 minutes.
Le Sang des bêtes, Georges Franju, 1949, 20 minutes.
Les Maîtres fous, Jean Rouch, 1955, 30 minutes.

The Large Syntagmatic Category functions in this study as a practical instrument of textual analysis because it opens up the question of segmentation: according to what principles does documentary film discern its units of meaning and place them in sequence? It permits us to evaluate the homogeneity of the documentary "genre" and to measure the degree to which this code of the classic narrative cinema structures the order and sequence of images in the documentary film. Are the texts to be analyzed consistent with the classic fiction film in regards to their syntagmatic structures? Or do they reveal a discursive order that belongs properly to documentary? How does documentary in its textuality mark out its difference from classic fiction?

In approaching this analysis, I fully anticipated inconsistencies in this "collective text," whose "air of family resemblance" is clearly less strong than that of other cinematic genres. The results of analysis were nonetheless unexpected. Broken into large syntagmatic units, the filmic chain reveals a radical heterogeneity of the texts. Far from displaying the structural consistency associated with genre, these eleven films emerge as surprisingly eclectic. In order to expose the formal eclecticism of this group of films, I will begin by reordering the corpus according to the proportion of narrative syntagmas each film contains. Here narrative is understood to apply to any sequence of shots that relates the chronology of any real or imagined event. Hence, the narrative syntagmas include the following chronological types: the alternate syntagma, the scene, the episodic sequence, and the ordinary sequence. The nonnarrative syntagmas include the following achronological types: the parallel syntagma, the bracket syntagma, and one chronological type, which denotes no succession in time: the descriptive syntagma. (In ranking the films, I have eliminated the autonomous shot from consideration. It is clear in the films analyzed that the autonomous shot functions at times as a narrative unit and at others as a nonnarrative unit, but the problems of classification go beyond the immediate concerns of this study. The autonomous shot is not in fact a syntagmatic unit at the same level as the other types that make up the Large Syntagmatic, i.e., it is not a concatenation of shots.)

Since all the nonnarrative syntagmas are "intrinsically rare" in the classic narrative film, as the narrative syntagmas are "intrin-

49

sically common" (with the exception of the alternate syntagma), it is reasonable to argue that films containing a high proportion of narrative syntagmas conform more closely to the syntagmatic ordering of the fiction film than do films with a high proportion of nonnarrative syntagmas. Table 2.1 presents the rearrangement of films in the corpus, the most "narrative" film appearing at the top, the least "narrative" at the bottom. Notations indicate the number of occurrences of each syntagmatic type.

The order of the table reflects a diminishing ratio of narrative to nonnarrative syntagmas based on the number of each type present and not according to its duration, i.e., the length of the filmic chain occupied by each type. The results are therefore somewhat rough; a method of measurement that would combine frequency and duration would give a better basis for comparison. However, the ratios on which the table is based are accurate enough for the purposes of this study, with one exception. Jean Rouch's *Les Maîtres fous* (1955) presented problems in analysis: The filmic chain seems to resolve itself into enormous undemarcated "ordinary" sequences that occupy the majority of the film's running time (for a discussion of this apparently anomalous system, see chapter 4). Thus we place *Les Maîtres fous* in rank with *Night Mail* (1935) and *Nanook of the North* (1922) as the most narrative of the films analyzed.

Scanning the table of frequencies, it is quite obvious that the films are surprisingly divergent in the way they call upon the large syntagmatic code. Compare the frequency of syntagmatic types of films that figure at the top of the table with those of films at the bottom. On the basis of this inventory, is it not reasonable to assume that films like *Night Mail* or *Nanook of the North* show a closer kinship in their syntagmatic organization with examples of the classic narrative film than they do with documentaries such as *The City* (1939) or *The River* (1937), with which traditional criticism has grouped them?

An attentive reading of these films certainly suggests that this is the case. But analysis also reveals that order and sequence in any film forms a complex system whose elements achieve a balance we can call textual economy. Each text has its individuality, its own way of disposing and displacing the syntagmatic codes. In the following analysis I will attempt to study this corpus of films as a spectrum within which degrees of similarity and difference can be distinguished. Thus, in order to speak of the films in general, certain features of their singularity must be considered. How are the syntagmatic types distributed within the text? In what kinds of patterns? How do they fit into the unfolding of the scenario? What

Table 2.1
Frequency of Syntagmatic Types

	insert	autonomous shot	parallel syntagma	bracket syntagma	descriptive syntagma	alternate syntagma	scene	episodic sequence	ordinary sequence
Night Mail	4	4	0	1	3	0	4	0	16
Nanook of the North	3	1	0	0	5	0	1	0	18
Les Maîtres fous	0	0	1	2	5	0	0	0	7
Le Sang des bêtes	0	3	0	1	4	0	1	0	5
The Battle of Britain	26	37	0	36	24	9	9	0	53
Land Without Bread	2	4	0	0	14	1	4	1	6
Listen to Britain	6	7	0	4	11	0	12	0	0
Rien que les heures	5	6	2	12	4	2	9	0	0
Fall of the Romanov Dynasty	12	12	2	23	17	4	0	0	19
The City	0	0	1	21	9	1	1	0	11
The River	6	0	0	13	3	1	0	0	5

kind of "story" do they tell? Do they perform the same functions as in the fiction film? What kind of "lacks" do we see in the ordering of sequences? How does each film's textual economy compensate for such lacks?

Keeping in mind the individuality of each text, I am able to make a number of general observations about order and sequence in these documentary films.

(1) *The displacement of narrative syntagmas as the dominant syntagmatic types is a significant tendency in this group of films, since eight of the eleven films exhibit this displacement to one degree or another.*

It is already apparent that at least at this level of organization, documentary films are generally less narrative than fiction films; some are radically less so. There is, this study suggests, a general resistance to narrative within the documentary film: a textual activity that works against the kind of order and sequence we find in the classic fiction film. If there is an activity, there is also a discursive agency—a documentary voice which emerges and withdraws, dissimulates and asserts itself. What are the signs of this resistance? How can this textual activity be described?

(2) *A "moderate" displacement of narrative syntagmas tends to operate in favor of the descriptive syntagma.*

As the table of frequency of syntagmatic types indicates, the texts that exhibit this tendency include *Le Sang des bêtes* (1949), *Land Without Bread* (1932) and *Listen to Britain* (1942). Here moderation is the structural result of description's "natural" ancillary relationship to narrative. Description, which is a mode of discourse, may interrupt narrative; it may never replace it. As Gérard Genette notes, "Purely descriptive genres never exist, and we can hardly imagine a work where the narrative acts as auxiliary to the description."[12] Narrative asserts its dominance even over the quantitative superiority of description.

The function of the descriptive syntagma in the three films we have mentioned is rather precisely defined by Genette in the distinction he draws between narration and description: "Description, because it lingers over objects and beings considered in their simultaneity and because it envisages the actions themselves as scenes, seems to suspend the flow of time and to contribute to spreading out the narrative in space."[13] Thus, the descriptive syntagma represents a basic change in the character of events these films portray. It is a pause in the forward movement of narrative. Infinitely more passive, the descriptive syntagma diffuses action. It suspends the immediate causal links between the motifs; it weakens motivation: the succession of shots no longer imitates the chronological unfolding of the story. In the descriptive syntagma, we perceive the coexistence of events without reading them as sequential.

Let us look in schematic fashion at the functioning of the descriptive syntagma in *Le Sang des bêtes*. Franju's classic documentary, which takes as its subject the slaughterhouses of suburban Paris, is organized around four central narrative syntagmas, each of which evokes the techniques of the slaughter of a species of beast: horse, bullock, calf, sheep. The film appears to unfold according to a rigorously defined chronology: dawn to dusk in the abattoirs. On reflection, however, we find that this quite specific referential frame is "arbitrarily" drawn. It is not defined by the trajectory of events that flow one from the other, moving toward closure, but by a simple limit of duration. It has unity of time, but not unity of action in the classic sense. If the temporal consecutiveness that orders the individual narrative syntagmas "follows" the orderly progress of the slaughter and dissection of the individual species, this motivation, this causality fails to produce any meaningful chronological link between the large syntagmatic units. In fact, if we look at the major divisions of the scenario, there is nothing beyond the logic of themes that moves us from one slaughterhouse to the next. Thus the narrative syntagmas do not relay each other—narrative continuity does not in effect cross Large Syntagmatic boundaries. The narrative segments succeed each other, but they establish their succession on the basis of their resemblance: each new syntagma repeats, with differences, the motifs and gestures of the preceding one(s).

I call this structure episodic because the narrative movement is confined to the smaller units of discourse. As analysis will show, the encapsulation of narrative is a general characteristic of the classic documentary film. In *Le Sang des bêtes*, each major narrative syntagma is linked to a descriptive syntagma that precedes it in a loose suprasegmental unit:

Table 2.2.
Four Segments from *Le Sang des bêtes*

	IMAGE	SOUND
1 descriptive syntagma	Les abattoirs de Vaugirard: passage of a suburban train; movement of trucks on the avenues; the slaughterhouse with its	Commentary: "At the Porte de Vanves, there is also the Vanves slaughterhouse. The municipal establishment, despite

	IMAGE	SOUND
	immense statues of bulls; an inscription: "A Emile Decrou, propagateur de la viande de cheval (1821–1901)." (5 shots)	the emblem of the bull, specializes in the slaughter of horses."
2 autonomous shot (dissolve)	A still life of the tools of the trade. A hand enters the frame to display each instrument as it is named.	Commentary: "The tools of the trade are, according to the animal, the jonc or reed, the English cleaver, and the pistol which fells the beast by detonation.
3 ordinary sequence (dissolve)	A beautiful white horse is led into a shed where it is destroyed by the pistol; its throat slit, the horse is hoisted into position and flayed by the butchers. One worker, at first seen in profile, moves across the floor sounding his wooden leg. (18 shots)	Following the percussive noise of the pistol and the animal's fall, the commentary names the successive stages of butchery: bleeding, hoisting, skinning, the "delicate" work of flaying. "It was while flaying a horse that Ernest Brayet severed his femoral artery and had to have his right leg amputated."
4 unidentified syntagma (fade-out)	The smoking head of a butchered horse; the old photo of a man standing, pipe in hand, beside a slaughtered horse; the covers of an ornate book close over the screen. (3 shots)	"This black horse was butchered by Alfred Marquant, recognized as one of the Meilleurs Ouvriers de France. It was Oedile de Marquant, his grandfather, who founded the art of flaying at the end of the century."

The passage we have transcribed here is immediately followed by a second descriptive syntagma that evokes the Parisian *banlieue* around the Canal de l'Ourck. In turn, that is followed by an ordinary sequence which recounts the slaughter and butchering of cattle in the nearby abattoirs of the Porte de Pantin.

Thus the descriptive syntagma functions as in the classic narrative film to "situate" the action, but it also operates textually to demarcate the film, isolating each major narrative progression and interrupting the story's linear movement. The demarcation of the episode in this passage is redoubled by punctuation: the continuity of the segments, reinforced by dissolves, leads us to the fade-out and the ironic image of the book that brings the episode to closure.

The spatial diffusion of the descriptive syntagmas suspends the flow of time and produces moments of relaxation from the increasing tension of repetition that the narrative sequences provoke. In this alternating structure of narrative and descriptive syntagmas, Franju does not set up a simple juxtaposition of modes and spaces, but rather an interpenetration, suggesting a profound correspondence between oppressive suburban landscapes and aggression against innocent animals. The descriptive syntagmas constitute, therefore, not only the situation and demarcation of the narrative but its expansion in space.

Land Without Bread and *Listen to Britain* share with *Le Sang des bêtes* certain structural features that are tied to the strong presence of segments in the descriptive mode. Narrative in all three films is relatively passive. Narrative syntagmatic units are textually isolated, and the films lack the linear development one associates with the classic fiction film. Rather, there is an erosion of the distinction between narration and description: the spatialization of narrative.

A final remark. In all three films, the agency that binds together the large syntagmatic units and produces the coherent movement of the scenario is extradiegetic, i.e., it originates outside the events the films' images represent to us. It may be embodied in a voice, as in the bitterly ironic commentary in the style of a travelogue in *Land Without Bread;* or it may remain invisible behind a rhetoric of forms, as we will see in *Listen to Britain* (see chapter 3).

(3) *The radical displacement of the narrative syntagma tends to operate in favor of the bracket syntagma.*

This tendency is the more marked the more radically a given film departs from the frequency of types found in the classic narrative film. In our sample, the least narrative films—judged according to their Large Syntagmatic ordering—contain the highest proportion

55

of bracket syntagmas. Reading from the bottom of Table 2.1, *The River, The City, Fall of the Romanov Dynasty,* and *Rien que les heures* all display in varying degrees of dominance the bracket syntagma as the most frequent type. *Listen to Britain* appears as an exception (it will be the subject of analysis in the next chapter). Also, it should be noted that *The Battle of Britain,* despite the predominance of the ordinary sequence, contains a substantial number of bracket syntagmas that resemble in their structure and function the bracket syntagmas we find in the other film of historical representation, *Fall of the Romanov Dynasty.*

These films all appear to resist the narrative organization of sequences that is absolutely crucial to the functioning of the fiction film. It is reasonable to anticipate then, on the level of the image track either the signs of textual disintegration or the clear signs of another order that has come to supplant narrative sequence. In the initial phase of analysis—the task of grouping the shots into identifiable units of meaning—I encountered already a symptomatic problem: the bracket syntagma must be defined in the broadest possible sense if it is to admit all the syntagmas that have been so classed. A bracket syntagma is identified as any achronological autonomous segment which displays no systematic alternation of images and which is ordered according to a principle other than temporal. The definition is suspiciously vague and predicated on negative attributes. Achronological, nonnarrative, lacking any specific pattern or structure, is the bracket syntagma a real ordering of the image track? Or are these uncertain, equivocal syntagmas the sign of the textual disintegration of the image track? Let's examine the problem in the context of larger filmic structures.

(4) *The tendency toward the displacement of narrative syntagmas coincides with the tendency to abandon the narrative ordering of the image track at the level of the scenario.*

What syntagmatic analysis ultimately discovers is that narrative is always present in documentary, whether it constitutes the core of the film or performs apparently more modest functions. However, if documentaries cannot do without narrative, few are "purely" narrative; none among the films studied here are. Classic documentary film always combines different modes of discourse, and this mixing of voices is perhaps its most salient formal feature. It seems quite likely in fact that a typology of documentary films is possible precisely on the basis of the "weight" narrative carries in documentary films in relation to that borne by a second ordering principle, which I call discursive. This weight can be measured, not simply by the preponderance of narrative or nonnarrative ordering—in this analysis, the amount of the syntagmatic chain occupied by narrative or nonnarrative large syntagmatic units—rather, we must first of all consider the textual level at which narrative prevails. When we speak of a film as being "narrative," we are first of all referring to the dominance of narrative at the higher levels of the text, i.e., in its larger syntagmatic units. "Narrative" documentaries resemble fiction films in that their scenarios take the shape of the unfolding of a story. The films we perceive as nonnarrative are not films without narrative; rather, they are films whose narrative elements are confined to the smaller syntagmatic units. In such films, another often didactic voice asserts its mastery over the order of the text.

Night Mail, Nanook of the North, Les Maîtres fous and *The Battle of Britain,* and in large measure *Fall of the Romanov Dynasty* all appear to function at the level of the scenario in the manner of the classic fiction film: the succession of their discourse—the unfolding of the chains of images—imitates the chronological unfolding of events. The spatio-temporal references are in fact quite specific: 1) *Night Mail* recounts the Postal Express's run from London to Scotland from dusk to dawn; 2) *Nanook of the North* follows the movements of an Eskimo family across the expanses of Hudson Bay and through the evolution of the seasons; 3) *Les Maîtres fous* describes the rites of a sect called the Hauka in a jungle compound near Accra from Sunday morning to nightfall; 4) *The Battle of Britain* evokes the events of the attempted conquest of Britain by German forces between August 1940 and the winter of 1940–41; 5) against the background of a class analysis of Russian society and the tsar's regime, *Fall of the Romanov Dynasty* narrates the events leading to the coup d'état, from May 1913 to the brink of the October Revolution.

Of the five films, only *Night Mail* possesses that general self-sufficiency of the fiction film that allows us to suppose that the "events are chronologically recorded as they appear on the horizon of the story."[14] This is due in large measure to a strategic suppression of the commentary as a narrative voice (See chapter 4). *Night Mail* conforms to the narrative structures of the fiction film at two levels: 1) in the construction of its "sequences," i.e., at the large syntagmatic level; 2) in the ordering of the scenario, which positions the large syntagmatic units within the dramatic movement of the film according to the narrative unity of time, place, and action. I would therefore identify *Night Mail* as a *classic narrative documentary.*

At the level of the scenario, *Nanook,* on the other hand, has a distinctly episodic structure: the large syntagmatic units have a tight internal continuity; the relation *between* these "sequences" is much looser and less specific. It is significant to recall that André Bazin cited the narrative sequences in *Nanook* as models of cinematic realism: for him the spatial and temporal integrity of the sequence of the seal hunt stands as exemplary.[15] The narrative syntagmas are in fact long in duration and unusually continuous. Each ordinary sequence constitutes a minor dramatic progression, describing, within a circumscribed space-time, an isolated event in the Eskimos' lives: hunting walrus, spear fishing, building an igloo, and so forth. The sense of internal temporal continuity that each sequence possesses is particularly striking because the progression of syntagmas serves to denote a complete cycle in Nanook's life and a full revolution of the seasons. Thus, the large syntagmatic units tend to be highly encapsulated: the relatively precise indications of spatial and temporal continuity within the syntagmatic units contrast with the relative lack of specific elements of continuity between syntagmas. No specific logic of action and causality emerges within one sequence to carry us effortlessly forward to the next. A consistent use of punctuation further reinforces the effect of the film's disjunctive narrative. The opening and closure of eighteen of the twenty-eight autonomous segments are demarcated by fade-in/fade-out, and three narrative units larger than the segment are punctuated in this fashion.

In contrast to the diegetic syntagmas, whose coherence depends on their "faithful" representation of a continuous space-time, the nondiegetic inserts are self-consciously narrative. From outside the diegesis they provide the information that links the sequences together and gives the scenario its narrative coherence. Thus they compensate for the lack of continuity between large syntagmatic units by contextualizing the events, i.e., localizing them in space and time. These inserts occupy strategic locations in the text at the sites of the major divisions of the scenario, which they largely effect. Maps situate us geographically and long written texts mark the progress of the story: the changes of season and the movement of the characters in space.

Nanook of the North stands as a model of a second type of documentary that I will call *episodic narrative,* defined by the two features already noted: 1) diegetic continuity at the level of the large syntagmatic units remains more or less faithful to the fiction film model; 2) an extradiegetic "voice" intervenes to produce the continuity of the scenario. As we have seen, *Le Sang des bêtes* has a similar episodic structure, although this structure is already equivocal: the four parts of its scenario stand only superficially in a narrative relation to each other. Moreover, Franju's film is considerably more discursive in that Jean Painlevé's commentary works as an often redundant and always ironic exegesis of the image. I would add *Listen to Britain* to this list of films with episodic narratives, despite that film's lack of linearity at the level of the scenario. As I seek to demonstrate in the next chapter, Humphrey Jennings's film uses a complex system of rhetorical structures to bridge its "episodes" and to create this diegetic illusion of Britain at war.

In *The Battle of Britain* the mode of narration is considerably modified. The spoken commentary participates fully in the act of narration. It not only creates the bridge between the large syntagmatic units, it assists in producing the continuity of the "sequences" themselves. The image track in the compilation film is, almost by definition, elliptical. Even when the filmmaker sacrifices respect for the field of reference—this is certainly the case in Capra's film, which abounds in imaginary constructions of all sorts—the assemblage of fragments can only mimic the *montage* figures and the techniques of continuity that are essential to narration in the classic fiction film. As André Bazin clearly analyzes in "A Propos de *Pourquoi nous combattons*," the gaps in the image chain of Capra's wartime documentaries are sutured by an "invisible" commentary which relays the image-text and specifies its narrative message.[16] (See chapter 4 for a developed analysis of these discursive interventions.)

The Battle of Britain belongs then to a third class in my typology, which I call *elliptical narrative* (elliptical only with reference to the image track). As analysis suggests, elliptical narratives are characterized by discursive interventions at two levels: 1) in the articulation of the general movement of the scenario; 2) in the production of the continuity of the autonomous segments. Esther Shub's compilation film *Fall of the Romanov Dynasty* demonstrates that in the film of historic representation the archival material is rarely complete enough to evoke events in the manner of the fiction film. The extraordinary number of intertitles attests to the constant intervention of a discursive agency which (among its other functions) compensates for the hiatuses of the filmed record. Shub's film is not only a historic narrative, it is a discourse on history.

We encounter similar problems in the case of the classic ethnographic film. It is often the function of the commentary to compensate for the inadequacy of the filmed record and in many cases to produce the intelligibility of the sequence of images. It is the particular function of the spoken ethnographic commentary to identify for the spectator the motifs that appear in the image and to situate them on a chain of time and causality. Thus in *Les Maîtres fous,* the voice-over tends to weave the film's continuity at all levels, especially in the lengthy narrative sequences that evoke the successive stages of the rituals carried out by the Hauka in their jungle compound. (See chapter 4 for a discussion of the function of language in this film.)

In all the films I have classed as either episodic or elliptical narrative, one can measure each text's distance from the classic fiction model by the level at which the discursive voice intervenes and by its force of mediation. As we will see, the degree to which the large syntagmatic units maintain their integrity is one indication of the film's adherence to "pure" narrative forms.

I would propose a final type of sequence and order in the classic documentary, which I call *discursive.* It is useful to refer to Gérard Genette's distinction between narrative and discourse (which is in turn a reformulation of Benveniste's) as described in "Boundaries of Narrative."[17] Genette draws a sharp opposition between the objectivity of narrative and the subjectivity of discourse. Objectivity is the lack of reference to a narrator, i.e., his or her apparent absence from the text; subjectivity involves the signs of his or her presence in the act of narration. All the films I am discussing possess spoken commentaries or intertitles, which are always extradiegetic marks of the narrator's presence; they are all, therefore, discursive to one degree or another. Elliptical narratives, as I have described them, are in this sense often as discursive as they are narrative: *Fall of the Romanov Dynasty* and *The Battle of Britain* contain numerous examples of spoken, written, and graphic discourse. In the films I will qualify as discursive, however, there will be a fundamental shift in the site of enunciation. It is no longer the function of the commentary or intertitles or rhetorical devices to shore up the narrative; the discursive agency fully assumes its functions as enunciator, one of which is to subordinate the narrative to the image-text.

Discourse is, as Genette says, "the natural mode of language, the broadest and most universal form, by definition open to all forms."[18] Discursive films are not therefore primarily governed by narrative sequence or narrative's semantic limits. Other orders, other meanings are possible. This is not to say that narrative is absent; rather, it is assimilated as an integral part of that discourse. Let's look briefly at examples of this integration of discursive modes.

Land Without Bread, Buñuel's evocation of the misery of existence in the isolated villages of the Hurdanos, belongs in the mode of bitter irony to the genre of the travelogue. Nothing, it would appear, could be more narrative than this genre, which attaches images from the observer's memory to the precise chronology of his peregrination. But the travelogue is also by nature highly discursive. It relies on the strong presence of an enunciator—the traveler—who assumes responsibility in relation to the audience for the order of discourse. The travelogue assumes, necessarily, the dominance of language over image. In *Land Without Bread,* the presence of the enunciator, embodied in the commentary of the presumed traveler, serves to denarrativize the image track, weakening the spatio-temporal references that produce continuity in the fiction film. Narrative syntagmas occupy less than half of the filmic chain. The representation of events is increasingly elliptical and often purely illustrative, serving as the fragmentary denotation for the narrative, which the commentary voices. The characters and their actions are all prisoners of the episodic fragment, which appears to have no forward movement of its own. The verbal notations of the movements of the "observer," the film party, from one village to the next produce the spatial and temporal articulations: "Going to the village square, we found. . . ." "One day we met these two Hurdanos taking a load of hides to Alberca." It is also the observer—materialized in one shot as a member of the film party attempting to intervene on behalf of a sick child—who invites the spectator to see: "Look at this infant," "See how thin this precious layer of soil is." Thus this enunciating presence imposes his order of discourse and takes charge of the unfolding narrative. It is not surprising that we encounter in this film a kind of crisis of demarcation. The visual sequences have an ambiguity of outline: lacking clear spatio-temporal references, the image-text fails to produce a sense of diegetic continuity.

In the broad outlines of their scenarios, *The City* and *The River,* perhaps the best known of the American "problem solving" documentaries of the 1930s, are clearly discursive films. *The River,* for example, traces the history of the Mississippi, but the spatio-temporal references are subordinated to the discursive logic of the film: the history of abuses of the river and its surrounding land leads us toward the resolution that modern science and the voice of the commentary propose: the Tennessee Valley Authority. Similarly, in *The City* immense descriptive and narrative passages evoking the modern industrial city prepare the way for a blueprint for urban renewal, ecstatically evoked in the script by Lewis Mumford and Henwar Rodakiewicz. As we descend to the smaller textual units, we find the signs there also of the displacement of narrative. I have already noted the preponderance of bracket syntagmas in *The River* and *The City*. I need now to examine in some detail two other features of these films that appear to have most radically abandoned narrative order at the level of the large syntagmatic units.

(5) *The tendency toward the displacement of narrative syntagmas as dominant types coincides with a tendency toward an increasing ambiguity of the types themselves.*

In the classic fiction film nonnarrative syntagmas constitute momentary breaks in the linear plot line. These syntagmas, which Metz describes in his typology, derive their meanings in large measure from their place inside narrative, and many documentaries conform to this basic economy of the narrative system. Others, however, seem to "choose" nonnarrative syntagmas to the relative exclusion of narrative types, in certain cases forming long, narratively undifferentiated strings of shots. Such films do not simply break at intervals with the forward movement of action and event; they disrupt basic patterns and structures that are at the heart of the functioning of the fiction film.

The more films "choose" syntagmatic types other than narrative, the more all the types tend to lose the features that distinguish them in the classic fiction film. Such deviant texts open links in the chain of images, dissociating the shots from the linear work of narrative. Their scenarios cannot as in the classic fiction film be reduced to a chronological unfolding. Without the spatio-temporal references according to which the syntagmatic units of the narrative film are articulated among themselves, i.e., without the causal logic of plot, what autonomous (and isolated) segments denote becomes highly ambiguous: how can we determine the precise temporal character of syntagmas that do not take up their place in a chain of narrated events? In the absence of narrative linearity, how do we determine the mode of the syntagma that is cut off from a chronology at the level of the scenario? On what basis, for example, do we distinguish the linearity of a sequence (leading to what?) from the simple spatial juxtaposition characteristic of the descriptive syntagma?

At the same time—and for reasons that are immediately apparent—this uncertainty of syntagmatic form brings with it a problematic ambiguity of demarcation. How do we define the boundaries of a form that is unclear? Metz provides us with three criteria for establishing the demarcation of the large syntagmatic units: a major change in the course of the plot, a change in cinematic treatment (one syntagmatic type supersedes another), or punctuation (dissolve, fade, and so forth) marking the syntagmatic boundaries.[19]

But when spatio-temporal references are intermittent or disjunctive, how do we determine a change in the course of the plot? If we are unable clearly to identify the type of a syntagma (or are uncertain even of its syntagmatic status), how are we to pinpoint shifts in cinematic treatment? Punctuation is, of course, generally unambiguous, but what if the films possess few if any marks of punctuation—as is the case with the films we are studying? These problems lead us in a circle, precisely because the criteria for demarcation are quite often interdependent.

In analyzing *The River,* we found the bracket syntagma to be the dominant type, occupying more than one-half of the filmic chain. The analyst is confronted with long catenae of images that appear to lack the orderly articulation—the continuity—which characterizes sequence in a narrative text. Can we in fact maintain that the bracket syntagma, as it is manifested in this film, is an autonomous ordering of the image track? We must remember that in the fiction film the bracket syntagma is always a momentary retreat from a dominant narrative order, in the nature of a parenthetical statement. But in *The River,* this form takes up a central position in discourse. Does the dilative "bracket" syntagma not reflect in fact a more permanent withdrawal of spatio-temporal references, which leaves the image in a position of subordination? This disordering of the image at the level of the Large Syntagmatic—the displacement of the ordering function to a position outside the image track—is evident not only in the dominance of the "bracket syntagma" over other syntagmatic types, but also in the ambiguity of all syntagmatic types. Let's look at a few of the problems of classification encountered in analysis.

It is not always possible to distinguish clearly between narrative and descriptive syntagmas: does the sequence of images on the screen signify a chronological unfolding, or does it refer to a primarily spatial relationship? Segment nine of *The River,* for example, appears initially to be in the descriptive mode: the loading of a steamship on the Mississippi described in its various aspects without specific reference to the consecutiveness of the activities portrayed. However, the ship's departure, represented in the final two shots of the syntagma, imposes retrospectively a chronologically sequential reading. Segment two describes the course of the Mississippi from its source to the delta. The succession of images represents a movement through space (the geographical outlines of which have just appeared on the map of segment one). The sense of consecutiveness is weak, and yet the shots have a causal-chronological sequence: water runs across the earth, becomes rivulets, feeds streams, which swell the river at the delta. If we consider the relationship of the motifs as spatial, it is the representation of a geographical space, quite different from the spatial coexistence denoted by the descriptive syntagma in the fiction film.

The bracket syntagma is not always clearly distinguishable from narrative types. Segment seven, for example, alludes, through a repetitive series of motifs, to the gradual deforestation of the northeastern United States: images of thickly forested land, followed by images of trees being felled, carried by log runs and rivers to their destination—the sawmill. The ordering of the subsegmental units is achronological, each one being composed of shots that accumulate examples of a single motif with no reference to spatial or temporal continuity. The succession of these subsegmental units, however, does trace in abstract fashion a distinct chronology, which is that of the phases of lumber production.

Certain bracket syntagmas are not clearly distinguishable from descriptive syntagmas: they evoke a sense of simultaneity between motifs and a certain spatial coherence. Segment fifteen, for example, represents the devastation caused by a flood on the Mississippi. The succession of images is heterogeneous, i.e., not ordered according to specific relationships in time or space: the images show inundated farms, rescue boats, food lines, tent cities, and so forth. Yet the relationship between the shots is not conceptual; it is based on a reference to a specific space-time. The shots represent a moment—these are images of a particular flood—and are linked by the spatial coexistence that integrates samples of an almost geographical space.

Certain syntagmas, whose boundaries and textual unity are clearly indicated, contain concatenations of images ordered according to more than one principle. The apparent unity of these structurally heterogeneous syntagmas contradicts one criterion for determining demarcation: the change in cinematic treatment cannot be considered, in these cases, as sufficient to constitute a syntagmatic break. Segment four, for example, begins with an alternation in series between shots of work in the fields and shots of river boats on the Mississippi. The initial syntagmatic order does not correspond to the classic alternate type (neither series displays a relationship of consecutiveness between its shots, and the series are not related to each other chronologically); nor is the alternation based on the symbolic opposition characteristic of the parallel syntagma. Yet the alternation is unmistakable in the segments' first ten shots. The eleventh provides the temporal-causal relationship that apparently motivates the alternation: workers load the products of the field onto a river boat. This shot, which at first appears to be just another in the series of alternating images, inaugurates a distinct subsegmental ordering in the descriptive mode: eleven shots that evoke the various aspects of the loading of the boat with no reference to their consecutiveness. The last four shots of the segment, however, mark out the line of a minor narrative progression, the steamship's departure: the ship's whistle, smaller craft on the river, the churning water behind the paddle wheel.

As these examples begin to show, the identification of both narrative and nonnarrative syntagmas in a text that is not governed by the narrative economy of the fiction film is often problematic. Detached and encapsulated, the small units lose their sense of narrative purpose. The narrative syntagmas, which quite often close in upon themselves, are not linked in a linear series, and consequently the bracket and descriptive syntagmas cannot be distinguished by the manner in which they interrupt the temporal consecutiveness of the text. Identification must often be made largely without reference to the surrounding text, according to the perceived modality of a syntagma's ordering. It is generally the case that the more the conceptual ordering of a text tends to dominate the spatio-temporal references, the more all syntagmas tend to be read as conceptual. In the case of the narrative syntagma, the viewer tends to read consecutiveness as frequentative, and in the case of nonnarrative syntagmas chooses the conceptual reading over the spatial. The end term of the tendency toward syntagmatic ambiguity is the (necessarily partial) decomposition of the syntagmatic unit. This lack of order can be seen in certain "insufficiencies" of the image track: the tendency we have noted in many films toward the fragmentary representation of events on the visual track (the "elliptical" ordinary sequence) or the many examples of massive, undemarcated syntagmatic units, in particular, bracket syntagmas.

(6) *The tendency toward the ambiguity of types manifests itself structurally as an ambiguity of function: the classification of a given syntagma (as narrative or nonnarrative) does not necessarily determine that segment's function at the level of the scenario.*

There is, in effect, a structural expectation—determined by the historical production of forms—that the modal character of a large syntagmatic unit will decide its role in the larger units of the scenario, just as the development of the scenario conditions the choice of syntagmatic types. Narrative sequences align themselves in a chain of actions and events that constitute the story line. The descriptive syntagma dissipates that linearity by considering ob-

65

jects in their spatiality. The bracket syntagma is nonnarrative, "a kind of filmic equivalent of conceptualization." And so forth. We anticipate that each syntagmatic type will exert its influence on the filmic flux; more precisely, that the succession of syntagmatic types will constitute its ebb and flow.

And yet, analysis demonstrates that this meshing of structures, which is absolutely essential to the functioning of the fiction film, does not always occur in documentaries. We have already seen in *The City* and *The River,* the most "conceptual" films of the group, that narrative syntagmas can be subordinated to the discursive logic of these texts. We also described in *The River* apparently anomalous syntagmatic units that are constructed according to more than one principle of ordering. Other examples are to be found in *Land Without Bread, Le Sang des bêtes,* and *Rien que les heures.* For the purpose of demonstration, let's examine a film that is to a large extent narrative at the level of the scenario.

If much of the first section of *Fall of the Romanov Dynasty* prepares us with a class analysis of the causes of social upheaval (segments one through thirty), the central sections of the film, unequivocably narrative, evoke the events of world war and the February Revolution (segments thirty-one through eighty-nine). A close examination of the text, however, reveals profound ambiguities—ambiguities that concern, in particular, the primary division in Metz's General Table of the Large Syntagmatic between achronological and chronological syntagmas. In some cases, it is difficult to establish the character of a given syntagma because the relationship between the shots or subsegmental units (consecutive, simultaneous, symbolic, conceptual?) is ambiguous, or because the syntagma is too fragmentary to allow a clear determination.

However, what specifically concerns me here is that the defining feature by which an achronological ordering is distinguished in the fiction film—the lack of any precise "temporal relationship between the facts presented in the different images"—does not always, in the case of *Fall of the Romanov Dynasty,* determine the way nonnarrative syntagmatic units function at the level of the scenario. Analysis in fact reveals that syntagmas whose ordering is nonnarrative are capable of operating as narrative units in the linear progression of the film. A large proportion of segments I have identified as bracket syntagmas because of their internal structure are an integral part of the narration of historical events. As units, these syntagmas are nonnarrative in structure: the shots or subsegmental units lack the signs of linear chronological development. Rather, they are perceived as vaguely simultaneous—as representing events that coincide in a synoptic historical time. Despite this sense of simultaneity, they differ from the descriptive syntagmas in the following ways. First, the motifs of the image do not have a relationship of spatial coexistence (spatial disparity is rather the case). Second, the syntagmas clearly represent events crucial to recounting the story of revolution in a distinctly narrative mode: the international mobilization of soldiers for war, war in the air and at sea, defection at the front, and so forth. These bracket syntagmas share features of the type: 1) the motifs presented in the image lack precise temporal relationships; 2) they are allusive, i.e., none of the shots or subsegmental units is treated with "full syntagmatic breadth"; 3) they are "samples of a same order of reality," revealing a presumed kinship within a category of facts. However, these syntagmas are not purely "conceptual"; rather, they are properly diegetic and represent, in the manner of a synecdoche, an abstract historical space-time. This "narrative" bracket syntagma shows an affinity, by certain features, with the alternate syntagma: the relationship within a series (when the units are not single shots) is one of consecutiveness; the relationship between the series is one of simultaneity. It lacks, however, the alternating structure and therefore the narrative continuity of the alternate syntagma.

Let's describe a typical occurrence of this type. Segment thirty-seven, whose intertitle "THE NATIONS ARE SET IN MOTION" clarifies the relationship between the subsegmental units, is composed of sixteen shots divided into approximately eight subsegmental units (there is considerable ambiguity even at this level). The syntagma represents the international mobilization of forces in preparation for war. The lack of spatial coherence and narrative linearity is apparent: parades of soldiers in different national uniforms, departures of trains in different countries, Mussulmen on horseback, members of the Foreign Legion, and so forth. The subsegmental units are clearly allusive ("brief scenes" that have the potential for narrative expansion). The syntagma, taken as a whole, represents by a series of "actions" viewed as simultaneous a particular historical moment. The analysis of the progression of the film's scenario shows that functionally this syntagma has a narrative, not a conceptual character. Syntagma thirty-seven stands in a linear relationship to syntagma thirty-eight, a bracket syntagma that represents, with the same discontinuity in space and lack of temporal precision, the movement of the mobilized troops into their positions in the field. Syntagmas thirty-seven and thirty-eight are analogous in their narrative function to syntagma forty, which I have classed as an ordinary sequence. This syntagma is composed

67

of thirty-nine shots grouped into small units of narrative exposition, and, like syntagmas thirty-seven and thirty-eight, it is a narrative condensation representing events in the battlefields of the war. But in this case the lack of apparent discontinuity—the presumed coherence in time and space of the succession of images, which is not specifically contradicted in the motifs or by punctuation—permits the spectator to read the syntagma as a single linear progression.

This analysis applies equally to the descriptive syntagma, whose internal ordering does not necessarily determine how it will function at the level of the scenario. A number of the descriptive syntagmas, despite the clearly descriptive character of their ordering (lack of consecutiveness, apparent spatial coexistence), do not interrupt the film's forward movement and constitute rather part of the chronology of events. Segment fifty-three, for example, representing women working in a factory, is composed of three shots that lack any sense of consecutiveness and appear to evoke the integral space of a single shop floor. On the level of the film's narrative progression, this syntagma represents an event, specifically established by the intertitle: "THE GOVERNMENT REPLACED THE MOBILIZED WORKERS FROM THE WAR PLANT WITH WOMEN."

As a tool for analysis, the Large Syntagmatic, this superior code of sequence and order, has allowed us to examine the narrativity of films that have traditionally been classed as nonfiction. What we have discovered is that documentary is ambivalent toward narrative. On the one hand, all the films in this corpus are governed by narrative ordering at one level or another of the text. On the other hand, documentary films necessarily mark out their distance from the sequential structures of the classic fiction film. The displacement of narrative syntagmatic types and the ambiguity of types and their functions are signs of a general and complex shifting among codes, both cinematic and extracinematic. As this analysis begins to suggest, each documentary text sets up its provisionary equilibrium among the codes: the "lacks" that appear in the sequential ordering of the films at the level of the image track are necessarily compensated by the fullness of other codes. Codes which are, it is reasonable to assume, quite exceptional in the fiction film, since they represent another discursive agency. This agency is most obviously manifested in the commentary and in an articulation between language and image which is not the same as that of the fiction film. However, the documentary is not simply, as one traditional definition would have it, a "film with a commentary." Each documentary has its textual strategy, what we will call its rhetoric.

3

A Figurative Strategy: *Listen to Britain*

Problematic of the Documentary Text

What can be read in the complex textuality of the documentary film? Are there signs in documentary texts of their place in the "border regions" of the dominant institution, the feature film? Does the documentary film both embrace and resist the signifying structures that the fiction film has set in place? If so, how does documentary exhibit the signs of this textual ambivalence—the affirmation inseparable from its negation—that it expresses for fiction?

As syntagmatic analysis already suggests, documentary is a mixed form, a discourse that admits a plurality of voices; its most striking feature is its textual heterogeneity. We can in fact read in most of the films produced in the classic period (roughly 1935 to 1955) the signs of a historical lag: faced with the technological and aesthetic revolution caused by the fiction film's conversion to sound, documentary remains unwilling and unable to become a talking cinema in the true (synchronous) sense. It is a crucial fact that weighs heavily on the formal structure of documentary films. Viewing the great documentaries of the late thirties, one is often struck by the films' eclecticism: a kind of mutism that recalls the silent period; archaic remnants of rhythmic and intellectual *montage* rub shoulders with "naturalist" editing and the sound film's evocation of the full diegetic space. For technical, economic, and, perhaps most importantly, ideological reasons, documentary resists the evolution of cinematic "language" in this period, thus marking out its textual difference from fiction.

Documentary's complex textuality poses crucial questions of exegesis. What is the part of fiction in documentary and what belongs to other discursive agencies? How does each documentary text use narrative and yet mark out its distance from the fiction film? How can we describe the textual system in films that are intra- and intertextually heterogeneous?

I'll begin with a simple reformulation of the basic problem: the message of the documentary is rarely enclosed within the film's narrative project. Documentaries do more than simply tell stories, even stories of a particular kind. For the analyst, describing the narrative structure in documentary films does not account for the global structure of the text. How could it, since even a cursory examination of the films we are considering shows that narrative in documentary is often both dispersed and fragmented? Even as viewers we are aware of quite perceptible shifts in register—even breaches at the most radical points—which mark the limit of narrative and the beginning of something else, some other discursive form. We reach a point in the study of documentary when narrative analysis stops short because it can no longer account adequately for what is happening within the text.

And yet we cannot say that documentary demands a separate semiotics, because we are faced with the simple fact that documentaries are full of narratives and that in telling their stories these texts quite "naturally" call on the signifying structures that the fiction film created for its own uses. In fact we often discover within documentary texts the realization of the fiction film's "plenitude" of expression, the operation of cinema's well-oiled machinery of representation.

Let's suppose, then, that in documentary there is a supplement of meaning: something more to be said, or something to be said more specifically, which can only be said by disrupting in one way or another the coherent narrative signified of the classic fiction film. This something more comes, by definition, from outside the diegesis. It discloses a second symbolic position, another agency at work, whose most obvious manifestation is the commentary. Despite its integration into the filmic system, the commentary remains resolutely extracinematographic: a voice from elsewhere—from whatever area of recognized expertise—which the films "uses" without reworking. A nearly universal aspect of documentary practice before the early sixties, the commentary remains a snare. It always risks overturning its delicate integration into the textual system; it is capable of asserting its superior semantic power, its capacity to order and define. Its self-sufficiency splits the apparent relations of complementarity which the fiction film is at pains to construct between the signifying elements. Its presence is then both necessary and in excess: nothing is more apparent than the documentary's modal ambivalence.

70

Thus the documentary message demands a supplement which must be added to the "plenitude" of representation, the coherent diegetic whole, the specific organization of the image and sound tracks that the classic fiction film sets in place. The supplement is external: it comes from outside "cinematic" discourse in order to complete it. It works against two different types of deficiency within the text: 1) the incapacity of the codes of narrative cinema alone to produce the documentary message, and therefore the necessity for an addition of meaning; 2) the documentary's incapacity to produce the seamless discourse of the fiction film, and therefore the necessity to supply a supplement to fill the gaps in the text. In the second case, the supplement is compensatory; it makes up for "absent" signs. It links, articulates, and sutures. In the first case, the supplement carries documentary's discursive message; exceeding the boundaries of narrative, it conceptualizes, contextualizes, and historicizes. One function of the supplement works to reestablish the endangered coherence of the text. The other works to incorporate, in the most material sense, extrinsic elements that originate elsewhere in other social discourses.

I am suggesting, then, that documentary is a mixed discursive form, i.e., that it seeks to integrate (to make a whole of) distinct fields of expression, to hold them in suspension. On the most general level, documentary disturbs the broad and ancient division between *mimesis* and the rest of literary production. As Gérard Genette recalls in "Boundaries of Narrative," *mimesis* consists in "an imitation by a narrative of scenic representation of a real or a fictional action exterior to the person and utterance of the poet."[1] The rest belongs to the vast discursive realm of direct expression and includes lyric poetry as well as scientific, philosophical, and moral texts of all kinds. As Genette suggests, the second, "natural" mode is open to all forms: a scientific text, for example, can incorporate elements of a narrative without compromising in the least its scientificity. Narrative, on the other hand, is defined by exclusions and restrictions; by what it cannot permit without ceasing to be itself. Thus, as Genette points out, there is a fundamental lack of symmetry: narrative easily becomes a part of discourse; discourse within narrative remains a foreign body, "a sort of cyst, easily recognized and localized": "Discourse can 'narrate' without ceasing to be discourse. Narrative can't 'discourse' without betraying itself."[2]

I hasten to add, however, that cinema is not literature and that within cinema a very different balance of forces exists. In literature an equal division of the field can be drawn between mimetic and

71

discursive, an "equal" body of works with distinct forms can be attributed to each. In cinema, such a distribution, such an equality, is not possible for historical and semiological reasons that have been delineated from the beginning of this study. To be discursive means to come from outside the dominant forms of cinema. Cinema can not be, in the first instance, didactic, philosophical, scientific, or propagandistic without disrupting the signifying practices set in place by the historical development of the fiction film. Analysis of the operation of the documentary text begins by describing this disruption.

A second opposition (the first in Genette's text) concerns the classic distinction between narrative and dramatic poetry as expounded in Plato's *Republic* and Aristotle's *Poetics*. The distinction is founded on a fundamental difference in modes of imitation. In dramatic poetry, representation is imitative in a very precise sense: according to the conventions of scenic representation, gestures and acts of speech appear to belong to characters rather than to the author. In narrative poetry, the acts of characters are described in voice of the narrator and the speech of characters is consigned to "indirect" discourse. In Plato's classification there is a mixed mode that allows for the possibility that within narrative characters can claim their own voices and speak directly, as in theater. The shifts in the mode of representation occur persistently in narrative literature—the enunciative to-and-fro between narrator and protagonist is accomplished with ease and seems to pass largely unnoticed by the reader. In the mixed narrative, representation—of place, action, and character—and the presentation of speech are homogeneously verbal. The voice of the narrator may give way to the speech of characters without any rupture, precisely because of the homogeneity of the signifier.

The boundaries between imitation and narrative in cinema are much more marked. In the fiction film, the image track with the support of diegetic sound—dialogue, noise, music—is quite able to represent setting, character, and event without the apparent intervention of an enunciating voice. Consequently, when such a voice of narration emerges, it exhibits its extradiegetic character, asserting its verbal power over the production of a diegesis. The narrative voice-over in cinema is more radically extradiegetic than the narrative voice in literature because it signals not simply a change in register between modes of representation, but a change in the signifying material itself. On the imitative plane, all elements are by definition diegetic and constitute a simulacrum of reality, a "direct" representation of phenomena that exist apparently outside of language. On the narrative plane, all elements are extradiegetic and are "mediated" and "transposed" in language.

We know that the codes of the classic fiction film work to integrate the heterogeneous filmic signifier and to efface the marks of a narrative presence. In documentary, however, shifts in modes of imitation from one dominant register to another are commonplace and fall with an emphasis that would be inadmissable in the fiction film. Furthermore, in documentary's classic period, the opposition diegetic-extradiegetic was reinforced by a phenomenological division: the imitative plane (i.e., everything that belongs to the image, including sound) is the domain of acts; the narrative-discursive plane is the domain of the word. The image is mute, and dialogue, in the sense given to it in the fiction film, is exceedingly rare.

Thus the commentary—in its narrative and discursive functions—is the most conspicuous example of supplementation in the documentary film. Indeed, the most apparent sites of shifting occur at the points of rupture where one agency asserts itself over the other. However, the play of supplement and compensation is complex and open to permutation. It is in fact this play in its specific arrangements that constitutes a documentary film's textual system: each text constructs its own system of checks and balances, traces out its specific *ligne de partage* between discursive agencies.

As Christian Metz points out in *Language and Cinema,* the filmic system is not a passive result of a combination of codes; the filmic system is itself an agency:

> What we are considering now are not the partial systems *integrated* by the film, but the activity of *integration* (or of disintegration)—the process of composition or "writing"—by which the film, relying on all of these codes, modifes them, combines them, plays them one against the other, eventually arriving at its own individual system, its ultimate (or first?) principle of unification and intelligibility.[3]

The textual agency plays on the codes, since it evokes them; it also suppresses them as codes in the interest of constructing its own system. The textual system can be described as a "passage from one code to another," the activity that works both with and against the codes:

> The system of the text is the process which *displaces* codes, deforming each of them by the presence of the others, contaminating some by means of others, meanwhile replacing one by another, and finally—as a temporarily "arrested" result of this general displacement—*placing* each code in a particular position in regard to the overall structure, a

displacement which thus finishes by a positioning which is itself destined to be displaced by another text.[4]

When Metz speaks of the filmic system as displacement, he is referring to a general principle of psychological economy:

> Displacement, in the basic sense of the term, is the most general principle of all psychical activity, the expression of the energetic and economic hypothesis which lies at the heart of analytic thinking. It is the ability to *move across* (= to "displace energy", as Freud says) to pass from one idea to another, from one image to another, from one act to another.[5]

In cinema we are talking about the displacement of "limited and controlled quantities of energy." The filmic text is a production of the waking state and is therefore subjected to a logic: to the dictates of coherence and order that define secondary process. Textual energy is bound; its discharge is circumscribed by the specific considerations of intelligibility, i.e., the filmic codes whose paradigms control, in their fleeting, historical way, what can be said at any given moment on the syntagmatic chain. Thus, if each filmic system is unique in the way it mobilizes the codes, it also obeys constraints that cinema has made part of its institution: a particular kind of text must be produced, which is delivered under specific conditions and reserves a special place for the spectator. A certain arrangement of the signifier is necessary to maintain the plenitude of the diegesis: a careful integration of sound and image, a grafting of materials constantly readjusted and realigned but always giving out onto a homogeneous narrative signified—the story for which all else is sacrificed.

From the beginning of this study the working hypothesis has been that documentary shares with the classic narrative film many of the latter's basic signifying operations. As analysis has confirmed, the Large Syntagmatic Code effectively describes textual organization of many documentary films at that level of the image track. It is beyond the scope of this study to undertake an exhaustive inquiry into the working of all the codes the documentary text mobilizes. I propose, rather, to continue this investigation of the classic documentary through the analysis of a single film, wagering, somewhat paradoxically, that more can be discovered about documentary in general by a close reading of one film than by a necessarily more static and limited description undertaken from the point of view of the codes.

I will begin then with a single textual system and an analysis that takes as its object the displacement of the codes which constitute that system. My concern is of course much larger. I am looking for textual operations, combinations that reveal, below or beyond the surface of the text, certain laws of their functioning. I want to locate the point at which I can begin to abstract a problematic of the documentary text. The difference I am looking for, therefore, is not simply that which distinguishes between the textual systems of films—the irreducible difference between films that belong nonetheless to the same clearly delineated group. I want to know what differences exist between the films that belong to the classic narrative cinema (from 1935 to 1955) and those that belong to the classic documentary cinema, which I have defined (not arbitrarily, I believe) as those films produced especially in Britain, the United States, and Canada during roughly the same period.

The textual system is, as Metz remarks, "the agency which *displaces* the codes, deforming each of them by the presence of the others." The documentary text, like all textual systems, is at once constructive and destructive: it uses the codes, constructs itself upon them, and destroys them in an active work of restructuration. So in this ambivalence, this "double and unique movement," the codes are simultaneously mobilized and suppressed. Nothing could better characterize textual system in documentary. But there is something more in this constant work of integration-disintegration, something that goes beyond narrative (although it constantly retreats). Something that jeopardizes the univocal text and makes it into a divided game.

As semiological study has confirmed, a text produces meaning by selecting within paradigms of choices produced by that historically specific reworking called the moment of the code. Like all discourse, documentary does not draw upon a static set of formal possibilities. Rather, quite pragmatically, documentary can only choose what has in a sense already been chosen: those figures and structures whose return and repetition in filmic texts of a given period and a given society have determined their readability. The work of the cinematic institution is this social circulation of texts. Of course there are documentary films that choose to resemble the fiction film in the pattern of their codes; textual systems in these films come close to reproducing the seamless body of narrative diegesis. However, such films often incite—and not just recently— certain accusations in critical discourse: they are indicted for *mise en scène,* reconstitution, manipulation, fictionalization. Unlike these stigmatized texts, the classic documentary constructs a system of textual rifts—rifts that are visible precisely because they are measured against the "ideal" (absent) text of the classic narrative film. The fact that the documentary text produces itself paradoxically within and against the codes of the fiction film is the clearest sign of the dominance of that cinematic institution.

In the weaving of each documentary text (to use Barthes's metaphor), we hear "off-stage voices," emanating from a virtual space, a "mirage of structures": the filmic codes that documentary adopts and organizes. Simultaneously, we hear other voices speaking from a different space—this time a clearly marked space of enunciation—voices that pull at the fabric of the text. Rifts in the stereographic space of the text appear at the most crucial (and weakest) jointures of the filmic signifier. They reopen the question of the hierarchy of the signifying materials: the primacy of the moving image and the ancillary status of the codes of sound, in particular the potentially powerful codes of spoken and written language. The documentary text tends to transgress the boundaries that guarantee the univocal character of the fiction film. It jeopardizes the carefully articulated organization of the filmic signifier and consequently the "transparent" narrative signified, the story it exists to produce. Elements of the sound track can break their ancillary relation to the image in order to tell a story of their own. From being single and homogeneous, the diegesis can become (always episodically) plural and heterogeneous within the well-defended limits of textual unity.

In documentary, plurality is also produced by breaks in another syntagmatic chain—temporal sequence, the film's chronology. In "Vraisemblance et motivation," Gérard Genette distinguishes between the apparent and the functional logic of narrative. The elements of narrative discourse move in a causal sequence, each successive event seeming to take root in those that precede it. According to Genette, this motivated sequence masks the functionality of narrative, which always moves backward along the chronological chain, justifying the means by the end:

> These *backward* determinations constitute precisely what we call the arbitrary of narrative, that is, not at all its indetermination, but determination of the means by the ends, and, to put it more bluntly, *of the causes by the effects*. It is this paradoxical logic of fiction which obliges us to define each element, each unit of the narrative by its functional character, that is, among others, by its correlation with another unit, and to account for the first (in order of narrative temporality) by the second, and so forth.[6]

The documentary text rarely exhibits this functional economy characteristic of the fiction film (its presence is more pronounced by definition in films that conform more closely to the narrative model). Motivation, the causal alibi that seems to emerge effortlessly from the narrative telling, is precisely what is lacking at certain jointures of the text: the segmental units do not call each other into being in an inexorable logic of time. Rather, segments tend toward closure, the short-circuiting of their narrative potential. They also call for a supplement: the textual energy for their binding must come from outside, in the form of the intervention of another voice.

Thus documentary departs in a partial and episodic manner from the kind of referential illusion, the constructed universe of the story, which the fiction film exists to produce. When documentary suspends the great principle of narrative film—the spatial and temporal articulations that constitute its prevailing structures—it must bridge these gaps in the text. Spoken or written language frequently fulfills this discursive function, but documentarists have often derided as uncinematographic films that rely on prolix commentaries. Humphrey Jennings, in particular in *Listen to Britain* (1942), takes pride in the absence of any sort of mediating language of this kind. We can anticipate, then, in this "poetic" film the existence of other structures of mediation that rely on figurative, not referential relationships. Indeed, it seems that documentary retains an arsenal of "small-scale" rhetorical figures that assert themselves against the transparent logic of the classic fiction film. Against is, of course, too strong a word. There exists a kind of rhetorical play in documentary: a figurative movement, a constant circulation that dislocates and reestablishes the nodal point of the text, its point of integration and textual unity.

In the following transcriptions, notations for the soundtrack will indicate a sound's source (on or off screen), its apparent distance (close, medium, or long sound take), and, where relevant, its synchronous or asynchronous relation to the image.

IMAGE	SOUND
Title (fade-in) The barrel of an antiaircraft cannon crosses the frame from lower left to upper right; a violin in upper frame, its neck crossing the cannon barrel. In the lower center frame: the RCA sound insignia. The title, then the credits succeed each other in dissolve.	Sounds of a crowd in movement: voices, shouts, footsteps, a dog barking. A crescendo of noise rises to meet the level of a bugle tune that sounds from the beginning of the shot. Marching drums recede, as does the noise of the crowd (off, nonsimultaneous).

Title

The Emblematic and the Real

There is the flatness of the graphic plane, a two-dimensional space on which an emblem is traced: "a drawing or picture expressing a moral fable or allegory [*Oxford English Dictionary*]."[7] There are in fact two emblems: The cannon, which stands for the military, the British resolve in war, and for courage; and the violin, which stands for domesticity, inner life, sentiment, heart. The two representations are also obviously poles of an antithesis: irreducible opposites whose intersection on this plane specifies the symbolic matrix of the film. The first product of their union is already present: the two bars of a bugle tune. It is an expansion, a measure of time. It is also a fragment: it is cut like the shots that follow from the full score, ideal and absent. The film will produce a field within which these emblematic figures can emerge and disappear in a constant exchange between the symbolic and the real. The film has the repetitive structure of theme and variation: variation being that newness within which we recognize the return of the same. The emblem is pure statement; the film, the living manifestations of this figure of antithesis, is embodied in the "real."

Both emblems are also producers of sound, as the exhortation of the title and the prominence of the RCA insignia seems to underscore. Paradoxically, the soundtrack in no way attempts to support or animate the title image. Rather, it juxtaposes against the graphic flatness of the titles an autonomous three-dimensional sound field that possesses the attributes the image lacks. The sound is struc-

78

tured in planes; it has depth of field; its volumes and timbres shift and change; it evokes movement in space and time; it possesses narrative character. This juxtaposition suggests the double intent of the film: to present the real and to evoke the figure. This discourse intends to bring together, to mingle the terms of the mythical opposition that sets the lived against the intelligible (Roland Barthes). The film's strategy is to find (to frame) the figurative within the real; to present the figurative as real.

Listen to Britain. The title is programmatic, even polemical. It proposes to rid the text of an encumbrance, the spoken commentary, and to permit direct access to the phenomena of the world of reference. The soundtrack here serves as a foretaste that promises to place the spectator in his accustomed relation to sound (and image) in cinema without the alienating mediation of the word. The title signals the film's rejection of a technique—the linguistic message—for anchoring what Barthes calls the "floating chain" of the signified: "The [linguistic] text directs the reader through the signifieds of the image, causing him to avoid some and receive others; by means of an often subtle *dispatching*, it remote-controls him towards a meaning chosen in advance."[8] The propaganda film depends on the repressive function of the text—the elimination of ambiguity at all cost. In *Listen to Britain*, Humphrey Jennings's strategy appears to be to relinquish control and to allow his film to run the risk of ambiguity. It is easy to understand the reaction this propaganda film provoked among certain elements of the documentary movement. Edgar Anstey referred to the film in *The Spectator* as "the rarest piece of fiddling since the days of Nero."[9]

IMAGE   SOUND
Descriptive syntagma:

Shot 1

1
Upper branches of trees blow in   Wind in the trees (on) blends
the wind.   with the noise of passing
                                     airplanes (off, established
                                     retrospectively).

Shot 2

2
Cornstalks blow in the wind.   Wind (on); crescendo of
                                     airplane noise.

| IMAGE | SOUND |

Shot 3

3
Two spitfires seen against the sky.

Crescendo of airplane noise (on).

Shot 4

4
Wheatstalks blow in the wind.

Decrescendo of airplane (off) allows reemergence of the noise of wind (on).

Shot 5

5

Two women and an older man   Decrescendo of airplane noise
working in a field look up, then   (off); noise of the wind (on).
return to work.

Shot 6

6

Two sky-watchers look upward   Noise of spitfires (off).
through binoculars.

IMAGE	SOUND

Shot 7

7
The two men (as in shot 6)   Noise of spitfires (off).
observe the sky from a bunker.

Shot 8

8
Four spitfires seen against the   Noise of airplanes (on).
sky.

IMAGE	SOUND

Shot 9

9
The observers' bunker in the middle of a field; a harvester at work (axis match).

The noise of spitfires is more distant (off) and yields to the noise of the harvester (on).

Shot 10

10
The harvester.

Noise of the harvester (in close-up).

Shot 11

11
Spitfires against the sky.

Noise of spitfires (off, in long shot). Noise of the harvester (decrescendo). Beep of radio signal begins over end of shot (off, asynchronous).

Shot 12

12
A house stands behind a white fence; a lamp glimmers in a window.

Noise of spitfires (off, in long shot). Beep of radio signal (off, in close-up, synchronous?).

13

| A window of the house (12) in near darkness with the lighted lamp. A man draws the curtains. | —This is the BBC home and forces news, and this is . . . (in close-up). Noise of spitfires (off, in long shot). |

Montage and Metaphor

Textuality in *Listen to Britain* is structurally ambivalent: the text embodies two distinct intentionalities and allows two readings. One is consistently dominant, let us say manifest, because it is the reading that orders the text and performs its concatenations. The other is latent: it lingers at the edge of awareness, never really forgotten and prepared to reemerge at a sign from the text. The first reading is diegetic. It is the dominant reading in that it asserts itself given the slimmest basis in the text. The spectator tries the narrative reading first. He or she knows that in cinema contiguity on the chain of images "normally" refers to contiguity in space and time. The syntagma has a metonymical force; narrative enjoys a kind of natural imperative. Each fragment should take its place in a chain whose logic is the simple measure of proximity: the repertoire of sequential orderings that Noel Burch describes as temporal and spatial articulation. The other reading is adiegetic. We define it first in its negativity: it exists insofar as it dispels the referential illusion. It breaks apart the temporal-spatial narrative signified in order to hold the pieces in another configuration. It is a supplemental reading in that it disrupts a (diegetic) order that is perceived as whole and sufficient and whose pathways are engrained by so many readings in the consciousness of the reader. We could call this reading discursive because it involves the recognition of certain textual operations; the text has marks of enunciation—the emphatic signs—which inform the reader of a discursive presence.

I have identified this segment as a descriptive syntagma, which, as Christian Metz indicates in his analysis of the Large Syntagmatic Category, is ordered according to a principle of spatial coexistence. The film gives us to understand through specific textual signs that the places represented in shots 1–13 are in a relationship of spatial proximity to each other and stand for a coherent referential space. We could describe this space as a segment of the trajectories of the spitfires, whose uninterrupted presence on the noise track is a sign of spatial continuity. There are, of course, other signs. We can point for example to the pattern of alternation that links the subjects (the workers in the orchard in shot 5, the sky-watchers in shots 6, 7, 9) with the object of their vision (the spitfires in shots 3, 8, 11). It is this classic technique of point of view that works to bind the fragmentary shots into a spatial continuity. We could add the other techniques of *montage* that operate here: matching screen direction (3, 8, 11), matching of positions (6, 7, 9), and so forth—the firmly established resources of the editor's craft.

We recognize however that the production of the diegesis does not proceed with the apparent self-evidence we find in the classic fiction film. It is manifestly a work; it overcomes obstacles. It weaves together a scene whose elements, in another reading, are intended to take positions in a quite separate play of difference and resolution. There is a rhetorical structuration that is superimposed upon but stands behind the diegetic text. It is a work of textual condensation that is always on the point of divergence. The rhetorical and diegetic move along the same pathways, but at the critical moment of concatenation they bind the text in quite different ways.

The rhetorical structuration of the segment proceeds by the division—and redivision—of syntagmatic elements into oppositional couples. The first antithesis introduces a cosmography, a division into spheres that stands as the initiatory principle of difference: earth and sky. The second: an opposition in a paradigm of social activity: civilian and military. Thus, we can see a first pattern of alternation that groups the sequence of shots in order to establish a geometry of space: 1, 2 / 3 / 4, 5, 6, 7 / 8 / 9, 10 / 11 / 12, 13. A second alternation cuts across the first to establish a second symmetrical division into opposing elements, spheres of social productivity: 3/ 5 / 6, 7, 8, 9 / 9, 10 / 11.

The film does not however simply present the oppositional couples; it continually synthesizes them. The text works tirelessly at its taxonomies: it compares and contrasts, establishes distance and proximity, in order to demonstrate the (partial) identity of the terms. If it presents the cosmic distinction between earth and sky, or the social distinction between military and domestic labor, it does so in order to bring them together and efface their lines of demarcation. This is the film's symbolic project: the British nation is at once diverse and unified. It is divided into spheres of activity, into social classes, into town and country, into sexual roles; yet it has the organic integrity of a body and the functional harmony of its parts. Like the conjoining of earth and sky, the British nation is a cosmic organism. The film's strategy is to project the signifiers of difference onto each other in order to produce an identification in which one category of facts is perceived as assimilable to another.

The film's diegesis is ultimately subordinate to the symbolic activity: it exists as a field within which the identificatory process takes place. With its pragmatic logic of time and space and its sequential progression, it naturalizes the laying out of the terms of antithesis. It is also the innocent place of synthesis: the terms are bound together because they are projected into the same space. Shot 9, for example, is a clear point of symbolic articulation within the sequence. The alternation (diegesis), which is also a juxtaposition (rhetoric), gives way to the synthetic shot: an axis match of shot 7, it reveals in deep focus the unexpected presence of the sky-watchers' bunker in a wheat field that a mechanical harvester is in the process of working.

Here the terms of the figure (the antithetical *comparanda*, the activities of peace and war) share quite literally the ground (the *tertium comparationis*). Paradoxically, the "realism" of the shot points up its underlying figurative character: we are dealing with a metonomy. But let's be clear in distinguishing terms here. *Montage* in this sequence, whether between shots or between planes of the image, is diegetic in that it links elements in their spatial-temporal unfolding (as it does elsewhere in cinema). *Montage* is metonymical only insofar as the narrative unfolding it produces permits a refolding of the text: a rereading that articulates the terms of the metonymic figure. Narrative editing is not, as such, a metonymic act. It does produce the base (the relation of proximity) against which the figure cuts its form. Narrative *montage* and figurative *montage* are distinct articulations, even though, as can be demonstrated in this segment, they often coincide.

To sum up, we have noted thus far the following configurations: 1) diegesis: the concatenations of the descriptive syntagma establish the coexistence of all elements in a spatial field (the first principle of unity); 2) antithesis: provokes a redivision of that field into antagonistic elements; 3) metonymy: reproduces the unity of the sequence on a figurative level through contiguity, that is, "direct contact" between the terms of antithesis. This contact produces yet another figure: paradoxism, the transgression of the bar that separates the antithetical terms.[10] And yet, as I have attempted to make clear, the semantic relationship that the text seeks to produce between the different "objects" bound in the figurative operation is

88

one of analogy: the terms of the antithesis, which make an outward display of difference, are linked by a common essence. That is, across the metonymic network that establishes a spatial transfer between terms, a metaphoric chain is cut—the final articulation in this symbolic exchange.

At this point I need to clarify how metaphoric operation will be understood for purposes of the analysis of this film. In *Listen to Britain* we are dealing with iconic metaphors: there are, almost literally, no words in the film. As a long critical discussion among scholars has made clear, rhetorical categories, which are almost all defined in relation to language, cannot be applied to figurative operations in cinema without considerable caution. Christian Metz has described the pitfalls of such an application in his discussion of "The Problem of the Word."[11] As classic rhetoric conceived it, metaphor refers to a "symbolic 'work' of referential resemblance" that results in "a compression, a concentration . . . within a single word (a word actually pronounced or written), that is to say when the vehicle, but not the tenor, was expressed in the sentence (for instance, 'that pig' for 'that repulsive person')."[12] Thus, in the linguistic metaphor, a relationship (resemblance) is established between the elements of two signifieds, according to the classic schema (see the accompanying figure).

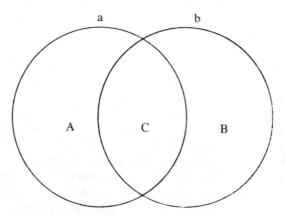

A = a group of traits belonging to signified a
B = a group of traits belonging to signified b
C = a zone of intersection, traits held in common by a and b

(See Group μ "La Chafetière est sur la table," *Communication et langages* 26 (1976): 44 and *A General Rhetoric* (Baltimore: The Johns Hopkins University Press 1981), 108-9.

The metaphoric operation takes place within the zone of intersection—"an encounter between like and like"—and leads in the direction of a substitution. It may end in a trope, rhetoric's consummated figure: signifier a has taken charge of the signified of b, for which it may substitute in discourse.

Can the figures that analysis discovers in *Listen to Britain* be properly called metaphors in this sense? I have to answer no. What I will describe are not figures in the rhetorical sense, and they are certainly not tropes. As Metz points out, in cinema we are not often confronted with tropological figuration. One term has not taken the place of the other, although an exchange between the literal and the figurative has at least been initiated. Normally the two terms stand in syntagmatic relationship to each other. Figures in *Listen to Britain* resemble what rhetoricians call the metaphor *in praesentia* in that the terms (one literal, the other figurative) coexist in the text. They are manifest elements and have a syntagmatic character (as opposed to the paradigmatic character of the tropological metaphor). But this resemblance is only partial, since the figures in *Listen to Britain* do not maintain a distinction between the levels of the figurative and the literal, the former at least tending to substitute for the latter. One term is not an extradiegetic supplement that descends into the text. Both are diegetic and constitute part of the narrative signified; both are figurative as they have equal status in the figurative operation (the tenor and the vehicle are meaningless descriptive terms here). Moreover, these figures are not ornaments in the rhetorical or musical sense. They do not embellish a text whose basic structure is already given (in the fiction film: the narrative unfolding of the plot). The figurative articulation is an autonomous and crucial syntagmatic ordering—an ordering that is at least as important as the diegetic one, which it rivals.

Let's consider a second model for the iconic metaphor. In their analysis entitled "La Chafetière est sur la table," the "Group μ" of the University of Liège examines the problem of analyzing a visual object that seems to be the product of a metaphoric substitution.[13] The object of their study is an image appearing in a Belgian advertising campaign for *Chat noir* brand coffee. It represents the strange iconographic combination of a cat and a coffee pot. It is a single object, clearly defined by its contours and the chromatic contrast between the object and its background. Yet, within it, two forms coexist in perception: certain traits belong to the "cat" (feline ears, eyes, mouth), others to the coffee pot (geometric form, steam). The object's coherence is due to a zone of commonality: certain traits are shared features—we might call them elements of resemblance.

The contours of the two "bodies" are congruent, the tail is also a spout, and so forth. Thus the authors can establish a chart of such traits indicating which are the exclusive properties of the cat or the coffee pot and which ones fit into a zone of ambiguity. The strangeness of the representation resides in its "mixed" character: the two forms both coexist and contradict each other. Thus, "Group μ" points to an important difference between the linguistic metaphor and this composite image in which the work of condensation, as Christian Metz says, "extends beyond the work of metaphor, while retaining something of it."[14] It is worthwhile quoting the text at some length:

> In the linguistic metaphor, the relation of intersection is established between two groups of elements belonging to the level of the signified, which we have elsewhere named the explicit [manifeste] and implicit [conçu] degrees. In discourse, only the signifier corresponding to the explicit degree appears, the implicit degrees being inferred by the context. . . . In the iconic realm, what is explicit and perceived is a new global object, which usually does not correspond to a single known form. The mechanism is thus radically different.[15]

As we will see, figures in *Listen to Britain* have something of the metaphoric about them because they propose a comparison between two referents on the basis of a zone of intersecting traits. These figures are also like the "composite structure" of the advertising image analyzed by the "Group μ" in that the resemblance between the terms is initially a resemblance of the signifier: a physical characteristic—gesture, movement, and especially sound—is the trait that the objects appear to possess in common.

Let's return to the text. I have already described the work of juxtaposition (the production of antithetical couples: earth-sky, domestic-military labor) which in effect sets up the terms (a, b) that tend to coalesce (however imperfectly) in the figure. The figurative strategy aims to establish a relation of similarity between oppositional motifs of the image track. This work is metaphoric in that it proposes the identification of two referents (a and b in Figure 3.1) on the basis of certain common features (C). Unlike the classic metaphoric operation, both terms are present in nearly complete integrity on the syntagmatic chain, except for the feature the motifs hold in common, or rather that the viewer ascribes first to one, then to the other, in a subtle play of recognition and misrecognition. The text does not move toward a substitution, one term does not take the place of the other; such a movement is contrary to the figurative strategy, which is to mediate the opposition.

91

In this segment the feature held in common is not a characteristic at all but an aural object belonging to the sound track. A noise: it attaches itself to three sources: the movement of trees and fields of grain (wind) in shots 1, 2, 4, 5; the spitfires (engine motors) in all shots of the segment, but anchored in shots 3, 8, 11; the harvester (engine motors) in shots 9, 10, 11. The work of identification is here a quite literal process of recognition in which the terms of the metaphoric "figure" appropriate the feature (the noise). This process relies on the specific character of the aural object, the codes of the spatial treatment of sound, and the cinematic codes that order the relation between on-screen and off-screen space.

At this point I need to open a parenthesis in this analysis in order to examine the nature of the sound object and the theoretical problems it poses in cinema.

In his study of the aural object, Christian Metz analyzes what he calls the "ideological undermining of the aural dimension": sound has a very weak existence as an object in western culture. In the metalanguage of sounds, it is not the aural profile ("buzzing," "hissing," "whistling," and so forth) which constitutes identification for the western ear. Rather, it is the recognition of the sound source. A designation such as "roar," for example, lacks the identificatory precision that the simple naming of the source ("surf," "jetplane") provides. Thus Metz is able to conclude, "Ideologically, the aural source is an object, the sound itself a 'characteristic.'" In what Metz calls the "primitive substantialism" of our society, there is a rigid distinction between objects and the "secondary qualities which correspond to attributes applicable to these objects."[16]

One of the physical characteristics of the aural object that distinguishes it from the substantive object is its more diffuse presence in space. Unlike visual objects, sound objects need not be anchored to a precise location in order to be perceived: the observer detects a sound even in the absence of its source, which may be masked or too distant to be visible. In cinema, this difference in spatial definition accounts for certain powers of representation in the sound film. A voice or a noise can "appear" (in the auditorium) without its source appearing in the image. Sound thus plays an important role in the structuration of space that is specific to film: it evokes a source from which it has been detached (the off-screen voice of the classic shot-reverse-shot being a prime example).

The attribute evokes the object. Like all theoreticians of *montage,* the documentarists of the classic period were quite aware of the "detachability" of the sound object. In his article entitled "Creative Use of Sound," John Grierson, commenting on the GPO's acquisition of a sound unit, states, "Sounds, of course, have not the same precise significance as visuals. . . . The point is that once you start detaching sounds from their origins you can use them as images of those origins." This detachability gave sound the capacity not only to evoke a space momentarily absent from the image, but to create a presence whose "space" could remain unmaterialized. Noel Burch calls this space "imaginary" (as opposed to "concrete"). Grierson is quite aware of the evocatory power of this presence-absence of sound when he speaks of the autonomous aural object: "Another curious fact emerges once you start detaching sounds from their origins, and it is this. Your aeroplane noise may become not the image of an aeroplane but the image of distance or of height. Your steamer whistle may become not the image of a steamer but of isolation or darkness."[17]

We should add, following Metz, that sound is never in fact "off." It is never sequestered in the invisible segments of space that surround the image. Sound is either present or absent. When it is present, it cannot be contained within the limits of the screen, even if its "source" is there. Diffusing itself in the ambience of the theater, it can refer to space the image does not represent and extend the boundaries of the diegesis. It has in this sense a plenitude that the image lacks. And yet the conventions of audio-visual composition are conceptualized according to the primacy of the image: the specificity of the visible prevails over the spatially ambiguous sound. The relationship established between sound and image is of course a matter of a reading, an interpretation by the spectator, who "locates" the sound in response to specific indicators: the image materializes a source; the sound gives the signs of its spatial existence (volume, timber, balance, resonance). In light of Metz's analysis of the aural object, it is not surprising to note that the image, with its power to "anchor" sound, dominates the indicators of spatiality that belong to the sound itself. This is an almost irresistible process of attribution that has the force of verisimilitude. And yet, it is in this real gap between the specificity of the image and the ambiguity of sound that the reading can achieve a certain pluralism: a confusion of sources, a reinterpretation, the doubling that lays the basis for figuration.

As I will try to show, one of the major textual strategies in *Listen to Britain* consists in the manipulation of the syntagmatic relations between sound and image. As a basis for analysis it would be helpful to review the categories of off- and on-screen sound—the spatial placement of sound sources in relation to the visible field of the image—in Daniel Percheron's excellent taxonomy, "Sound in

Cinema and Its Relationship to Image and Diegesis."[18] A sound may be "on," i.e., its source may be located within the space represented in the image; or it may be "off" if its probable source cannot be located in the image. As Percheron points out, off-screen sound opens a rich paradigm of possibilities. Off-screen sound may be extradiegetic insofar as it supplements the narrative signified (the commentary and the musical score are the most pervasive examples in documentary film). Off-screen sound may be diegetic, i.e., function in the direct representation of events. However, off-screen diegetic sound may be asynchronous in relation to the image: although it is intended to be read as diegetic, it conflicts with the space-time represented in the image. Off-screen sound may be synchronous, that is, understood as existing in the spaces adjacent to the screen. It is of course this last category of off-screen sound that is the most frequent in the classic narrative film.

The symbolic trajectory in the initial segment of *Listen to Britain* is complex. Our analysis discerns below the diegetic sequence a web of signs bound together in relationships that are antithetical, metonymical, and, finally, metaphoric. The figurative operations occur at the level of the diegesis: all terms have a "realistic corre-late" and function diegetically as well as symbolically. As we have shown, the feature held in common is a sound: continuous, rela-tively weak, frictional, it has the ambiguous character of an aural object:

> *Shot 1:* Attribution. The aural object attaches itself to its source: moving branches of trees.
> *Shot 2:* The sound is still anchored in the image, but a "doubling" has become perceptible. Through the codes of the spatial treatment of sound, the noise of the spitfires becomes increasingly distinguishable from the noise of the wind. An increase in volume, modification of timber and reverberation, which constitutes an aural traveling shot, signifies the approach of the planes.
> *Shot 3:* The image of spitfires anchors the second layer of sound appearing in shot 2, in fact produces the spectator's apprehension retrospectively by materializing the source and defining its texture in close-up.
> *Shot 4:* A rebalancing of sounds takes place corresponding to the spatial field determined by the image. The noise of wind in a cornfield is once again foregrounded, and its resemblance with the noise of the distant spitfires is restated.

Thus, as this analysis indicates, the symbolic exchange is initiated through an exchange of the signifier. A physical property is at-tributed to one object, then to another, without compromising cinematic realism. Each phase in the emergence of the figure has its diegetic alibi. The "identity" of the sound in shot 1 is "caused" by distance, which, following the codes of the spatialization of sound, muffles the distinctive features of the spitfires' engine noise. The doubling of the noise track in shot 2 is produced by the shift in sound texture of the approaching airplanes, and so forth.

It is easy to see that the same analysis can be made of the (textually productive) confusion between the spitfires' engine noise and the harvester in shots 8–11. The aural object is at first perceived as singular, then doubled and recombined through the progressive elucidation of the space of representation that the narrative sequence provides. The textual gains are considerable. Cinematic realism is preserved. There is no manifest figurative level—nothing extradiegetic intervenes. The enunciator does not mark his presence in the text. For the spectator, the figurative activity is subliminal, i.e., it functions below the threshold of immediate apprehension. And yet the figurative intention becomes clear on reflection. Who could deny that this textual working aims at producing metaphors that can, in fact, be formulated in linguistic terms? Doesn't the spectator speak to him- or herself unconsciously of "tillers of the sky" and "soldiers of the earth," thus performing the symbolic work of the sequence? Subliminal but nonetheless real, the figurative activity achieves a textual transparency. It dissimulates itself behind the codes of *montage*, whose central aim is to produce a seamless representation of the "real." Verisimilitude covers over the mechanism of symbolic articulation.

IMAGE	SOUND
Descriptive syntagma: 2	

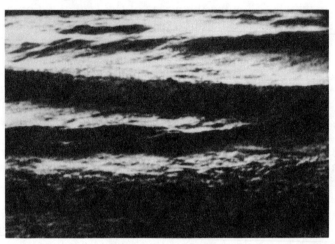

Shot 14

14 (dissolve)
Ocean waves unfold on the shore.

—[This is the BBC home and forces news. Here is the news, and this is . . .] Joseph McCloud speak . . . (fade-out) Noise of airplanes (off, in long shot).

Shot 15

15
Two men seated on a bench look out to sea.

Noise of airplanes (off). Dancehall music (off, in long shot, synchronous?).

Shot 16

16
A man wearing a helmet is silhouetted against the sea.

Dancehall music (off, in long shot, synchronous?).

Shot 17

Explanatory Insert: 3
17
Shadows of figures pass across the poster.

Dancehall music (off, closer).

IMAGE   SOUND

Shot 18

Scene: 4

18

Dancers move across a crowded dancefloor.

Noise of dancers: shuffling feet, voices, whistling (on). Dance music (source is off).

Shot 19

19

A young couple sits at the edge of the dancefloor talking. Passers-by cross the screen.

Speech: ". . ." (on, masked). Voices, laughter (on, masked). Noise of the crowd (off). Music (off, in long shot).

IMAGE	SOUND

Shot 20

20

The young couple (as in shot 19) engaged in conversation, the woman manipulating an object in her hands (axis match).	Speech: "It's your fault . . ." (female voice, on, masked). Voices, laughter (off). Music (off, in long shot).

Shot 21

21

A young man is speaking to a woman (partially off).	Speech: "Could I see it?" (male voice, on). Noise of the crowd (off). Music (off, in long shot).

IMAGE   SOUND

Shot 22

22
Dancing couples sing along   Speech: "Roll out the
with music.   barrels . . ." (sung, on).
                                    Noise of the crowd (on, closer).
                                    Music (off, closer).

Shot 23

23
Dancing couples circle the   ". . . now's the time to roll the
floor. Danceband in   barrels, 'cause the gang's all
background.   here." (Source is on)

100

IMAGE   SOUND

Shot 24

Autonomous Shot: 5
24
Two sentinels against a metal   Dancehall music (off, in long
barrier. The man at the left puts   shot; fade-out at the end of the
on his helmet and both look out   shot).
to sea and the setting sun (fade-
out).

Linear Text/Plural Text

I have skirted the problem of segmentation in the analysis thus far. But there clearly is a problem, even in the first segment. In his "Introduction to the Structural Analysis of Narrative," Roland Barthes defines a sequence as "a logical succession of nuclei bound together by a relation of solidarity: the sequence opens when one of its terms has no solidary antecedent and closes when another of its terms has no consequence."[19] In his article on demarcation, Christian Metz undertook to define this binding together of nuclei we call the autonomous segment according to the relationship of certain codes within the filmic text: "The analyst of the classic film is correct to consider as a single autonomous segment any passage from a film which is not interrupted by a major change in the course of the intrigue nor by a sign of punctuation nor by the abandonment of one syntagmatic type for another."[20] Now it is precisely when one examines the textual markers that, far from resolving into solidary units, the "segments" reveal apparently insoluble intratextual conflicts. Is it possible to maintain, for example, narrative continuity in the concluding shots of segment 1? The two shots represent a house in the near darkness of dusk. The change in lighting, the presence of a lamp in the window, the curtains being drawn seem to denote a leap forward in time, although no other textual markers motivate this apparent ellipsis. Moreover, the noise of the spitfires—the sign that binds the shots of the segment together—continues to impose its continuity on the sequence of images.

But then the noise of the spitfires outruns its function and spills over the line of demarcation that clearly separates segments 1 and 2: we move from the darkened window to an image of waves unfolding on the shore. This is obviously not a simple technique of continuity since the sound flows well into shot 15. Rather, this noise seems to disengage itself from the image and assert a degree of diegetic autonomy. Also, what do we make of the sound of a BBC "home and forces" broadcast interjected into shot 13? Are we meant to imagine a "source" beyond the darkened window? Why then does the broadcast continue into segment 2 where it fades out quite inexplicably? Finally, how are we to interpret the (distant?) strains of dancehall music that seem to jar against images of the sea watch and upset our sense of verisimiltude? In shots 13–16 the sound track is split into its constituent elements—speech, noise, music—none of which seems realistically speaking to complement

102

the image. Nor can we be sure that the three sounds are meant to coexist anywhere but in this textual space.

The effect of conflict, even rupture, is particularly apparent here because of the way I have cut the text for analysis. I have assumed a bias—the bias of the classic narrative film—which privileges the image and diegesis, defined as the narrative articulation of the space represented by the image. *Listen to Britain*—and doubtless most classic documentary films—present methodological problems for analysis. Here, to begin with, there are problems with the notion of the shot. Classic film criticism conceives of the shot as that primary division of the visual chain that determines the film's syntagmatic order. This notion of the shot can only be applied to films that respect the primacy of the image and the ancillary function of the other materials of expression, in particular those of the sound track. To identify and isolate the shot in *Listen to Britain* becomes quite problematic because the elements of the sound track assume a real textual autonomy, i.e., an existence as independent discursive units. The BBC broadcast, for example, is certainly an acoustic shot that has its own integrity, bridging as it does, two shots, and two segments, on the image track. Similarly, the noise of the spitfires continues to exist on the sound track even when it has lost all support in the image. It constitutes, in fact, an acoustic "segment" that spans visual segments 1 & 2.

We are thus confronted with two aspects of textuality in *Listen to Britain* that transgress laws of the classic narrative film: 1) that elements of the sound track can have an independent textual activity and form units that are not defined or are only partially defined in relation to the image; 2) that a textual plurality is possible based on the "rediscovered" separateness of the materials of expression. It is possible, for example, at the brief textual moment that is visual shots 14 to 16 to identify four (at least potentially) distinct representations. Image: ocean waves unfolding on the shore, the sea watch; speech: the BBC broadcast; noise: the spitfires; music: the strains of "Roll Out the Barrels"—elements that coexist without for the moment coalescing. As we will see, this plurality will be partially repressed in the process of reading, but the text's "openness" allows for the complex if fleeting counterpoint that characterizes certain "sequences" in *Listen to Britain*.

We are immediately caught in a paradox. For, despite the text's often complex counterpoint, the image persists in defining quite clearly the boundaries of its own syntagmatic units. Within each segment, the text passes from one shot to the next following the codes of continuity and *montage* that belong to the fiction film. However, when we move to the next higher level at which the segments take their place in the general ordering of the scenario, we encounter unmistakeable breaks in the narrative sequence. Each syntagmatic unit closes back on itself. Each is, narratively speaking, quite self-contained and appears to exhaust its meaning, although the specific narrative moments the film evokes continue to unfold, we assume, elsewhere in a reality to which the film makes no further reference. Moreover, the syntagma's sense of completion is often marked by insistent and redundant punctuation—fades, dissolves, contrastive cuts. What signs are there for example to carry us across the syntagmatic boundary that separates shot 13 from shot 14, segment 1 from segment 2? How are we to measure the narrative proximity of the darkened window and the shoreline at sunset?

The linearity of *Listen to Britain* is no more than apparent (I will deal with this appearance in a moment). Its story line is cut up, its pieces bracketed. The terms of what Roland Barthes calls the proairetic codes (the pragmatic codes of action) are weak; they exist in the mode of denegation. The narrative thrusts itself forward only to recede; traces a trajectory, then closes it off. The segment in the classic fiction film is also an autonomous unit, narratively self-sufficient, its edges clearly defined. But it is at the same time a link in the sequence of events that is the story. If the classic segment displays a narrative wholeness at the syntagmatic level, it is fashioned so as to fit into the larger narrative movement of the scenario: the chain of sequence and causality that is the structural legacy of novelistic fiction.

By abandoning linearity, the film text also sets aside the structuring activity organized by the hermeneutic codes. The hermeneutic work depends on the forward movement of narrative, even though it acts against it by setting up delays—obstacles, deviations, half-truths, falsehoods. Thus narrative is never a simple unfolding; it is also the gradual and halting resolution of enigmas, a suspense that creates expectation in the reader and dispatches him along the labyrinthine pathways that lead to "truth." "Its structure is essentially reactive, since it opposes the ineluctable advance of language with an organized set of stoppages: between question and answer there is a whole dilatory area whose emblem might be named 'reticence,' the rhetorical figure which interrupts the sentence, suspends it, turns it aside."[21] But in *Listen to Britain,* the text does not hold us in suspense or generate expectation. It discloses itself: there are no enigmas to resolve. Each syntagma is complete, semantically whole. Every element has its explanation—brief, implicit, often depending on the already-solved mysteries of ideology, the strong presence of cultural codes.

How can we describe a textual economy that seems, by comparison with the (apparent) dynamic of the fiction film, to tend toward stasis? How does the text displace itself?

Segment 2. I have identified it as a descriptive syntagma, but in the absence of real narrative progression, such modal distinctions become increasingly uncertain. At best we can speak of the sense of place, the sea watchers' minimal gestures, the apparent inconsequence of the brief actions. Two elements seem to link this segment to the first: the noise of the spitfire, as we have already noted, and the repetition of a motif—the sea watchers have relieved the sky watchers of segment 1. There is a new element, however; on the music track we hear a ballroom dance tune. Is it asynchronic, emanating from outside the scene? Or is it synchronic, coming from an off-screen source whose distance establishes the music's tonality and volume? This is the second example in so many segments of this use of an ambiguous sound source. A closer reading of the segment will show that the mechanism is the same and operates for the same purpose.

Segment 3: an explanatory insert. The words on the poster, the shadows that cross the frame, and the new aural presence the music has acquired situate us in space. We are outside the ballroom at Blackpool. Retrospectively, we redefine the spatial field of segment 2, lending it depth of sound field and locating it in relation to the spaces of segment 2 and the ballroom we are about to enter.

Segment 4: scene: "the scene reconstructs a unit still experienced as being 'concrete': a place, a moment in time, an action, complex and specific."[22] This is the first of twelve scenes in *Listen to Britain,* some of which are grouped in larger narrative progressions: segments 4, (7, 8, 9), 13, 16, 19, 21, (24, 28, 31, 33). The scene is a nodal point (a point of concentration): the only occurrences of that "spatio-temporal integrality experienced as being without 'flaws.'"[22] The scene has great density. It expands without gaps; it is confined in space: the scenes all take place in enclosed interiors (ballroom, railway car, canteen, concert hall). Each scene represents a musical performance, the music's measure guaranteeing the scene's continuity. The scene is a textual contraction: the film slows its forward movement, the action achieves its most specific development. The opposite textual principle is embodied in the bracket syntagma, where each episode is cut off from its potential expansion. And yet, paradoxically, the scene is as episodic as a unit within the global structure of the film as the "brief scenes" that are bound together in the bracket construction: "occurrences that

105

the film gives as typical samples of a same order of reality, without in any way chronologically locating them in relation to each other in order to emphasize their presumed kinship within a category of facts that the film-maker wants to describe in visual terms."[23] The structure of the scenario mirrors the structure of the bracket syntagma.

Shot 18: the swirling movement of the dance floor, the music's increased volume, and the noise of shuffling feet, laughter, whistling take the place of the quiet stasis of the preceding segments. Contrast and continuity. Diegetically, the appearance of the sound source in the image and the aural realism of the complex field of noise, music and voices move backward on the filmic chain to endow the sound fields of segments 2 and 3 with narrative verisimilitude. The promise is fulfilled: the imaginary has become concrete, a bridge is thrown across the syntagmatic boundaries. The "fractured" space of the signifier gives way to the synthetic space of the diegesis: a suprasegment is created. "The classic film is thus marked by a tendency toward units which are often superior to the segment (suprasegment or macrosegment). These units are often called sequences (in every day as well as professional language), and they often correspond to units in the scenario. They are generally determined by a global unity of time, place and action."[24]

Segment 5: autonomous shot. We return to the sea watch. Shot 24 is an axis match of shot 16: they reflect each other across segment 4 and enclose the ballroom scene: "Following a sort of internal tautology, segments connected in a suprasegment rhyme strongly within this new unit. What is notable about this operation is how it concentrates the rhyming effects in the narrative succession."[25] A "minor dramatic flow," this suprasegment appears to conform to the repetition-resolution that characterizes narrative progression in the classic fiction film.

As Raymond Bellour's work on narrative structure demonstrates, the classic film ceaselessly repeats itself as it leads to its resolution. The suprasegment is by definition a unit within which elements reflect each other with particular insistence, but repetition, as Bellour makes clear, also operates globally to sustain the progression of the story across the "ordered reservoir of similarities." This mirroring of elements, particularly complex at the subsegmental level, is at the heart of the intimate working of the text: "The level of units smaller than a segment is where the multiple play of echoes which structures and defines the progressive resolution of the textual system is systematized."[26]

It is easy enough to demonstrate that the principle of repetition and resolution operates in *Listen to Britain:* textual repetition is in fact extraordinarily intense not only within the suprasegment but between subsegmental units that echo each other across the text. We can, for example, point to the strong elements of symmetry that link segment 1 to the suprasegment we are now studying. Consider only the most conspicuous elements of this repetition. The first image of waves breaking on the shore (shot 14) adds the final term to the cosmography (earth and sky) initiated in segment 1. Domestic labor—cultivation of the earth—is replaced by domestic leisure—the ballroom at Blackpool. The sky watch gives way to the sea watch and the first relay occurs in a series of exchanges between the figures of vigilance. We will soon meet the signalman who watches over the troop transport train, the maternal figure whose glance secures a schoolyard of dancing children, the military patrol that safeguards the domestic space of an English village.

But we already encounter a difficulty. Repetition is not of the same order as in the fiction film. In the classic narrative film, repetition depends on the text's global continuity, i.e., a stable configuration of characters and the linear development of the plot: ". . . the schema of familial relations which constitute the space of narrative."[27] In *Listen to Britain,* analysis quickly demonstrates that narrative continuity sustains repetition only within the very circumscribed space of the syntagmatic or suprasegmental units. The mirror effect of segments 2 and 5 is one example of narrative repetition (identity of character and setting, similarity of gesture, temporal sequence), but it is a faulty one. Beneath the artifice of continuity (the off-screen strains of music that link these segments to the intercalated space and temporal development of the Blackpool ballroom scene), we see the editor's hand and the gesture of a rhetorician. Is this constructed space referential or figurative? From beneath the diegetic the emblematic emerges. The sentinels enclose textually the space of the ballroom because they stand on either side on the filmic chain. They have the symbolic presence of stone lions at the temple gates.

At all other levels, outside the rhyming effects that belong to these brief "dramatic" developments, the situation is very clear: the discontinuity of the narrative signified does not permit repetition of the sort that is most characteristic of the fiction film. In *Listen to Britain* symmetry is produced at varying intervals across the textual space between like elements—motifs that hold features in common with other motifs. They resemble each other abstractly

107

without reference to a narrative world of sequence and causality. The human figures repeat each other in the structural manner of the actant. They are functionally similar, but their actions are without specific narrative effect.

Segment 4 is composed of six shots of the ballroom at Blackpool. Shot 18 and shots 22 and 23 allow us to examine at varying distances the crowded dance floor and the passage of anonymous dancers across the frame. In the center of the segment, however, we have an example of focalization: from the turning crowd seen in long shot there emerge in medium and medium close-up two groups of seated figures engaged in conversation. After establishing the first fully coherent space of the film, the camera centers our attention on individual "actors." Three shots (19, 20, 21) frame and reframe the speakers in this circumscribed and private space. As spectators of the fiction film, we anticipate our entry into the subjective game of point of view, which the shots, by their composition and articulation, seem to promise. Shot 20 is an axis match of shot 19. It brings us closer to the soldier and the young woman, stimulating our expectation. Shot 21, which frames one of the two interlocutors, seems excerpted from a classic reverse-angle series and gives a structural promise of repetition. The film appears on the verge of establishing a second subjectivity—in addition to the spectator's—the subjectivity of the character. It is the character that has the power to capture and orient the spectator's look, to initiate the secondary identification whose cues come from the well-worn codes of editing.

However, in this segment as elsewhere in *Listen to Britain*, focalization is abortive. The characters are quite literally masked—masked in the technical sense. The acoustic "realism" of the scene allows only a partial focalization of speech. Thus, the snatches of conversation ("It's your fault. . . ." "Could I see?") are all but suppressed by the noise of the ballroom that invades the frame. The promise of intimacy and knowledge is not kept: the figures slip back into the anonymous swirl of the dance floor and never reappear. Like all the human actors who perform the acts of the film's diegesis, they are cut off: prisoners of the single shot or the syntagma. Unstable, fleeting, incapable of development or complexity, these figures never achieve the status of character, as Roland Barthes defines it:

The character is a product of combinations: the combination is relatively stable (denoted by the recurrence of the semes) and more or less complex (involving more or less congruent, more or less contradictory

108

figures); this complexity determines the character's "personality," which is just as much a combination as the odor of a dish or the bouquet of a wine.[28]

In *Listen to Britain* the human actors have no past, no intelligible evolution, no psychological complexity. They are rather examples of what Barthes calls the "figure": "The figure is altogether different: it is not a combination of semes concentrated in a legal Name, nor can biography, psychology or time encompass it: it is an illegal, impersonal, anachronistic configuration of symbolic relationships."[29] The figure is a "symbolic ideality," a mere site where the cultural codes take on a body. Thus these briefly focalized "individuals" give us the flattened signs of their cultural existence. In this segment, they are youth with its associated semes of exhuberance, innocence and optimism—traits that they hold briefly before passing them on to other figures, other relays.

What interests us here in particular is the question of textual economy. As Barthes points out, the character is a subject and therefore a subject of attribution. He or she is the sum of attributes lodged under the sign of a name; in cinema, we should add, there is also a body. Once "identified," this Name-Body exists independently, and its appearance evokes all the semes that have been attributed to it. A kind of shorthand, a textual condensation is essential to narrative fiction:

> In the novelistic regime (and elsewhere?), [the Name] is an instrument of exchange; it allows the substitution of a nominal unit for a collection of characteristics by establishing an equivalent relationship between sign and sum: it is a bookkeeping method in which, the price being equal, condensed merchandise is preferable to voluminous merchandise.[30]

In documentary's classic period, the absence of characters generates real problems of textual economy. This is an historically specific problem. We should recall that *Nanook* is, structurally, nothing but a succession of attributions: Nanook the hunter, Nanook the builder, and so forth. In the place of the complexity of the character, we find another kind of shorthand: the perpetual reference to cultural codes, in particular to human typologies of the most enduring (rigid) sorts: the typology of the ages of man, the typology of sexual roles, of human industry, and so forth. The actor's body carries the blatant signs of social stereotype. A binary work of connotation takes place that divides the human sphere into worker-soldier, mother-child, plebeian-royalty, peasant-city dweller.

109

Even the occasional reversal of roles (e.g., woman as worker) involves the most superficial of ironies. Roland Barthes says: " 'Life' then, in the classic text, becomes a nauseating mixture of common opinions, a smothering layer of received ideas."[31]

IMAGE	SOUND
Segment 6: Descriptive syntagma	
25 (fade-in)	
Columns of miners carrying lanterns in the dark.	Noise of machinery (fade-in, on and off).
26	
Columns of miners move along a tunnel.	Reverberating noise of steps in an interior space (on, change in sound texture).
27	
Columns of miners move along a tunnel.	Noise as in 26 (on).
28	
Row houses set against a darkened hillside.	A sharp banging noise at the beginning of the shot (off, asynchronous). Ambiant noise (on).

Shot 29

29	
Elevator machinery at the entrance to a mine shaft, dark against the sky.	Noise of miners' work (crescendo from long shot to close-up; off, synchronous?).

IMAGE	SOUND
Segment 7: scene	
30	
A signalman looks out of the tower window.	Noise of machinery (off, synchronous?).
31	
A train signal flips up.	Noise of the switch (on).
32	
A night landscape. A train enters frame left and moves to center frame.	Noise of the train (crescendo) and application of brakes (from off to on).
Segment 8: scene	

Shot 33

33	
Inside a railway coach two soldiers sing while one of them plays a guitar.	Speech: "Oh, give me a home where the buffalo roam . . ." (sung, on and off). Music: guitar accompaniment (on).

IMAGE   SOUND

Shot 34

34
Two passengers seated opposite
each other are engaged in
conversation.

Speech: ". . . big electric
lamp . . ." (on). ". . . where the
deer and the antelope
play . . ." (sung, off).
Guitar as in 33 (off).

Shot 35

35
Two other soldiers sing while
one plays the guitar.

Speech: "Where never is heard
a discouraging word . . ."
(sung, on and off). Voice from
conversation (34) continues
(off).
Guitar as in 33 (on).

IMAGE	SOUND

Shot 36

36
Two passengers engaged in
conversation (as in 34).

Speech: "Remember Tommy
and the . . .?" "Oh, yes, do I!"
"Wasn't it a great night?" (on)
Voices with guitar continue the
song (off).

Shot 37

37
Two soldiers singing (reframe of
33).

Speech: "Home, home, on the
range . . ." (on and off). Guitar
(on).

IMAGE	SOUND

Shot 38

38
Accordion player.

Voices continue the song (off).
Accordion (close-up, on); other
instruments (off).

Shot 39

39
A soldier singing (man from
right frame in 35).

Voices singing (on and off).
Instruments (off).

Shot 40

40
Two soldiers singing. The
soldier at the right lights a
cigarette (as in 33).

Voices singing (on and off).
Yodel (off). Guitar and
instruments (off).

Segment 9: scene
41
The dark signal tower window.
A figure appears (as in 30).

Voices singing with musical
accompaniment (off, in long
shot which fades). Noise of
switches and train (in close-up
which masks the voices).

42
The train pulls away in dark of
night.

Noise of train (gradual
decrescendo, on).

43
Train signal flips up (as in 31).

Noise of train (off, in long shot).

44
The train moves into the
distance.

Noise of train (decrescendo,
on).

Segment 10: descriptive syntagma

Shot 45

45

Two men work at the nose of an   Noise of the shop floor (on and
airplane under construction.   off).

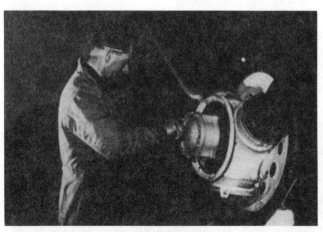

Shot 46

46

Single worker at the nose of the   Noise of the shop floor (off).
plane (axis match of 45).

117

| IMAGE | SOUND |

Shot 47

47
General view of the shop floor.   Noise (on).

Segment 11: autonomous shot

Shot 48 (fade-out)

48
An airplane takes off in a dark   Noise of the shopfloor (off,
landscape. The taillight marks a   asynchronous) in acoustic
pattern against the sky (fade-   dissolve with the noise of the
out).   airplane take-off (decrescendo,
                                       fade-out).

To bind/to separate

Segments 5–6: A new beginning, a turn of the page. For the first time, no element bridges the boundary; the narrative movement of the suprasegment (2–3–4–5) has come to a stop. Textual demarcation is clear and redundant: the punctuation (fade-in/fade-out) reenforces the change in the motif of the image (from the sea at Blackpool to the dark mine tunnel). The documentary text works at producing continuity: it motivates the passage from shot to shot, from syntagma to syntagma. But it must also simultaneously cut the textual volume into meaningful units (units of meaning).

I have already cited the three criteria put forth by Christian Metz for the demarcation of the autonomous segment in the classic narrative film: a major change in the course of the plot, a sign of punctuation, a change in syntagmatic type. Only punctuation—dissolve, fade, iris—has a material presence and is inscribed in the signifier. Shifts in the course of the plot or in syntagmatic types are produced as necessary parts of a reading. The ebb and flow of the story line is established, as Stephen Heath indicates, "according to the simple criteria of unity of action, unity of characters, unity of place; it has no analytic status other than that of allowing reference to the film as narrative."[32] As we have attempted to show, it is precisely these classic unities that fail at critical moments to bind the documentary text and carry it forward. The second sign of demarcation—shift in syntagmatic type—is also predicated, more than may at first be apparent, on the perceived continuity of a story line. In the absence of the global units of action and character, how do we distinguish the linearity of narrative from the simple spatial arrangement of the descriptive mode? How do we determine what is chronological and what stands outside any logic of time? What logic underlies for example the *montage* of industrial or urban landscapes in the documentary films of the 1930s? (Van Dyke's and Stiener's *The City* poses very complex problems of segmentation.)

These are far from purely academic questions. Without segmentation, without the logic that binds shots together into segmental units, the film is incoherent; it has no meaning. A closer look at segments 6, 7, and 8 will show how this binding and separating takes place in *Listen to Britain.*

Segment 6: descriptive syntagma, an evocation of place. Three shots—the play of moving lanterns across the dark frame—trace the miners' descent into the mine, and these are followed by two shots that show us a vast landscape of row houses and the structures at the entrance to the mine shaft. A slight textual breach occurs: the noise of the miners' labor is heard in crescendo against

119

the exterior shots. This is the equivalent of an acoustic traveling shot: our ears descend into the mine with the miners, while our eyes examine the industrial landscape above. Asynchrönism, counterpoint, a gap, but a measurable one. The sound has been freed from its source, which exists nonetheless in the image's proximate space.

Segment 7: scene. The boundary with segment 6 is established only retrospectively. Shot 30 appears at first as the continuation of segment 6: the motifs of the image track (the signal tower in 30 seems to follow in series the mine shaft structure in 29), the match in lighting, and most convincingly the apparent continuity of the noise track all suggest the spatial contiguity of the two shots. The off-screen sound in shot 30, whose source is established in segment 6 as the miners' labor, is reidentified only in shot 31, which shows us the switching of a railway signal. Thus this momentary "confusion" between tapping picks and the noise of railway switches allows an initial narrative reading across the syntagmatic boundary. It is a "false" reading in which identity and resemblance are confused and then sorted out. *Listen to Britain* abounds in this kind of figurative play: the final measures of a Mozart concerto are "matched" with the high-pitched noise of a machine shop; the rhythm of a locomotive is mimicked by the percussive music of a marching band, whose drum rolls "blend" subsequently with the noise of a steel foundry. Some of these "false" matches create as in the case at hand the momentary illusion of identity; others, as we will see, make a display of their figurative character.

Acoustic matches resemble optical effects in that they depend on a work of the signifier. The film proposes to compare motifs in two segments by establishing a resemblance between certain of their physical properties. A sound resembles another in pitch, texture, volume, cadence. By examining syntagmatic boundaries in *Listen to Britain,* we can identify three types of acoustic matches, or, rather, three ways of articulating these matches on the syntagmatic chain. (1) By a process of misapprehension-correction, the spectator attributes a sound to one source when it belongs, the film soon clarifies, to a second (the example at hand: the transition between segments 6 and 7). (2) The two sounds "reflect" each other across a syntagmatic boundary without there being any "mixing" of their signifiers (the rhythmic noise of a locomotive is replicated by the rhythm of a marching band). (3) The two sounds blend in an acoustic dissolve in an opposing movement of crescendo-decrescendo, one sound fading-in, the other fading-out (the orchestral music dissolves into the noise of the machine shop). If their surface

120

articulations are different, the three types clearly have a common figurative origin.

It would be tempting to classify these textual articulations as punctuation: they fall at the syntagmatic boundary and they appear to give a special textual emphasis to the moment of demarcation. However, punctuation cannot be defined by simple reference to its materiality: a lapdissolve, visual or acoustic, is not by nature punctuative. It must also function as punctuation in the text. We need to examine the character of these textual articulations. Physically speaking, the visual or acoustic fade ("normally" of course they occur together) separates more than the lapdissolve, which creates a passing combination of two images or two sounds. The dissolve "hesitates" on the edge of textual division. It is displacement in that it emphasizes the passage from one shot to another by displaying its own functioning. But, as Metz points out, the dissolve is also condensatory.[33] For a fleeting moment two images or sounds blend on the screen or in the auditorium, a bit in the manner of Freud's collective figures. The question is then what function is primary in these articulations in *Listen to Britain*.

In the majority of cases, the punctuative function—to separate the autonomous segments—has already been assumed by the image track. The division of the visual text is not emphatic but quite clear, even if it is established retrospectively, as in the case of the boundary between segments 6 and 7. The straight cut and the juxtaposition of space (the concert hall-the waterfront, the locomotive in its railway yard-the military parade in a city street) operate to demarcate the syntagmatic boundaries by a kind of degree zero of segmental punctuation. Such articulations have become the norm in the classic fiction film where narrative logic easily carries the spectator across the breach in temporal-spatial continuity. This flow of the narrative text proceeds with an apparent self-evidence. Actions generate each other in sequence as if the course of the story obeyed an imperative located outside discourse in a "reality" that somehow preexists and therefore determines the narrative sequence. This is verisimilitude as we understand it in the tradition of contemporary narrative. As Tzvetlan Todorov suggests, the laws of discourse hide behind a putative reality that governs its every gesture: "In our day, another meaning has become predominate: we speak of a work's verisimilitude insofar as the work tries to convince us it conforms to reality and not to its own laws. In other words, verisimilitude is the mask which is assumed by the laws of the text and which are meant to be taken for a relation with reality."[34] The contemporary narrative possesses a functional economy. It gives the impression of self-sufficiency, of a textual automatism that suppresses all signs of intervention. As Gérard Genette suggests, verisimilitude is based on the reduction of motivation defined as that which is necessary to dissimulate the text's functioning. The value of a narrative unit is measured according to its functionality. Ideally in modern fiction, motivation is implicit, it costs nothing.

The transparency of the fiction film depends on this constant opening onto the narrative signified. The dissolve as punctuation, for example, is highly codified and bound to a stable signified (that is, the passage of time). In *Listen to Britain*, the dissolve and the fade frequently mimic the punctuative function of those figures in the fiction film. The dissolve that initiates segment 2 and the fade-out/fade-in that separates segments 5 and 6 are examples of a kind of sleight of hand. With reference to the fiction film and by a kind of force of habit we read these figures as narrative articulations. At the same time, we are quite aware that the film does not operate narratively at that level—cannot operate narratively if it is to produce its message. These articulations are textual. The discourse uses them to move us from one topic to another, not from one time to another. To move us, to reposition us, without allowing us to experience the gap as rupture. Similarly, the film's celebrated "poetic" effects—in particular the rhetorical devices that occur at the segmental boundaries—are part of the film's work of continuity. In all these cases, this work of continuity is economically costly. In varying degrees, it makes a display of its textual markers.

Looking back over the segments we have just studied, it is easy to see a particular strain, a textual strain, at the points of articulation that link the autonomous segments together at the level of the scenario. At the smaller levels of the film's discourse, in the linkage of shots that produces the autonomous segments, continuity is relatively effortless, that is, it is highly codified. At its most manifest level, the film exploits those same codes of *montage* that are at the heart of the functioning of the fiction film. But if we examine the major points of suture in the textual body, we discover a traumatic zone where the text expends enormous energy. When it is able, the film produces suprasegments by the force of diegetic implication, often to the point of straining our credulity. But even this narrative flow is quickly exhausted, and the film once again approaches a point of rupture. At these moments, as we might expect, motivation becomes a strategic textual problem. In the classic documentary film, it is typically the commentary that intervenes to suture the film's splitting, to impose coherence and continuity. But *Listen to Britain* is a *tour de force*. It rejects the expediency of language in favor of less conspicuous and less alienating textual devices. With a virtuosity that is the contrary of codicity in cinema, *Listen to Britain* imitates, always imperfectly, the "seamless" body, the "beautiful closed object" that is the fiction film.

Segments 8 and 9: scenes. In segment 7 narrative motivation appears abandoned. The chain is broken: the three shots of the signal tower compose another unit that enters the paradigm of human industry, as indicated by the figurative device I have described above. However, at the boundary between segments 7 and 8, we already have the sign of a reinitiated narrative continuity: the sound of singing voices from off-screen call segment 8 into being. A dissolve—this time quite classic—introduces us into the interior space of the railway car of a troop transport train. A narrative suprasegment has begun, with its unity of time, place and action.

Once again within this narrative suprasegment the rhyming effects are quite strong. Not only is there consistent internal rhyme, but the suprasegment is a structural and thematic repetition (with differences) of the suprasegment 2–3–4–5 (the sea watch, the Blackpool ballroom). The signalman like the sea watchers stands in the position of sentinel, enclosing the space of the transport train. The segments repeat the pattern exterior/interior/exterior, reinforced by the same shifts in lighting, dark/light/dark. The central segment is a musical performance—the soldiers' nostalgic "Home on the Range" is an echo of the music from the Blackpool ballroom. Moreover, segment 8 quite precisely repeats the narrative focalization analyzed in segment 4: individual "characters" emerge, snatches of conversation, masked by collective singing, can be overheard (shots 34, 35, 36). The arrival and departure of the train, symmetrically balanced in the succession of shots, brings the suprasegment to a perfect closure.

Segment 10: descriptive syntagma. An abrupt cut takes us from the gentle descrescendo and darkened frame of the train disappearing into the distance to the brightly lit floor of a noisy aircraft factory. A rupture, a break in the narrative continuity occurs. The film's paradigmatic work reasserts itself. We reposition ourselves and link the suprasegment 7–8–9 conceptually to the paradigm of human industry (transportation).

Segment 11: autonomous shot. Figuratively, the airplane substitutes (metonymically) for the productive labor represented in segment 10. It is also a clear repetition by analogy of shot 44: like the train, it disappears in a darkened frame. The decrescendo of the noise track is accompanied by a fade-out that marks a pause in the text.

Thus, the text weaves together its disparate elements using all its powers of comparison, of narrativity, its rhetorical and figurative devices, optical and acoustic, linkages of all sorts, as well as all the resources of analytic editing. "If the text is subject to some form, this form is not unitary, architectonic, finite: it is the fragment, the shards, the broken or obliterated network—all the movements and inflections of a vast 'dissolve,' which permits both overlapping and loss of messages."[35] Structurally, the text proceeds by imbrication: the conceptual overlays the diegetic, the narrative reemerges from beneath the symbolic, analogy fashions a chain of resemblances that binds motifs together across segmental boundaries. One textual principle can fade and another comes to take its place in a constant action of relay. The filmic system is a network, but, paradoxically, one without any sense of the systematic. We might call it a patchwork: it covers over with the materials at hand the gaping holes in its discourse. The functional law of the text is pragmatism.

Where does analysis begin? I chose to examine *Listen to Britain* from its beginning and to follow its unfolding. That choice was to a certain degree arbitrary and motivated by the investigative character of this reading. Without having dealt with the film's most brilliant moments, the analysis begins to encounter redundancy— permutations of the "same" textual operations—which suggests that we have uncovered the film's textual strategy, at least for the levels that have been the object of our analysis. Should analysis stop here? I believe it is worth considering, schematically, one further "suprasegment," an immense syntagmatic development that occupies more than one quarter of the film's textual space: 57 of the film's 213 shots, divided into 12 autonomous segments (numbers 23–34). I am referring to the well-known "sequence" that takes place at London's National Gallery.

Continuity for the sequence at the National Gallery is established by the time of a performance: Myra Hess plays the first movement of a Mozart piano concerto in the gallery's concert hall. The concert succeeds a music hall performance ("Flannigan and Allen") in the popular milieu of a canteen. Despite contrasts in tone and the milieus represented, the two sequences resemble each other strikingly in their insistence on a rigorously "theatrical" space: a perfect frontal division between the public sector and that belonging to the performance. The utter stability of the space is in part due to its rigid geometry, the immobility of the "actors" within it, and the classicalness of the *découpage*. Recurring long shots assure us of the integrity of this referential space. The symmetry of the framing—almost all the "detail" shots whether of the players or the audience are taken in medium close-up—reinforces the scene's

Canteen Show: "Flannigan and Allen"

sense of equilibrium. Further, the return to the same points of view, doubtless in part motivated by the technical constraints of shooting, contribute to the sense of continuity. There are thirteen shots showing us Myra Hess and members of the orchestra, but only five camera set-ups. Finally, there is the orderly progression of the point of view shot: the audience fixes its gaze on the performers, the performers present themselves to be seen. The look out of the frame (series A) followed by its object (series B) sets up a structure of alternation, one of the most predictable (highly codified) in the classic cinema.

In this sequence of shots, sound plays its suturing role: in the visual absence of the performers it reminds us of their "presence" off-screen and it motivates with seeming naturalness their return to the image. Sound endows the flatness of the screen with a fictional depth and dimension, giving us the signs of another (contiguous) space. It helps create the impression of organic unity that belongs to the scene: "a spatio-temporal integrity experienced as being without 'flaws' . . . a place, a moment in time, an action, compact and specific."[36] Through its displacement the camera can break up the scene, reduce it to a catena of "partial" views; but we reconstitute it in response to the signs of its plentitude. The spatial ambiguity of sound plays a particularly important function in this work of the diegetic reading.

The scene we have described is the center of the suprasegment. But it is not in fact a single scene. It "recurs" four times: segment 24 (including inserts 25 & 26), segment 28 (including insert 29), segment 31 (shown here as exemplary) and segment 33. It is "interrupted" by four segments intercalated in the series and forms with them a pattern of alternation at the level of the scenario. The four segments of the second series represent locations within the gallery or in its proximity:

Segment 27: architectural features of the gallery, in particular low angle shots of light flooded windows (4 shots).
Segment 30: visitors to the gallery, in apparent proximity to each other (9 shots).
Segment 32: empty frames of evacuated masterpieces (3 shots).
Segment 34: views of settings outside the gallery and in the nearby streets (13 shots).

126

What is immediately striking is the discontinuity of this alternation, the to-and-fro that *montage* establishes between the matrix of the concert hall and the various locations, which seem progressively distant from this point of origin. From a narrative standpoint, this discontinuity appears totally arbitrary. Nothing in the movement of the series sets up a chain of before and after, cause and effect. No movement of a character, no development of a plot justifies the displacements of the scene. No voice emerges to furnish an alibi for the apparent lack of internal motivation. Furthermore, the text sets up a modal alternation. The segments that take place in the concert hall have all the earmarks of the scene with its integral chronological development. The segments of the second series have little appreciable narrative character and seem to justify their concatenation by their co-presence within a more or less well-defined referential space. We have therefore identified these segments as descriptive syntagmas. But this modal alternation is not clearly defined. The descriptive syntagmas "borrow" some of the temporal markers of the scene; the scene, broken into pieces and juxtaposed to the descriptive syntagmas, seems to lose much of its sense of narrative purpose.

Let's look at how the film produces this modal ambivalence. Autonomous segment 23, which initiates the suprasegment with a shot of the neoclassical portico and dome of the National Gallery, already contains the opening orchestral notes of the Mozart concerto. This is an example of asynchronous sound—we could not, realistically speaking, be expected to hear the concerto from this position outside the concert hall. This "aberration" is however quite tame. Classic cinema abounds in this kind of asynchronism, which quickly resolves itself. The ear and the eye have not taken up different positions; their consonance has simply been delayed. The "harmony" of voices reestablishes itself in the fullness of the scene viewed in long shot. In segment 27, however, we are once again outside the concert hall, somewhere within the gallery: the archway leading to the gallery entrance and a series of light-flooded windows. But the spatial treatment of the sound of the concert has not been modified: volume, reverberation, the dosing of treble and bass, the "color" of the sound remain constant and continue to evoke our presence in the space of the concert hall. Is the sound asynchronic? Surely. And yet a certain coherence of space—we have not gone very far from the sound source—and a sense of simultaneity link the scenes within the concert hall to the motifs of those segments that take place on its periphery. Is the sound synchronous, representing an off-screen space that framing hides

Segment 31: Concert Hall at the National Gallery

Portico and Dome of the National Gallery

Scene of the Concert Hall

From Segment 27: Architectural Features of the Gallery

from us? If so, the film seems to ignore the codes of cinematic realism. Not only are the acoustic signs of distance lacking, the entire on-screen sound field that the image would seem to call into being is absent: where are the snatches of conversation, the ambient noises of movement in the gallery, of traffic in the streets? And yet, despite this lack of "realism," the continuous progression of the music track, which retains something of its diegetic status, functions to cover over the ellipses of the image. The "theatrical" space of the sound field lends its coherence to the fragmented space of the image. The whole produces something like a narrative effect.

Syntagmatic, Referential, Figurative

The sequence at the National Gallery is in the first instance, like all sequences, a syntagmatic fact: images and sounds are linked together on the discursive chain. In the classic cinema, this concatenation would lead with apparent self-evidence to a referential field where the textual combinations seem to fall away before presumably real relations in space and time. The classic text in fiction does not appear to signify, it refers: the signified dissimulates itself behind the "real." However, the situation in this sequence is paradoxical. We are not faced with the "lies" of fiction: the film does not ask us to take the actions and actors for what they are not. We quite willingly grant the "documentary realism" of the image, that is, of the individual shots. We place our faith in the integrity of the referent: this is the National Gallery, a concert has taken place, we are in the war-torn Britain of 1942. We know the images and sounds are "true," and all the same we do not give ourselves over completely to that regime of belief that the fiction film engenders. The codes that link the shots (subcodes of *montage*) and the codes that link image and sound (codes of audio-visual composition) have undergone a displacement. It is as if the referent, despite its documentary authority, is not fully in charge. The text lacks the self-sufficiency that characterizes narrative structure in fictional and historical texts and has come to signify the real: "The paradox comes full circle: narrative structure was evolved in the crucible of fiction (via myth and the first epics), and yet it has become at once the sign and the proof of reality."[37]

Like most documentaries of the classic period, *Listen to Britain* must come to terms with one of the major problems of historic discourse. The "document," except when it is produced with reference to a predetermined structure, is "imperfect": it has no place assigned to it on the syntagmatic chain. It does not as yet have the sense of destiny and moral purpose that can only come from its function within a larger discursive whole. Real events, which documentary films take as their referents, have no structure immanent within them. "Pure" documents lack finality and meaning, the articulated sequence and the closure that characterize all narrative, in fact all discourse. Documentarists, like historians, endow their material with meaning through a discursive act (performed at all stages of the film's production, not simply through *montage* in the limited sense), an act that produces a structure, i.e., a system of relationships between the assembled materials, images and sounds. As we have seen repeatedly in *Listen to Britain,* the documentarist has an obsessive urge to narrativize: to organize his materials in a discursive structure based on relations of space and time. As Hayden White points out, to narrativize events is to place them within a moral order from which they derive their meaning and their realism:

> It is the historians themselves who have transformed narrativity from a manner of speaking into a paradigm of the form which reality itself displays to a "realistic" consciousness. It is they who have made narrativity into a value, the presence of which in a discourse having to do with "real" events signals at once its objectivity, its seriousness, and its realism.[38]

Listen to Britain, like most classic documentary films, does not deal with the sort of coherent acts and individual destinies that the fiction film acquired as a legacy from the nineteenth-century novelistic tradition. Rather it seeks to recount a historical situation whose scope often exceeds the capacities of the filmic image and the powers of *montage.* Cinematic techniques did not develop to evoke the more "abstract" space of historical representation. We have already briefly examined the problem of character in *Listen to Britain.* Like many classic documentaries, the film sets out to portray collectivities, rather than "individuals" with their more or less complex features, and I have attempted to show how the absence of such novelistic characters affects the textual economy of the film. In the absence of these two stable commodities—continuities of action and character—how does the film produce the impression that the action is "one and whole like a living being"? (Aristotle)

The suprasegment we have been examining embodies the film's

Segment 33: Myra Hess and Her Audience

134

textual strategy. First, the scene stands as a "natural" symbolic matrix: it brings together within the integrity of a referential space the diversity of the body politic that elsewhere in the film has been created through the "artifice" of *montage*. The scene in the National Gallery concert hall insists on its spatial coherence—the division into symmetrical halves and the architectural limits—and the temporal continuity of a musical performance. Within this measured space and time, we see the signs of Britain's social multiformity—the fellowship of social types, including the royal party—aligned along the axis of their solidarity.

The moment of the scene is carefully chosen. It is intended to produce a great density of meaning. Totally significant, the moment radiates across the text: a culmination of all that has gone before, an ordering of everything that is to come. The scene is a microcosm, at once concrete and abstract: a specific set of actions and actors that stand for the whole of a social situation. We lose all sense of the arbitrary. Narration itself becomes a symbolic activity: to create the narrative continuity of the scene, linking the shots through the resources of *montage,* is to produce the notion of community, the metaphoric union of all divisions of British society. The symbolic is not secondary; it is the essential complement of the diegetic.

But the scenes that take place in the National Gallery concert hall are without narrative consequence, without signs of a hermeneutic work. Perfectly symmetrical and self-contained, they evoke an orderly, symbolic space, without issue. Here, as we have seen elsewhere in *Listen to Britain,* a sense of plenitude exists within the boundaries of the syntagmatic unit. Where are the elements of dissymmetry without which there is no narrative movement? How can the text transcend the limits of the scene without giving up its "wholeness"? How can it expand to embrace a global historical field ("Britain at war") that the film proposes to represent? How can the text produce this field as diegesis? Like many documentaries, *Listen to Britain* could fall back on the resources of language. Language with its superior semantic powers is quite capable of narrativizing the historical field. Historiographic texts evoke real events in their detail or link them to historical generalities, or pass between levels of representation with an ease the filmic text cannot emulate. But it is precisely in the name of cinematographic specificity that *Listen to Britain* rejects that discursive option.

Textual strategy in *Listen to Britain* consists in superimposing two distinct levels of discourse. In this suprasegment, the diegetic chain joins the scenes of Myra Hess's performance with the de-

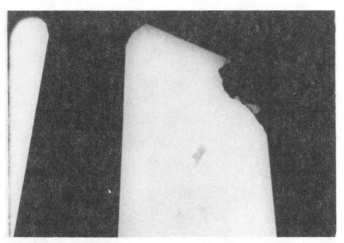

From Segment 34: Views outside the National Gallery and in Nearby Streets

scriptive syntagmas (27, 30, 32, 34) which we perceive as a spatial expansion of narrative. The second chain is a figurative network that weaves together the motifs of sound and image and makes them cohere in a symbolic structure. Thus, the suprasegment represents on the one hand an apprehensible space, measurable, rational, despite the narrative passivity that seems to characterize the segments that take place outside the concert hall. On the other hand, the segments of this alternation function according to a principle of opposition, which is in the first instance spatial, but which is ultimately figurative. Two antithetical terms are set against each other: exterior versus interior, and a chain of associations that the film work has endeavored to put in place has linked the terms of this opposition to sets of contrasted features: the exterior is linked to dislocation, diversity, discontinuity; the interior to domesticity, integration, continuity. Thematically, the film sets out to represent the survival under conditions of war of that domestic space—the family with its stable configuration—which is at once lost and refound. Against the images of distress and dislocation, the text proposes the familial community of the concert hall: Myra Hess, the last in a chain of maternal figures, commands the attention of her children. The text undertakes a symbolic work of incorporation: to annex all Britain to this domestic sanctuary. Thus in this suprasegment the text constructs a tension between two contradictory movements: to open up and to enclose. The film's strategic problem is to negotiate this antithesis, to "domesticate the irreducible," as Roland Barthes would say.

It is this symbolic work that explains the insistent repetition of certain motifs: the entrance way to the gallery, the revolving door, the strangely vacant images of windows, the balustrades and archways that serve as frames in the exterior shots and mark off the architectural limits of place. But the main agent of this symbolic transgression between inside and outside is the sound track. Detached from its source, the music of the concerto continues to evoke the closed space of the concert hall over the disparate images of the gallery, its patrons, and the nearby London streets. We recognize here the work of metonymy, or, more properly, synecdoche: the acoustic part stands for the phenomenal whole. It is a transgression against diegesis, since the space of the image and the space of the sound are incommensurable and yet conjoined. The text stages "an original relationship between two coherences," a work of condensation that acts directly on the signifier. It is clearly not a case of diegetic music assuming an extradiegetic function, as can happen in the fiction film. In this pattern of alternation, the

Gallery Windows

Visitors Moving through the Gallery's Revolving Door

Gallery Visitors

From Segment 35: The Machine Shop

Segment 36: The Marching Band

From Segment 37: Workers Hammering Steel Ingot

From Segment 37: Steel Welders

145

The Concluding Images: Land, Sky, and Industry

146

Closing Title

music repeatedly reinvests itself with the reality of its source. The split in the materials of expression, the asynchronicity, and the paradoxical work of condensation the film produces are on the symbolic level entirely coherent: they constitute the work of figuration and take the place of the diegetic integration the text cannot achieve.

Beginning with the motif of the Mozart concerto, we can follow a chain of figurative operations that serve to bridge the syntagmatic intervals: acoustic dissolves that produce unexpected comparisons between apparently incongruous visual motifs. The final orchestral measures are "matched" by the high-pitched noise of a machine shop in segment 35 (nine shots). The noise of machinery and the pulsating rhythm of a locomotive synchronize with the marching band of segment 36 (one shot). The percussion of the martial music is echoed by hammers on steel ingots in the foundry in segment 37 (twelve shots). The hiss of steel welding dissolves into the strains of "Rule, Britannia," which links the last elemental images in a condensatory recapitulation of the whole text. In bringing the film to closure, figurative dissolves replace diegetic continuity; narrative causality gives way to poetic gesturing. This is the rhetorical version of the musical coda: a repetition of themes, an emphatic order, the final flourish. We recognize the stereotypic utterances, the commonplaces of propagandistic discourse. A familiar rhetoric, but from outside cinema.

147

This is the strategic textual problem of documentary: it "wants" to construct a textual system capable of "saying" anything, to give the filmic system the discursive power of language. At the same time, it cannot escape the moment of the code, i.e., it can only speak in ways that the cinematic codes have traced out in advance. As Christian Metz asserts, "Very often in the cinema it is the *saying* that determines absolutely what is *said*."[39] We take Metz's assertion in its most textual sense: documentary speaks the "language" of the fiction film, or it relies on verbal language (the commentary), or it depends on another rhetoric, like the one I have traced out here. Most often documentary achieves an uneasy compromise, a mixture of discursive forms. The more documentary films conform to the codes of the fiction film, the more we perceive them as "cinematic." Other discursive forms flood the documentary text with marks of enunciation which exhibit the signs of their presence.

4

Documentary Film: History or Discourse?

The documentary film depends for its specific effect on a particular placement of the spectator in relation to the image. As recent theoretical work particularly among French scholars suggests, the cinematic apparatus has a history whose origins are to be located in western representation as it was constituted in the period of Renaissance humanism.[1] The instrumental base—the set of technical processes that carry the film from its recording by the camera to its projection in the movie theater—produces an image whose construction derives from monocular perspective, the conception of pictorial space developed in the *Quattrocento*. In monocular perspective, the spectator applies to the flat space of the image the law of the constancy of the size of objects within the perceptual field. When an object is known to us through experience, we recognize in the process of perception the object's real size, however large or small it may appear on the retina. As viewers, we interpret the changes in the size of the perceived object not as changes in the size of the real object, but as the varying distances between the real object and the eye. The strategy of Leonardo's window is to lend the structure of the retinal image to the flat pictorial surface that the viewer is invited to read in depth. This illusory impression of spatial depth that monocular perspective evokes depends, therefore, on disavowal—the application of laws of perception to a field the observer knows is two-dimensional.

This representation of space supposes an immobile point of reference in relation to which the objects represented are disposed, the point inscribed in real space by the line of *perspectiva artificialis* from which the look is deployed. It is this point of reference that the subject (the "eye" of the subject) necessarily occupies:

149

The image produced by the camera cannot do otherwise than confirm and reduplicate "the code of specular vision such as it is defined by the renaissant humanism," such that the human eye is at the center of the system of representation, with that centrality at once excluding any other representative system, assuring the eye's domination over any other organ of the senses and putting the eye in a strictly divine place (Humanism's critique of Christianity).[2]

The viewer, then, in the tradition of western representation, identifies in the first instance with the "creator" of the image, whose place he or she assumes as subject in order to possess the image as object. In cinema, this position is occupied initially by the camera, the instrument that "sees" first, its frame establishing the vanishing point of perspective and its own emplacement. Hence the spectator takes the place of—identifies with—the absent camera and assumes the field of its vision as his or her own. The spectator thus becomes the transcendental subject, the locus of the production of meaning, the site of an ultimate signified. As Jean-Louis Baudry observes, "This system [*perspectiva artificalis*], a recentering or at least a displacement of the center (which settles in the eye), will assure the setting up of the 'subject' as the active center and origin of meaning."[3]

The placement of the spectator-subject of the fiction film also depends upon a certain disposition of the film-object as text: the narrative film appears as history, not discourse. I draw here on the linguistic distinction formulated by Emile Benveniste, which establishes two separate but complementary planes of utterance.[4] Historical narration is a mode of utterance in which the marks of the discursive act, i.e., the individual appropriation by a subject of the apparatus of *langue,* are not in evidence. To begin with, the historic mode suppresses the forms designating the subject of enunciation "I" and the discursive partner "you". As Benveniste asserts, this mode excludes all "autobiographical" forms: "The historian will never say *je* or *tu* or *maintenant,* because he will never make use of the formal apparatus of discourse, which resides in the relationship of the person *je:tu.*"[5] Discourse, by way of contrast, is defined by the exchange between "I" and "you," by the situation of dialogue: "What in general characterizes enunciation is *the emphasis on the discursive relationship with the partner,* whether he is real or imagined, individual or collective."[6] In discourse, as Benveniste describes it, the enunciating subject is present to his enunciation, and each instance of discourse establishes a "center of internal reference" within which a certain number of forms are engendered: the indicators of person, the personal and demonstrative pronouns (which refer only to "individuals," not to concepts); ostensive indicators, such as this/that, here/there (which demand the support of gesture); the system of tenses, whose foundation is the present, the time of discourse itself. All these forms are tied to the discursive situation, without which they could not signify. Beyond the specific forms that mark the enunciative act, enunciation also provides the conditions necessary for major syntactic functions: interrogation, intimation, assertion.[7] For Benveniste, then, a distinction is to be made between the elements of language that are fully constituted within *langue* and those that depend for their existence on the act of appropriation of *langue* by an individual speaker: "We must therefore distinguish entities which have their full and permanent status in *langue* and those which, arising from enunciation, only exist in the network of 'individuals' that enunciation creates in relation to the 'here-and-now' of the speaker."[8]

As Christian Metz points out, it is precisely the signs of the presence of an enunciating subject that do not exist in the classic narrative film: "In Emile Beveniste's terms, the traditional film is presented as story, and not as discourse. And yet it is a discourse, if we refer it back to the film-maker's intentions, the influence he wields over the general public, etc.; but the basic characteristic of this kind of discourse, and the very principle of its effectiveness as discourse, is precisely that it obliterates all traces of the enunciation, and masquerades as story."[9] In the case of the filmic image, enunciation is of a different order from that of language. Unlike the linguistic sign with its double articulation—its significative and distinctive levels—the iconic sign has an analogical character: it maintains a spatial relationship between its signifier and the referent. The linguistic sign acknowledges its distance from the field of reference; the iconic sign poses as a copy of the real. The filmic image seems quite incapable of manipulating the field it represents. It has no syntactic structures (the image cannot question or deny); it has no shifters in Jakobson's sense; it has no system of tenses (the image is always an utterance in the present). It lacks the discursive powers of language and appears to give us, quite "naturally," a pure recitation of events without the mediating presence of a "speaker." The image discourse we call film would seem a perfect vehicle for narration in the historic mode as Benveniste describes it: "It is sufficient and necessary that the author remain faithful to his historical purpose and that he proscribe everything that is alien to the narration of events (discourse, reflections, comparisons). As a matter of fact, there is then no longer even a narrator. The events are set forth chronologically, as they occurred. No one speaks here; the events seem to narrate themselves."[10]

The character of the filmic signifier with its radical suppression of marks of enunciation is conducive to the particular symbolic position that the spectator assumes in cinema. The spectator does not identify in the first instance with what the images represent but with the agency that makes them visible. The narrative in cinema is "a story from nowhere, that nobody tells, but which, nevertheless, somebody receives. . . ."[11] This someone, the film spectator—whose place is inscribed by the code of monocular perspective and whose object remains unappropriated—is able to assume an (illusory) position in relation to the film, which is that of the subject of enunciation. In the following passage Christian Metz evokes this subject-effect that the cinematic apparatus and the filmic text seem designed to produce:

> I'm at the cinema. I am present at the screening of the film. *I am present*. Like the midwife attending a birth who, simply by her presence, assists the woman in labour, I am present for the film in a double capacity (though they are really one and the same) as witness and as assistant: I watch, and I help. By watching the film I help it to be born, I help it to live, since only in me will it live, and since it is made for that purpose: to be watched, in other words to be brought into being by nothing other than the look."[12]

It is this placement at the locus of the production of meaning that constitutes the spectator's peculiar *visée de conscience* and the source of the special pleasure that cinematic narratives provide.

The conjunction of narrativity (with its particular mode of discourse) and the cinematic apparatus (with its particular inscription of the subject) is a historic fact. However, despite the predispositions that may be discerned—the seemingly perfect marriage of an instrument and its vocation—this historic union should not be taken for a natural fact. As historians of cinema have amply demonstrated, a period of experimentation was necessary (in the years between 1895 and 1915) before cinema "found" its social function as a machine for telling stories. The work of the "pioneer" figures—G. A. Smith and James Williamson of the "Brighton School," Edwin S. Porter, D. W. Griffith—served to separate filmic space from the static space of the theatrical scene. It was the mobilization of the camera and the creation of the codes of *montage* that allowed cinema to "signify according to laws of its own."[13] What has been called the discovery of the shot is inseparable from the notion of

152

sequence: the reintegration of the fragmentary shot into an arrangement that produces a continuity of a wholly different order. Historically speaking, the codes of sequence are the primitive base of cinematographic discourse, and they developed as a product of the search for a new "technique" of narrative that could meet the expectations of an audience steeped in the naturalism of late nineteenth-century novels and theater. As Noel Burch suggests, this basic motivation can be seen in all the advances that mark the primitive evolution of filmic discourse:

> Starting from the first premises of the alternating shots in the work of Porter and the British, and the earliest contiguity matches (matches of direction and eyeline), this evolution, through the increasing ubiquity of the camera, was ultimately to succeed in establishing the conviction that all the successive separate shots on the screen referred to the same diegetic continuum. In other words, the time spans represented were linked together by relations of immediate succession, simultaneity, or a more distant anteriority or posteriority; the spaces pictured communicated directly or at one or more removes; and above all the whole constituted a milieu into which the spectator might penetrate as an invisible, immaterial observer, yet one who not only saw but also "experienced" all that transpired there. [14]

This historical work that placed cinema in the clear line of descent of fictional narrative and inscribed the spectator-subject in a position of apparent power within the cinematic apparatus constituted the essential base for the cinematic institution. It was thanks to its formation as a social machinery for telling stories that cinema began to function according to its own laws of production and consumption and became, like all institutions, capable of perpetuating itself. The dominance of the cinematic institution should not be underestimated; it is not simply economic, it is semiological. Film "language" is inextricably bound up with narrativity: cinema developed as a distinct system of signification in order to tell stories. As Metz observes, the historic weight is enormous:

> Indeed the cinema is eminently apt to assume this role [of telling stories]; even the greatest demand could not have diverted it in any lasting way along a path that its inner semiological mechanism would have made improbable. Things could never have occurred so fast nor remained in the state we still find them, had the film not been a supreme story-teller and had its narrativity not been endowed with the nine lives of a cat. The total invasion of the cinema by novelesque fiction is a peculiar, striking phenomenon, when one thinks that film could have

153

found so many other possible uses which have hardly been explored by a society that is nevertheless forever in pursuit of technographic novelty.[15]

In analyzing the large syntagmatic category in documentary, we found that even departures from the classic model do not imply a radical displacement of narrative; rather, they involve the subordination of narrativity in certain films, in a textual sense, to the smaller units of discourse. In *Listen to Britain*, we saw how the documentary text can both repress and continue to exploit the codes of narrative ordering. Even when the text abandons the principle of narrative at the level of the scenario or even of the large syntagmatic units, the narrative-effect reemerges, irrepressible, in the sequential development of shots at the subsegmental level. Those films that appear the least "classical" in structure, i.e., those that lack spatio-temporal articulation at the level of the large syntagmatic or the scenario, contain not a single, continuous narrative but a proliferation of narratives, short in duration and restricted to the subsegmental level. Each brief narrative flow appears as abstracted from a larger narrative movement and contains the signs of its potential expansion in time and space. As Metz suggests, narrative exerts its hold over all filmic texts, even in those that take a paradoxical stand against it: "A narrative kernel remains present in nearly all films—in those where it constitutes the main point as in many others where the main point, even if located elsewhere, hinges on it in various fashions: on it, under it, in its gaps, sometimes in opposition to it."[16]

We are thus led to the conclusion that what distinguishes documentary from the fiction film is not the simple presence or absence of narrative. Narrative is never absent in documentary films, even if its presence is more or less marked. Nor can we ascribe a particular mode of narration to documentary, given the heterogeneity of texts this study has discovered. Certain documentaries closely resemble the fiction film in that they deploy its basic signifying structures at many textual levels; others mark out their distance by adopting these structures episodically or by restricting them to certain textual functions. Can we in fact assert that documentary represents a specific discursive form? If so, how can it be described? Further, how do we account for the effect the documentary text produces in the spectator? In what play of textual forces is the nonfiction effect rooted?

One of the distinctive features of textuality in documentary is the co-presence of two discrete planes of utterance, two clearly marked moments of discourse. The first is the discourse rooted in the image, which evokes a presumably coherent and autonomous world of time and space; the second is a discourse of language, which stands above and outside of the discourse of images. The most common manifestation of this linguistic agency is the spoken commentary. The voice of the commentary is the only material element that detaches itself from the image in a manner quite unlike that of the occasional voice-over of the fiction film, which situates the spectator within the universe of the story and thereby favors the spectator's access to his or her imaginary. In the narrative film, sound, even extradiegetic sound, supports the diegesis: "Meant to strengthen the verisimiltude of an anecdote, sound is merely a supplementary support of representation: it must integrate itself docilely with the mimed object; it is in no way detached from that object."[17]

This ancillary character of sound in cinema has its historic roots in the hegemony of the eye, which in western cultures, as Edgar Morin points out, has secured its dominance at the expense of the other senses, notably hearing:

The genesis of a language of the silent image, accompanied solely by music, could only be brought about with ease and efficiency in the heart of a civilization where the preeminence of the eye has progressively asserted itself at the expense of the other senses, in the domain of the real as well as in that of the imaginary. Whereas the sixteenth century, before seeing, "hears and smells, sniffs the air and picks up noises," as L. Febvre shows in his *Rabelais,* the cinema reveals the decadence of the sense of hearing (the dissociation of the sound source from the visual sources, the approximations of dubbing, the schematization of mixing, etc . . .) at the same time as it founds its empire on the concrete and analytic powers of the eye.[18]

In cinema, sound came to "complete" the moving image. Diminished in its powers of representation, it contributes nonetheless to the impression of reality evoked by the image.

A study of the cinematic signifier reveals a heterogeneity of materials—the animated photographic image, written text, speech, noise, and music—which are destined to be received by the spectator, or rather to be constituted within the spectator as one homogeneous narrative signified. Together the film-text and the spectator perform a work of integration on these disparate audio-visual elements, following the pathways traced out by the codes governing syntagmatic relations between sound and image in cinema. As Morin suggests, there is to begin with a fundamental irrecon-

155

cilability between the representation of visual and auditory space that is overcome by the preeminence of one sense over the other: sound in narrative film seeks its truth in the image. The fiction takes root, as Metz suggests, in the spectator's consciousness through the denegation at all levels of the reality of the signifier: "The fiction film is the film in which the cinematic signifier does not work on its own account but is employed entirely to remove the traces of its own steps, to open immediately on to the transparency of a signified, of a story, which is in reality manufactured by it but which it pretends merely to "illustrate", to transmit to us after the event, as if it had existed previously (= referential illusion)."[19] At the level of the sound track, the spectator denies the work of technicians, which has taken the place of the work of auscultation accomplished by the hearing subject in a real auditory field. In the movie theater, as Claude Bailblé observes, the spectator does not exercise his organs of hearing and his powers of intentionality (listening loses its active quality); the listener does not isolate what he wants to hear and push into the background (actually, the side ground: lateral inhibition of sound created by the movement of the hearer's head) what is "insignificant."[20] The spectator denies the artificiality of this constructed auditory space (what Bailblé calls the *perspectiva auricula artificalis*[21]) for the sake of fiction—in order to privilege the signified: "In today's cinema, where the spectator frees himself of all effort (he is like pure spirit) by taking up the position of the narrative agency, of the look of the camera, the apparatus must still relieve him of spatial exploration, of the work of the invocatory drive (in any case impossible in monophony) in order for the fiction to become fully transparent."[22]

The "more real" that the sound track adds to the impression of reality of the moving image hinges on a specific disposition of the spectator: he must take himself (while knowing he does not) for the first, the original hearer; he must "forget" the work of technicians, the "hidden" (but at the same time acknowledged) status of the auditory messages as discourse. This denial includes the denial of the separation of spaces in the movie theater: the screen as site of the image, the loudspeaker as site, or rather source, of the sound. The effect is one of the subordination of one space to the other: diegetic sound "finds" its source in the image, is anchored, identified by the image. It is in the image in order to constitute the fullness, the wholeness of the diegesis. Denial extends to the reception of all extradiegetic elements, whose primary quality is discretion. In the classic narrative film, extradiegetic elements of the sound track have ancillary status: they must serve or be silent. A commentary from outside the diegesis may intervene, or the voice of a character-become-narrator may surface from within the diegesis in order to situate the fiction. But once these voices have presented the spectator with his object, defined its contours or filled its gaps, they retire and leave the spectator to his pleasure. Extradiegetic music contributes to shaping the narrative and invests it with connotations. But although it directly manipulates affect in the spectator, film music is received in apparent passivity. Claudia Gorbman in her work on "Narrative Film Music" observes, "Most feature films relegate music to the viewer's sensory background, that gray area of secondary perception least susceptible to rigorous judgment and most susceptible to affective manipulation."[23]

The organization of the materials of expression in the nonfiction film is markedly different. The documentary film depends for its specific effect on the maintenance of a certain heterogeneity. This heterogeneity is due in the first instance to the coexistence within the filmic text of two distinct (and nonintegral) modes of expression, one historic, the other discursive. It is not simply a question of the mixed character of the filmic text—the fact that any film integrates codes that belong specifically to cinema and codes that come from outside it. The linguistic text of the commentary is not only extracinematographic, like the dialogue of the fiction film; it is rigorously extradiegetic. Released from the boundaries of narrative, it assumes autonomy as a discourse and deploys its own forces in the construction of the global message of the film. Thus the two modes of discourse produce a split in the materials of expression between the diegetic agency and the extradiegetic agency, or to put it another way, between what belongs to the image (including sound) and what belongs to the second, linguistic discourse. The nonfiction-effect takes root, then, in this dual structure.

However, the split is never constant. Rather, there is an oscillation between modes of expression in which the "objectivity" of narrative, created by the intermittent autonomy of the image-discourse, is reappropriated by the linguistic discourse: the voice of the commentary emerges to assert its authority, then retreats, only to reemerge again. In order to describe the nonfiction-effect produced by the documentary film, I must begin by describing this voice.

The spoken commentary is a discourse that displays marks of enunciation. It bears the signs of what Benveniste terms the "implementation of *langue* through an individual act of utilization."[24] It is a form of oral discourse (subjected of course to the work of technical processes by means of which the voice is in effect reconstituted). It is an utterance that presumes a speaker (even if he is no longer present) and a hearer (even if he or she remains unnamed in the dark anonymity of the movie theater). The most direct and immediate mark of enunciation is the phonetic materiality of the voice, the vocal realization of *langue:* "The sounds emitted and perceived, whether they are studied in the context of a particular idiom or in their general manifestations, as processes of acquisition, diffusion, modification—these are so many branches of phonetics—always originate in individual acts, which the linguist captures as much as possible as native performance, in the heart of speech."[25] The voice of the commentary posits itself as the subjective person and by this act posits the existence of a you, of a non subjective person, the one who receives the message. This is what Benveniste calls the figurative frame of enunciation. Two "figures" are posited, one the source, the other the objective of discourse: "But immediately, as soon as he asserts himself as speaker and assumes *la langue,* he plants the *other* in front of him, whatever may be the degree of presence he attributes to this other. Every enunciation is, explicitly or implicitly, a discourse, it postulates a hearer."[26]

The voice of the commentary is, of course, not the only speech in cinema. There is the speech of characters in the diegetic film, and it also possesses marks of enunciation, in fact, more so than the commentary. But for the spectator this speech is not so much heard as overheard. The voyeuristic spectator pretends to take unawares the images and sounds that are not meant (but he knows are meant) for him. Speech circulates within the represented space of the fiction; the figurative frame of enunciation is always enclosed within the fictional frame of narrative. The look "into the camera" and the interpellation of the spectator in speech are both perceived as violations (of the same order) of the separation of spaces in the movie theater. What distinguishes then the voice of the commentary is the fact that it addresses the spectator, that it crosses from the space of the film to the space of the auditorium. It constitutes itself as subject, thus implicating the other, and engaging itself in an intersubjective situation.

To the extent that the commentary exhibits its discursive relation to the spectator, it is possible to assert that documentary film alters the conditions of reception set in place by the fiction film and restores to cinema a certain measure of its reality, its reality as discourse. But such an assertion immediately calls for reservations. The commentary maintains, as I have noted, a complex and ambivalent relationship with the discourse of images, and its modal character, its status as discourse is never completely realized. Moreover, the marginality of documentary film is evident not only in the film texts but in their uneasy integration into the cinematic apparatus.

The spectator who is being addressed is caught in his position of spectator in the configuration of the movie theater: the disposition of the seating, the projector, the screen. This arrangement imposes on him his physical immobility and his passive position of reception. With the classic narrative film this passivity and immobility are the conditions of an (illusory) activity—the assumption by the spectator of the role of enunciator in the interest of another kind of movement: the play within the psyche of certain libidinal forces. In documentary, on the other hand, the spectator is apparently called upon to assume a different position. He cannot identify with the voice of the commentary as he does with the camera, because the voice addresses him (to whom else could the voice be speaking?). And yet the discursive situation is not complete. The spectator knows that he cannot address the voice because it (or rather its source) is elsewhere, situated on the other side of a chain of technical transformations: microphone > amplification > magnetic tape > optical track > loudspeaker. The position of authority that the voice of the commentary assumes is here produced within the apparatus itself: the spectator submits, accepts his position of reception, his passivity, the voice's authority (he remains seated); or, if he rejects it, he may walk out of the movie theater. He may withdraw, but he may never reply or contradict. The reversibility of discourse is not possible; the discursive "partners" cannot be "alternatively protagonists of enunciation." The figurative frame of enunciation is hence only partially constituted as it is in other discursive situations where reversibility has been suppressed (as in the televised political speech, for example).

What can be said about the linguistic discourse as vocal realization? The commentary in documentary film is a voice without a body, a subject without substance. Not only is the narrative voice off-screen—it can never appear in the image—it is without placement. It is by definition the voice that is not represented—that is not capable of representation. It is deprived of even the shadow of a body that the image could provide. The voice in classic documentary possesses the qualities that Roland Barthes attributes to writing: "Writing is that neutral, composite, oblique space where our subject slips away, the negative where all identity is lost, starting with the very identity of the body writing."[27] The neutralization

159

of the voice—its kinship with the voiceless enunciation of the printed page—is obtained by a work of normalization and resembles the work carried out by phoneticians who attempt to eliminate all individual traits of phonic enunciation in order to produce an average image of sound. The voice has been stripped of its grain, to use Barthes's word. It is not a person, it is a subject. It is not particular, it is general. It has in effect been desexed: always male, a universal, neutered he. It is without age, giving no sign of youth or old age. It is deprived of regionalisms, of sociocultural origins, of signs of class. It has no physical state (it is never out of breath or afflicted with pain), and the signs of its emotional state are largely muted (seldom joyful, upset, or afraid). Its environment has also been repressed: we do not know from where and under what conditions he speaks. The voice does not refer to himself explicitly as a subject: he never says "I," nor does he refer to the spectator as "you." The marks of enunciation are not emphatic. The speaker does not insist upon his relationship to his enunciation nor is his discourse centered on the hearer: the codes of implication of the discursive partner rarely intervene. We are faced, therefore, with a profoundly ambivalent phenomenon: the voice of the commentary asserts itself as the subject of enunciation (the film does not recount itself) while at the same time the marks of this enunciation have been largely effaced.

The assertion that the spectator does not identify with the voice of the commentary must then be reexamined, for it represents only one of the values (one pole of the ambivalence) compounded in this particular arrangement of the cinematic *dispositif.* It is in fact intended that the spectator identify with (take as his or her own) the discourse proffered by the voice of the commentary. If this were not so, what then would be the significance of the neutralization of the voice, of the emptiness of this enunciation? The process of identification, which always remains partially realized, is abetted by what can be described as an analogy of position between the spectator and the voice of the commentary.

In describing the relationship of the spectator to the characters of the fiction film, Metz analyses in the following way a certain play of secondary identification:

It can happen (and this is already another "notch" in the chain of identifications) that a character looks at another who is momentarily out-of-frame, or else is looked at by him. If we have gone one notch further, this is because everything out-of-frame *brings us closer to the spectator,* since it is the peculiarity of the latter to be out-of-frame (the

160

out-of-frame character thus has a point in common with him: he is looking at the screen).[28]

Now, the voice of the commentary, never embodied like the voice of the off-screen character, is by definition out-of-frame. The difference is of course that the voice, unlike the fictional character who is momentarily off, is not situated in that imaginary space contiguous to the frame. There is no play of the look within the diegesis, even though the voice is possessed of a look. The voice is also a spectator and it is looking at the screen. But from where? There is here the (illusory) beginning of a different repartition of the spaces of the movie theater. The voice, radically separated from the screen (the represented instance), comes to position itself on the side of the three-dimensional space of the auditorium: the garrulous spectator takes his place beside the silent one.

The signs of this positioning of the commentary are in the text itself. The voice is looking at the image since it names it, refers to it by means of marks of enunciation—he constitutes it as the "world of reference" that he holds in common with the spectator. The referents of the linguistic message are largely confounded with the representation of the image:

Image: Long shot, symmetrically framed, of a church-like structure.
Voice: "This is not a chapel edified to the glory of John the Baptist, patron saint of butchers, nor to the memory of his so gentle lamb. This is the auction house of the abbatoirs.

Le Sang des bètes

For the commentary as for the spectator, the image is an object, the "beautiful closed object which must remain unaware of the pleasure it gives us."[29] The voice of the commentary is "knowledgeable," it is a metalinguistic discourse in that it stands above the discourse of images, commenting, telling the images' "truth." But it is also sealed off from the image: the appearance within the frame of one of the filming party in Buñuel's *Land without Bread*—not the embodiment of the voice but the invasion of the image by that off-screen space that belongs to the narrating agency—is perceived as a strange and unanticipated disruption of the boundaries of the narrated.

In documentary cinema as in the classic narrative film, the spectator comes to occupy the position of the subject inscribed for him by the cinematic apparatus. But this emplacement is not entirely empty: it is already occupied by a voice. The spectator is not responsible alone, as in the historic mode of discourse, for the constitution of the film as meaning. The spectator of the fiction film, as Metz observes, is all-perceiving:

> All-perceiving as one says all-powerful (this is the famous gift of "ubiquity" the film makes its spectator); all-perceiving, too, because I am entirely on the side of the perceiving instance: absent from the screen, but certainly present in the auditorium, a great eye and ear without which the perceived would have no one to perceive it, the instance, in other words, which *constitutes* the cinema signifier (it is I who make the film).[30]

The spectator's primary identification is with the camera—the instrument that "saw" before, but is no longer there (represented by its double—the projector, situated "in back of the head"). The cinematic apparatus permits the spectator to fantasize him- or herself as the subject of enunciation. But in documentary cinema, the voice of the commentary is also a constitutive instance—it stands on the side of narration (of the production of meaning) and hence on the side of (beside) the spectator, his constant companion, his double. More knowledgeable than the midwife-spectator that Metz describes,[31] it also assists in the birth of the film as meaning. It functions not just so that meaning will be produced, but so that a certain meaning will be produced.

Hence the problem of the ambivalent position of the commentary. The conditions necessary to permit identification—the assumption by the spectator of the voice as his or her own—are never complete. The voice is after all material, it speaks from behind the screen, it is perceived as an integral part of the signifier. It shares with the other elements of the signifier the fact of being recorded, of being a "presence played in the mode of absence." The commentary is as fictive as any other element of the signifier; it is the shadow of a voice, part of the "imaginary that constitutes it as a signifier." However, the commentary is distinct from all diegetic elements: it exists within no perspective. Diegetic sound produces an impression of space (of depth, if not of laterality) through a varying play of volume and timber (in concert with the image, whose depth it mimics). The commentary lacks the three-dimensional perspective and the sense of acoustic spatiality that constitute the artificial depth of field of diegetic sound. It maintains, rather, a constancy of distance (volume and timber), a constancy that recalls the consciousness of the subject, "the constituting transcendental function to which narrative points back as its natural secretion."[32]

As we have seen, what characterizes the voice of the commentary as signifier is its neutralization, its absence of grain, and this neutralization is fundamentally an effacement of difference. The voice is emptied out so that it may be filled. It is transparent: if it is not possessed, then it is possessible. But never entirely. The spectator's identification with the voice stops far short of its apparent goal, in order precisely that the voice may retain its function. So the image and the commentary, history and discourse, identification and distantiation teeter in a delicate balance, and it is in this balance of forces that the nonfiction-effect is created.

The following transcriptions are taken from the corpus of eleven documentary films analyzed in chapter two and are intended to illustrate the discursive ambivalence that is essential to the work of the classic documentary film. The texts are quite diverse, and they evoke in their specific textual organizations the dialectic of subordination-dominance and the shifting modalities of enunciation that establish the symbolic position of the subject.

Transcription 1: *Night Mail*

Night Mail is a film with a strong narrative character. The spatio-temporal references that constitute the story are unusually specific and localizable: the film represents the mail run of the Postal Express from London to Glasgow from 8:30 P.M. to the dawn of the following morning. The major divisions of the scenario are distinguished as stages in the train's trajectory: 1) the express's departure and its journey toward the main junction for the Midlands (segments 1–13); 2) events surrounding the arrival of the Postal at the Midlands station (14–21); 3) the work of the postal employees aboard the express as it speeds toward Scotland (22–26); 4) the train's ascent into the highlands and its arrival in Scotland (27–32).

The train's journey in the first part is marked by the recurrence at more or less regular intervals of narrative syntagmas containing similar motifs: the train in motion and images of passing landscapes—classical representation of travel in the fiction film. These sequences are interspersed with narrative segments representing what we take to be typical scenes marking the Postal Express's itinerary (the delaying of a passenger train, the halting of work along the tracks) or scenes of work related to the train's passage (the functioning of switches, the positioning of retrieval and signal mechanisms). The continuity of the second and third divisions of the scenario is guaranteed not only by a strict narrative consecutiveness, but also by a circumscribed unity of place: the junction station and the interior of the Postal Express. The fourth division mirrors the first through a "repetition" of the motifs of the train's passage, which take on the rhythmic cadence of the commentary and music—the famous "coda" written by W. H. Auden and Benjamin Britten.

The following eleven segments are excerpted from part 1: the departure of the Postal Special.

Shot No.	Image	Speech	Noise/ Music
	1: Autonomous shot		
1	A carrier delivers a message to a clerk at his desk.	—Here's the departure message for the Down Postal. —Right. Thank you. O.K. (Reading into the telephone) Group control, Euston telegraph. 157 Postal left at 8:30 flat. 6810, 340 tons, 12 vehicles.	Background noise (on).
	2: Ordinary Sequence		
2	Aerial view of a train in movement (very long shot).	8:30 P.M., weekdays and Sundays, the Down Postal Special leaves Euston for Glasgow, Edinburgh and Aberdeen.	Background noise of the train (on).
3	Aerial view of tracks (very long shot).	The Postal Special is a fast express, but it carries no passengers. It is manned by 40 post office workers.	Train (on).

164

Shot No.	Image	Speech	Noise/Music
4	Aerial view of tracks (very long shot).	Half a million letters are sorted, picked up or dropped at full speed during the night, or carried on for morning delivery in Scotland.	Train (on).

3: Ordinary Sequence

Shot No.	Image	Speech	Noise/Music
5	The Station house: exterior (very long shot).		Ringing of bell (off).
6	Worker stands at lighted panel of train schedule cards (medium shot).	—Attention, B. —Attention, B to C. —Can you take Postal Special? —Can take Postal Special. (Voice-over of telegraph messages.)	Bell (on).
7	Telegraph lines (long shot).		Noise of telegraph equipment (off).
8	A second worker at another lighted panel (medium shot).	—Can you take Postal Special? —Line clear. (Voice-over)	
9	Dial switch: arrow moves down—line clear (close-up).		Noise of switches (off).
10	A worker operates switches (long shot).		Noise of switches (on).

Shot No.	Image	Speech	Noise/ Music
11	Switches; workers in background (medium shot).		Noise of switches (on).
12	Dial-signal (close-up).		Noise of switches (off).
13	Final switch is thrown (as in 11) (medium shot).		Noise of switches (on).
14	A signal flag goes down (medium shot).		Noise of the signal flag (on).
15	The dial (as in 12) (close-up).		Noise of switches (off).
16	An approaching train is seen through the station structure. A switchman enters right (very long shot).		Noise of the train (on).
17	Railroad landscape at night; a signal (very long shot).		Noise of the train and its whistle.

4: Ordinary sequence

18	Workers repairing a track at night (long shot).		Noise of tools (on).
19	Workers on the tracks (pan in long shot).		Noise of tools (on).

Shot No.	Image	Speech	Noise/Music
20	The foreman blows his whistle (medium shot).		Noise of the whistle (on).
21	Workers with picks (medium shot).	—Stand by! Stand clear! (off)	Noise of tools (on).
22	Workers move to the side of the track; the train passes (medium shot).	—That'll be the Postal, mates. —Right on time, ain't she, Joe? (on)	Noise of train's passage (off/on).
23	Workers standing in a group (medium shot).		Noise of the train (off).
24	Three workers (medium shot).		Background noise (off).
25	The train passing (long shot).		Noise of the train (on).
26	Workers (as in 24) (medium shot).		Background noise (off).

5: Ordinary sequence

27	A train in a country landscape (very long shot).	Four million miles every year.	Noise of the train (on).
28	Landscape seen from a moving train (long shot).	Five hundred million letters every year.	Noise of the train (off).
29	Telegraph lines seen from the moving train (long shot).		Train whistle (off).

167

Shot No.	Image	Speech	Noise/ Music
		6: Autonomous shot	
30	A railway worker at a telephone (medium shot).	—That you, Harry? You'll have to shunt the local. I've got the Postal on. Righto. (on)	Noise of the telephone (on).
		7: Scene	
31	A train pulling into a station; a conductor directing the stop (long shot).		Noise of the train (on).
32	View of the passengers in the slowing train (medium long shot).		Noise of brakes (off).
33	A man hanging out of a compartment window engages a railway worker in a conversation (medium shot).	—How long do we wait here? —At best a couple of minutes, mate, while the Postal Special goes by. There you are. Here she comes. (on)	Noise of a speeding train (off).
34	The faces of two workers, heads turning to follow the train (medium close).	—She's right on time tonight, mate. (on)	Noise of the train (off).
		8: Ordinary sequence	
35	The Postal Special in the countryside.	Trains from Lincolnshire, Derbyshire connect at Tamwell. Trains from from Warwickshire, Leicestershire connect at Rugby.	Noise of the train (on).

168

Shot No.	Image	Speech	Noise/ Music
36	Telegraph lines and the sky seen from the moving train (long shot).		Noise of the train (off).

9: Ordinary sequence

37	A man leading a horse (long shot).		Noise of hooves (on).
38	A haystack: the man in the foreground (37) looks at his watch and raises his head (medium shot).		Noise of hooves (off).
39	Country landscape (seen by the man in 38) (very long shot).		A distant train whistle (off).
40	The man (as in 38) (off). looking (medium close-up).		Whistle.

Insert

41	A village seen from the moving train (off) (very long shot).		The whistle (louder).
42	Train tracks; a package is thrown from the train and lands on the ground (long shot).		Noise of the train (off).
43	The Postal in a landscape (as in 39) (very long shot).		Noise of the train (on).

Shot No.	Image	Speech	Noise/ Music
44	The man enters the frame, stoops to pick up the package (medium shot).		Noise of the train (off).
45	A newspaper (seen, in close-up).		Noise of the train (off).
46	The man turns away from the tracks, shouts and waves (medium shot).	—Charlie!	
47	"Charlie" (seen, in long shot).	—Charlie! (lower and off)	
48	The man with the newspaper (medium-close shot).	—She come in at five to two.	

11: Ordinary sequence

49	The Postal approaching (long shot).		Noise of the train (on).
50	Landscape seen from the train (very long shot).		Noise of the train (off).

12: Ordinary sequence

51	Two postal workers descend a stairway in the dark (long shot).		Noise of footsteps (on).

Shot No.	Image	Speech	Noise/ Music
52	The two men (51) drop their mailbags on the side of the tracks (long shot).	At 34 points between London and Glasgow, postmen wait to deliver to the Postal Special. The mails have been roughly sorted. . .	Footsteps and background noise (on).
53	The two men on a dispatching tower set the net in place (long shot).	. . . by district. The postmen set up a net to catch the mail dropped by the train.	Noise of the maneuver (on).
54	The two men, who have redescended onto the tracks (long shot).	They strap up the mail in strong leather pouches.	Background noise (on).
55	The two men at the side of the tracks (reframed in long shot).	—There's something in these bags, all right, Bert. (on)	Background noise (on).
56	The men on the side of the tracks (reframed in long shot).	—Must be old Fred's cooper knife (on).	Background noise (on).
57	One worker climbs up the mail tower (medium shot).	The pouches are fixed to the standard by . . .	Background noise (on).
58	And places the mail pouch in the spring clip (close-up).	. . . spring clip.	Noise of the clip being placed (on).

Shot No.	Image	Speech	Noise/ Music
59	The worker climbing down from the tower (medium shot).		Background noise (on).
60	*Insert* The Postal approaches (long shot).		Noise of the approaching train (on).
61	The worker on the mail standard looks into the distance (medium shot).		Background noise (on).
62	*Insert* The Postal approaching (long shot).		Noise of the train (on).
63	The worker swivels the suspended pouches out over the tracks; the train approaches and the pouches are swept into the train (long shot).	A net is swung out from the train as it approaches. The impact releases the clip, and the pouches are swept into the train.	Noise of the train whistle, pouches being swept up (on).
64	The Postal moves into the distance (very long shot).	Those letters were posted in Bletchley half an hour ago.	Noise of the train, whistle (on).

The segments we have identified here all display a strong "classicalness," i.e., they conform to the syntagmatic types that Christian Metz describes in his study of the large syntagmatic category (see chapter 2). In fact, of the film's twenty-four segments (excluding autonomous shots and inserts) we count sixteen ordinary sequences and four scenes. *Night Mail*'s classical narrative structure is one sign of the dominance of the diegetic agency. Correlatively, we can expect to see a general effacement of the discursive commentary, even though the film has a clear didactic intention: each division of the scenario carries a certain body of "knowledge" to be communicated.

As in the fiction film, the production of a diegesis in *Night Mail* depends on a particular organization of the signifier in which sound supports the representation of the visual. The images, the noise track, and the speech identified as dialogue are so many coherent references to a world that seems to mandate their presence together on the syntagmatic chain. The noise track in particular complements the realism of the image by mimicking its spatiality and by dint of its own continuity covering over the fragmentation that is *montage*. Further, it fills out the diegesis by representing in continuity what has momentarily disappeared from the image. In these segments, the off-screen sound of the speeding Postal Special relates the space of the frame to the train's trajectory and creates, in this play between on- and off-screen space, a world of reference that remains largely imaginary. With the exception of the anamolous voice-overs verbalizing the telegraphic messages, dialogue, however infrequent, appears as it does in the fiction film: as mimetic speech that gives an auditory reality to the succession of characters and provides us with information essential to advancing the narrative. In brief, diegetic noise and speech, despite the latter's episodic character, deviate very little from the functions they perform in the fiction film.

The same cannot be said for the other linguistic discourse—the other plane of utterance—which stands resolutely outside the diegesis. Quite incapable of integration, the commentary asserts its separate status, and when it intervenes it produces a textual plurality that all the codes of the fiction film labor to suppress. How does the text manage these two distinct discursive agencies? *Night Mail,* which insists on the self-sufficiency of its narrative ordering, offers a discursive strategy that I would now like to examine.

The first quality of the commentary is discretion. It is quantitatively discreet: of the 240 shots that precede W. H. Auden's poetic coda, only thirty-three contain extradiegetic speech. In those segments where it appears, the commentary does not displace the diegetic elements. It takes the lead in fact only when the image has a lessened informational charge, i.e., in the sequences that represent the train's passage in nocturnal landscapes (segments 2 and 5 in our example). Even here the commentary does not occupy the full audio field, as is often the case in the classic documentary; rather, it allows for the continuity of the noise track, the image's constant companion. Thus the diegetic instance is represented as continuous, while the discursive instance is intermittent.

The commentary is also discrete in that it remains functionally distinct from the discourse of images, which narrates the passage of the Postal Special on the particular night in question. The commentary has in fact three functions. First, it is *narrative* insofar as it assists the advance of the film's action by providing narrative information that the image, noise, and dialogue do not carry. The commentary informs us of the train's destination (see shot 2), or links one action with another that has come before. It informs us, for example, that the pouches to be swept onto the train in segment 11 contain letters that have been previously sorted by district (see shots 52–53). However, this narrative function is ancillary, because the image and its associated sounds maintain their diegetic integrity. The commentary rarely refers—and always discreetly—to the here-and-now of the image. It names a place ("Crewe, the main junction for the Midlands") or specifies the duration ("The scheduled stop for the Postal Special is thirteen minutes") and the nature of the activity ("five hundred bags must be unloaded, engines changed, and some of the English crew changed for Scots"). Thus the commentary does not take possession of the image, as it frequently does in the classic documentary.

The second function of the commentary is what I will call *exegetic*. Speaking with the voice of knowledge, it identifies elements of the scene already present in the image but presumably not fully intelligible. Thus, most of the commentary in segment 12, which describes the technique of rapid mail delivery to the speeding train, is a gloss of events that the image represents ("They strap up the mail in strong leather pouches. The pouches are fixed to the standard by a spring clip.") This metalinguistic text elucidates the image, thereby controlling the process of intellection. This textual function is also rather infrequent; the only other extensive example in the film is the description in segment 19 of the sorting procedures carried out by workers on the speeding postal.

The third function I will ascribe to the commentary is *iterative*. The film's diegesis—the story told by the image track and its associated sound elements—represents a single occurrence: the Postal Express's passage into Scotland on a particular night. The film's plotline is in this regard perfectly linear. However, we cannot without distorting the filmmakers' intentions reduce *Night Mail*'s message to pure anecdote. The film does not simply narrate a singular event; it aims to evoke a field of occurrences always more general, more "historical," more abstract than the succession of specific events that form the narrative line in the fiction film.

174

In *Night Mail* the commentary performs its iterative function by using what Gérard Genette calls sylleptic formulations,[33] i.e., words added to the narrative text that indicate the frequency of acts. The first two segments of our example give us a perfect illustration of how the iterative expands narrative linearity. In segment 1, the clerk at Euston Telegraph specifies from within the diegesis the departure of the Postal Express whose progress constitutes the film's narrative thread: "Group Control? Euston telegraph. 157 Postal left at 8:30. Flat 6810. 340 tons. 12 vehicles." Segment 2 generalizes by giving this specific event a place in an iterative series of undetermined extension: "8:30 P.M., weekdays and Sundays, the Down Postal Special leaves Euston for Glasgow, Edinburgh, and Aberdeen." Thus we are able to read the narrative in the mode of habit and repetition so that the single occurrence stands for all the others the text does not represent. Similarly, the commentary in segment 5 ("Four million miles every year. Five hundred million letters every year.") and in segment 8 ("Trains from Lincolnshire, Derbyshire connect at Tamwell. Trains from Warwichshire, Leicestershire connect at Rugby.") broadens the temporal and geographical boundaries of narrative.

In *Night Mail* the discursive agency intrudes as little as possible in the conduct of the narrative. It is functionally discrete, a quite separate instance whose interventions are perceived as momentary infractions of the narrative hegemony. What belongs to the film's diegesis remains whole and inviolate. But however momentary and intermittent, the commentary produces a modal shifting, a change in focalization, because these separate textual agencies adopt quite different perspectives and demand quite different spectatorial positions. In the diegetic instance, everything happens as in the fiction film: the narrator has absented himself from the scene of enunciation and the story seems to tell itself. In the discursive instance, the spectator is called upon to identify with a voice that stands outside of the narrated. The discursive perspective is more distant (it alienates us from the experience of immediacy) and more knowledgeable (it sees far beyond the here-and-now of the actions unfolding).

The shift in modes in *Night Mail* is signaled by the shift in the status of speech. Diegetic speech (dialogue) is entirely contained within the fiction: the enunciator and his addressee are always represented as existing within the diegesis. The voice of the commentary, on the other hand, seems without a point of origin, and the figurative frame of enunciation is never closed: the position of addressee remains vacant. Moreover, this modal distinction is reinforced by an opposition between quite different characters of speech. The dialogue in *Night Mail* contains signifiers of class, of region, of the occupational hierarchy; that is, it realizes an often subtle representation of dialectical differences of all sorts. This "popular" speech contrasts, often quite ironically, with the neutralized voice of the commentary—the vacuity that is the sign of authority and truth.

The modal vacillation I have attempted to describe is quite subtle, a textual fluctuation that never threatens to override the narrative order. The strategy at work in *Night Mail* is rather to minimize discursive intervention in order to maintain the dominant historic mode. As Gérard Genette indicates, textual modulations do not necessarily alter a text's basic tonality:

> But a change in focalization, especially if it is isolated in a coherent context, can also be analyzed as a momentary infraction of the code which governs this context, without the code's existence being placed for all that in question, just as in a classical musical score a momentary change of key, or even a recurrent dissonance, is defined as a modulation or an accidental, without the tonality of the whole being contested.[34]

Purely exegetic, or simply introductory, or relegated to the "empty" syntagmas that mark the train's progress in a darkened landscape, the commentary has the status of parenthetical remarks inserted into already complete statements. In the film's final segments, the discursive text assumes a quite unexpected dominance. This poetic coda, written by W. H. Auden with music by Benjamin Britten, reverses the balance of forces. The image remains, but the noise track has been completely supplanted by the commentary and the musical score that imitate nonetheless the pulsating rhythm of the locomotive. The voice, still quite neutral, assumes a poetic diction, and at the film's closure, reasserts the full narrative power of language:

This is the Night Mail crossing the border,
Bringing the cheque and the postal order,
Letters for the rich, letters for the poor,
The shop at the corner, the girl next door.

Transcription 2: *Les Maîtres fous*

Jean Rouch's *Les Maîtres fous* is an ethnographic study of a "new religion" practiced by members of a sect called the Hauka. The narrative core of the film represents the execution of rites by the sect in a jungle compound near the city of Accra from Sunday morning to nightfall. The structure of the scenario is quite simple and consists of five major parts, representing the following: (1) Accra, the "true Babylon": the ethnic diversity, the conflict of traditional and modern, African and western, the polyglot masses who find work and distraction there (segments 1–3). (2) The Hauka sect: workers who migrate from the northern savanna to Accra's noisy suburbs and who worship the new gods of technology and power (segments 4–5). (3) The sect members' departure from Accra and arrival in the jungle (segment 6). (4) The unfolding of the rites, which are broken by only one segment (12) showing the pomp and circumstance of British colonialism, the model for the Haukas' perverse practices (segments 7–11 & 13). (5) The Accra salt market on Monday morning: images of the smiling demeanor of "happy" workers juxtaposed with images of these same workers as the possessed Hauka of the previous day's rites.

The transcription that follows begins with the Haukas' arrival in their jungle compound and represents the first phases of the ritual: segments 7, 8, and 9.

Shot No.	Image	Speech	Noise/ Music
	7: Descriptive syntagma		
67	Tree branches, then the building of the jungle compound, the statue of the governor (vertical pan down in long shot).	Colored rags flutter in the sky. They are the union jacks. Just below is a statue of the governor with his mustache . . .	
68	The face of the statue (close-up).	. . . his sword, his guns and his horses.	Background noise (off).
69	The "horses" (close-up).	The first part of the ceremony . . .	Voices, background noises (off).
	8: Ordinary sequence		
70	A man emerges from the jungle wearing shorts (long shot).	. . . is the nomination of new members. This man . . .	Voices and noise (off).

177

Shot No.	Image	Speech	Noise/ Music
71	A man in robes; then a seated group of men (discovered in pan, medium shot).	This man has been sick for one month; he has one fit after one other.	Voices and noise (on).
72	The man in shorts (as in 70) is examined by a man in a hat (medium shot).	He sleeps in the cemetery and digs up the corpses.	Voices and noise (on).
73	A group of participants (medium shot).	Everybody knows that this man is possessed by Hauka . . .	Voices and noise (on).
74	The man in shorts with the man in a hat (medium shot).	. . . and M—— [name inaudible] in his felt hat watches. He's not yet . . .	Voices and noise (on).
75	The man in the hat seen from behind; the man in shorts slips away (medium long shot).	. . . entitled to wear a pith helmet. In two or perhaps three months . . .	Voices and noise.
76	A seated group (medium shot).	. . . he will be initiated, when he asks to be, but for the time being . . .	Voices and noise.
77	The man in shorts returns (medium long shot).	. . . he has simply been . . .	Voices and noise.

178

Shot No.	Image	Speech	Noise/ Music
78	The man in shorts circulates with a "gun" (long shot).	. . . nominated. He takes out two wooden guns, which he strikes together to imitate the sound of gunfire.	Voices and noise.
79	A participant moves in a frenzied dance (medium long shot).	He straightens the elders.	Voices and noise.
80	The dancer falls (medium long shot).		Voices and noise.
81	The fallen dancer (medium long shot).		Voices and noise.
82	The fallen dancer gets up (medium shot).		Voices and noise.
83	Group of participants. Two men gesticulate (long shot).		Voices and noise.
84	Group of three participants in struggle (medium long shot).		Voices and noise.
85	The three men in struggle (medium long shot).		Voices and noise.
86	A group of participants; a man is prostrate, in a trance (medium shot).		Voices and noise.

Shot No.	Image	Speech	Noise/Music
87	The prostrate man (medium shot).	The nomination is over.	Voices and noise.
88	Trees, flagpole, union jacks, compound floor, participants (vertical pan shot).	M—— has hoisted another union jack.	Voices and noise.

9: Ordinary sequence

Shot No.	Image	Speech	Noise/Music
89	A man carries a long pole; several participants pass, move away (medium shot).	The second part of the ceremony is the public confession around . . .	Voices and noise.
90	Participants grouped around a tree (medium shot).	. . . the concrete altar. The guilty Hauka must confess their wrong-doings.	Voices and noise.
91	Part of the group (as in 90); one man holds a chicken (medium shot).	One say: "I've had intercourse with the girlfriend of one of my friends, and for two months . . .	Voices and noise.
92	The group of participants (medium shot).	. . .I've been impotent."	Voices and noise.
93	One participant making a confession (medium close shot).	Another says: "I never wash."	Voices and noise.
94	A confessor repeatedly throws himself to the ground and rises.	"I'm dirty. I'm not elegant."	Voices and noise.

180

Shot No.	Image	Speech	Noise/ Music
95	The man with the chicken (as in 91) (medium shot).	And another say:	Voices and noise.
96	A confessor squatting and shaking (medium shot).	"I don't care about the Hauka. Sometimes I feel they don't exist." One member was given a ram . . .	Voices and noise.
97	A man kneels with a ram; the altar (pan in medium shot).	. . . and a chicken.	Voices and noise.
98	A participant wearing a pith helmet and with a whistle in his mouth (close-up).	The penitents on one side and the others facing them.	Voices and noise.
99	A group of participants (medium shot).		Voices and noise.
100	The group of participants (medium shot).		Voices and noise.
101	Participants grouped around the altar (long shot).		Voices and noise.
102	Two men, one holding a chicken (frontal medium shot).	One of M——'s assistants holding the sacri . . .	Voices and noise.

181

Shot No.	Image	Speech	Noise/ Music
103	The two men, one swinging his arm (medium shot from the back).	. . . ficial chicken swings his arm to and fro to tell the gods:	Voices and noise.
104	The two men with the chicken (waist down, medium shot).	"We give you this chicken neither in front . . .	Voices and noise.
105	A man bending over the altar (medium shot).	. . . nor in back." The blood is poured . . .	Voices and noise.
106	The blood-soaked altar, conical shaped with black stripes (vertical pan up in medium shot).	. . .on the concrete altar and on the termite hill previously painted black and white and representing . . .	Voices and noise.
107	Two men at the altar (medium shot).	. . . the governor's palace. The penitents come before the blood-drenched . . .	Voices and noise.
108	The blood-soaked altar (close-up).	. . .altar to take the great oath. They swear . . .	Voices and noise.
109	Two men at the altar (medium shot).	. . .not to do it again. "If we do it again, we ask our Hauka . . .	Voices and noise.
110	A man looking down (medium close shot).	. . . to punish us by death."	Voices and noise.
111	The altar (close-up).	Then the penitents sent . . .	Voices and noise.

Shot No.	Image	Speech	Noise/ Music
112	The penitents move left (pan in long shot).	. . . outside the compound. They will have to be possessed . . .	Voices and noise.
113	Two men, one carrying ropes (medium long shot).	. . .before they are allowed back into the holy circle. In the spirit of purification . . .	Voices and noise.
114	A participant walks toward the camera (pan in medium shot).	M—— makes a libation of gin.	Voices and noise.
115	A participant in black (as in 114) pours the contents of a bottle on the trees (medium shot).	He pours it over the olive trees, the poles that hold the union jack . . .	Voices and noise.
116	M—— pours a libation on the pole (medium long shot).	. . .and the governor's palace.	Voices and noise.
117	A movie poster: "Mark of Zorro" (pan in medium close shot).	On the governor's palace: a telegram, movie poster for "The Sign of Zorro."	Voices and noise.
118	M—— takes objects from the niche (medium shot).	Above is the secretary general . . .	Voices and noise.
119	M—— squatting performs a rite with his hands (medium close shot).	. . . where M—— keeps sacrificial eggs. The sentry is mounting guard. . .	Voices and noise.

183

Shot No.	Image	Speech	Noise/Music
120	The sentry with wooden guns under his arms smiles (medium shot).	And M—— breaks the eggs over the steps and balconies of the governor's palace.	Voices and noise.
121	A hand performing a rite (medium close shot).		Voices and noise.
122	M——'s hand (close-up).		Voices and noise.
123	M—— seated, speaking the ritual (medium shot).		Voices and noise.

When I began to examine segmentation in *Les Maîtres fous* I encountered enormous difficulties. What disconcerts the analyst is the general lack of demarcation of the narrative on the image track: much of the text does not seem to be marked off into discrete syntagmatic units. Some of the segments I have identified appear in fact as amorphous strings of narrative development in which few marks serve to distinguish the various "moments" of the Hauka rites. Segment 13, for example, includes nearly a hundred shots (out of the film's 356).

In analysis I attempted to apply the three criteria for demarcation described by Christian Metz to which I have already referred: "The analyst of the classic film is correct to consider as a single autonomous segment any passage from a film which is not interrupted by a major change in the course of the intrigue nor by a sign of punctuation nor by the abandonment of one syntagmatic type for another."[35] In applying each of these criteria to the text of *Les Maîtres fous* I often reach an impasse. (1) The representation of events at the level of the image track is often so discontinuous that the criterion of major changes in the course of the plot is inapplicable. (2) There are no marks of punctuation of the traditional sort: fades, dissolves, and so forth: at best I was able to identify certain recurrent motifs (downward pans from the flying "Union Jacks" to the compound floor, for example) which seem to serve a demarcative function. (3) There are no discernible changes in cinematic treatment for much of the film's narrative development. I identified the main segments of the Hauka rituals as ordinary sequences (units of complex action in which many moments have been "skipped") simply because they are clearly linear and discontinuous. The question remains: are these in fact autonomous units of discourse?

As Michel Marie indicates, all film depends in great measure on language for the articulation of its discourse, in particular in organizing its narrative structure: "Film is structured by a body of discursive instances which language [*la langue*] mobilizes at every moment; this is how it works for the internal relationships of temporality, relationships of simultaneity, or consecutiveness, etc. Here it is the global relationship between the visual axis and the acoustic axis that we must consider."[36] In the organization of the filmic chain, language intervenes as the disposition of the shots and sequences, i.e., as *montage*. Through a set of subcodes of *montage*—codes of continuity—the film expresses relations of temporality and thus articulates the fragments of its discourse. But in the sound film, language also intervenes as speech, which brings with it all the resources of verbal temporality. In the fiction film speech *(parole)*, which is at the heart of film language in the sound period, assumes a major responsibility for structuring the narrative text. The intervention of speech takes two forms: dialogue, in the theatrical tradition of mimetic speech; commentary, the discursive voices that emanate from outside the diegesis.

In *Les Maîtres fous* there is a form of speech which, we suppose, finds its source in the image, but this "dialogue" presumably spoken by the participants of the rites, is largely masked and ultimately incomprehensible to the western audience to which the film is addressed. The participants' speech was in fact never intended to be deciphered. It constitutes simply part of the post-synchronized noise track whose flattened audio field lacks the spatial depth evoked by the image. Moreover, diegetic sound in *Les Maîtres fous* is functionally passive: it never motivates a change of shot by calling for the materialization of an off-screen sound source. This is why I made no attempt to note the spatiality of these diegetic sounds by specifying them as on- or off-screen. Voices, murmurs of the crowd, the ambient sounds of the congested streets, the cries of the possessed—all support, but without great conviction, the real-effect of the image.

The commentary, on the other hand, is not only extraordinarily pervasive, it acts as the constant agent of mediation. Its textual continuity rivals that of the image track, which seems to lose the ability to tell its own story. Nearly every shot in the film appears to call for the intervention of language. Constantly "speaking" the images, the voice of the commentary evokes the entire *mise en scène* and conducts the unfolding of the plot carefully marking the major phases of the action: "Colored flags flutter in the sky. They are the Union Jacks. Just below is a statue of the governor with his mustache, his swords, his guns and his horses. The first part of the ceremony is the nomination of new members" (shots 67–70). The commentary identifies the actors, narrates their actions, and even reiterates their words and thoughts in the language of the spectator: "One of Mountyeba's assistants holding the sacrificial chicken swings his arm to and fro to tell the gods: 'We give you this chicken neither in front nor in back.'"

The commentary does not simply assume the narrative function, overseeing the events' unfolding; it contextualizes the images by drawing on other fields of reference and other bodies of knowledge. The commentary plays the role of informant and ethnographer, giving us access to information the image does not provide. It not only describes the actors and their actions, it traces their personal history: "This man has been sick for one month; he has one fit after one other. He sleeps in the cemetery and digs up the corpses." And, adopting the voice of hermeneutics, the commentary interprets social action and gesture: "They are waiting for a dog. Why a dog? Because it is strict taboo, and if the Hauka slaughter and eat a dog, they will prove that they are stronger than the other men."

In relation to the image, the commentary is always in the broadest sense exegetic. As Roland Barthes points out, the photographic image because of its analogical plenitude resists meaning, and its polysemy is treated as a dysfunction, for which society seeks to compensate by means of techniques most often based on language, e.g., the caption of the press photograph.[37] In cinema, the spectator is presented with the full perceptual surface of the image, the visual object relayed by the codes of analogy. The photographic image possesses a high degree of iconicity and a lesser degree of schematization when compared with other visual arts whose iconic production is highly coded. As Christian Metz shows in his work "Le Perçu et le nommé," in front of the photographic image the social subject performs an operation of "subtraction" in which he or she isolates and retains the "significant" features of the represented object, thus transforming perception from a natural into a cultural phenomenon:

In ordinary perception, or in the perception of strongly representational images, it is the social subject, the spectator, who produces the schema

186

himself, by a mental subtraction of the non-pertinent features; in cases of schematization, it is a specialist (sketcher, etc.), an "addresser" who performs, in advance, the same subtraction, by giving it material form. The difference is that the process of abstraction and classification—the subtraction—intervenes in the first case at the level of reception, in the other at the level of production.[38]

The need to name—to secure the recognition by the spectator of the represented objects and actions by means of a nomenclature— becomes acute in the ethnographic film. Here identification (always social) of the photographed scene cannot be accomplished by the social subject alone. The spectators cannot isolate the pertinent features of the image because the complex process of cultural production on which recognition depends is alien to them. They cannot identify the discrete objects represented in the image because they lack the social knowledge of the pertinent features of visual identification and the corresponding semes of language. In ethnographic film, identification cannot be left to the intervention of language at the level of reception by the spectator but depends upon a work at the level of emission: the linguistic text acts as a universal commentator, offering a metalinguistic signified that dominates the image and, for western spectators, brings about recognition (or more precisely, replaces recognition). The commentary in the ethnographic film is radically metacodic, standing above the visual-linguistic codes of another culture. Ethnographic film casts the spectator in a position of dependency: without the commentary, signification does not take place. Hence language intervenes at every level of the film: it permits the naming of the image, it organizes, narrates, and connects the document with history and science. The language of the commentary is the constant and indispensable gloss of the image track. Without it, spectators could only experience the unsettling impression of representation without signification. With it, they achieve recognition and interpretation through the linguistic signs of their own culture, with all the distortion that such intellection entails.

Transcription 3: *The Battle of Britain*

The Battle of Britain is a historical narrative and as such takes as its field of reference a sequence of historically verifiable events, a "concrete reality" preexisting and "determining" the order of discourse. This compilation film contains more than twelve hundred shots culled from archival material and distributed among 195 autonomous segments, with a running time of approximately fifty-five minutes. Widely considered a masterpiece of the editor's craft, the film recounts the events of the attempted invasion of Britain by German forces between August 1940 and the winter of 1940–41. The scenario can be broken down into eleven major parts: (1) Nazi preparation for the invasion (segments 1–20); (2) British preparation of defenses (21–41); (3) German air attacks against British convoys, ports, and airfields and the defense launched by the Royal Air Force (42–75); (4) German air attacks on airdromes and industrial sites (71–91); (5) air attacks on London (92–107); (6) the massive attack of 15 September 1940 (108–33); (7) German air force night bombings of London (134–58); (8) RAF retaliatory missions against German military sites (159–67); (9) Nazi revenge: destruction of Coventry, 14 November 1940 (168–71); (10) the burning of London by incendiary bombings, Christmas 1940 (172–80); (11) definitive British victory against the German onslaught (181–95).

The following passage is taken from the third part of the scenario and represents the first stages of the Nazi assault against British ports and airfields and the RAF defense (segments 53–68).

Shot No.	Image	Speech	Noise/ Music
	53: *Autonomous shot (nondiegetic)*		
288	Map of England; animation of planes flying from Europe to drop bombs.	For the next week, the Germans attacked the coast cities from the Thames River to Waveland.	
	54: *Alternate syntagma*		
289	View off the wing of a Nazi plane (long shot).		Noise of air battle (on/ off).
290	A Nazi plane dropping bombs (very long shot).		Noise of air battle (on).
291	The site of bombing hits (very long shot).		Explosion of bombs (on).

Shot No.	Image	Speech	Noise/ Music
292	Nazi planes in the sky (very long shot).		Noise of air battle (on/ off).
293	The site of bombing hits (very long shot).		Explosion of bombs (on).
294	Site of bombing hits (very long shot).		Explosion of bombs (on).

55: Ordinary sequence

Shot No.	Image	Speech	Noise/ Music
295	A civilian bus moves along a country road (very long shot).		Background noise.
296	The bus driver looks out his window (seeing, in medium long shot).		Background noise.
297	A plane in the sky (seen from below, very long shot).		Noise of a distant plane (on).
298	The bus driver turns toward his passengers (medium shot).	—It's the Gerries! Take cover!	Background noise.
299	A woman looks out of the bus window (seeing, medium shot).		Background noise.
300	A Nazi plane in the air (seen, long shot).		Engine noise (on).

Shot No.	Image	Speech	Noise/ Music
	Insert		
301	The pilot of a Nazi plane (close-up).		Engine noise (off).
302	Pilot's hand on a gearshift (close-up).		Engine noise (off).
	End insert		
303	The driver standing beside the stopped bus (medium shot).		Noise of plane engine (off).
304	Bullets pierce the windows of the bus (medium close shot).		Noise of hits (on); plane engine (off).
305	Bus being riddled with bullets, (pan to) driver standing (as in 303).		Noise of hits (on); plane engine (off).
	56: *Ordinary sequence*		
306	Planes in the sky (very long shot).		Noise of planes (on).
307	The face of a Nazi pilot (close-up).	—Spitfire!	Engine noise (off).
308	The copilot (close-up).		Engine noise (off).
309	A plane in the air (very long shot).		Plane engine (on).
310	The pilot (as in 307, close-up).		Plane engine (off).
311	The pilot's hand on a gearshift (close-up).		Plane engine (off).

Shot No.	Image	Speech	Noise/Music
312	RAF planes in the air (long shot).		Plane engines (on).
313	RAF planes (long shot).		Plane engines (on).
314	RAF planes (long shot).		Plane engines (on).
315	RAF planes (long shot).		Plane engines (on).
316	RAF planes (long shot).		Plane engines (on).
317	RAF planes (long shot).		Plane engines (on).
318	Nazi pilot looking (seeing in close-up).		Plane engines (off).
319	An attacking British plane (seen in long shot).		Plane engine (on).
320	Smoking Nazi plane going down (very long shot).		Noise of the descent (on).

57: *Descriptive syntagma*

321	View of a downed Nazi plane. Graphic: "180 Planes" (zooms out in long shot).	Hitler paid off with 180 more planes.	Music begins.

Shot No.	Image	Speech	Noise/ Music
322	View of another downed Nazi plane (long shot).		Music.
323	View of a third downed plane.		Music.

58: *Autonomous shot (nondiegetic)*

Shot No.	Image	Speech	Noise/ Music
324	Map of the English coastal area. Animation: "Southhampton" and "Plymouth" zoom out; smoke rises from the cities.	Then the Luftwaffe battered the great port towns of Southampton, Plymouth . . .	Music.

59: *Bracket syntagma*

Shot No.	Image	Speech	Noise/ Music
325	View of the rigging of ships with planes flying above (long shot).	. . . trying for a knock-out . . .	Music.
326	A ship (long shot).	. . . before the flow . . .	
327	Boxes labeled "Made in U.S.A." (medium shot).	. . . of supplies from overseas . . .	Music.
328	Boxes labeled "Safety cartidges" (medium shot).	. . . became more than a trickle.	Music.
	Insert		
329	A burning port (very long shot).	The ports took a terrible pounding . . .	Music.
330	Docks; unloading in progress (long shot).	. . . but they couldn't be knocked out.	Music.

Shot No.	Image	Speech	Noise/Music
331	A plane being unloaded (long shot).	Cargoes went on being unloaded . . .	Music.
332	Worker at the controls of a crane (medium long shot).	. . .with the protection of the . . .	Music.
333	A tank being unloaded (long shot).	. . . RAF overhead.	Music.

60: *Autonomous shot*

334	RAF planes in the air (long shot).	Battling the Spitfires and Hurricanes in the air wasn't panning out.	Music.

61: *Autonomous shot (nondiegetic)*

335	Map of England.	So Goering switched his main attack to the fighter airfields! Dover, Deal, Folkestone.	Music.

62: *Ordinary sequence*

336	A plane dropping bombs (long shot).	Maybe he could destroy the planes . . .	Music.
337	Aerial view of the ground (very long shot).	. . . on the ground.	Music.
338	Nazi planes on a bombing mission (very long shot).	He bombed the airfields . . .	Music.
339	Aerial view of the ground (very long shot).	. . . and the fields were hit.	Music.

Shot No.	Image	Speech	Noise/ Music
		63: *Bracket syntagma*	
340	RAF planes in a field (very long shot).	But the planes were saved.	Music.
341	A country house with a farmer and his wife seated outside: (pan to) an RAF plane (long shot).	For Britain, unlike Poland and the Low Countries, didn't make the mistake of bunching its planes on the runways. The planes of the RAF were scattered and hidden.	Music.
342	A plane hidden in the trees (long shot).	Only a few in any one field, and those in the far corner.	Music.
343	Planes seen through the trees (long shot).		Music.
		64: *Autonomous shot*	
344	Spitfires in the air (very long shot).	The Spitfires still went up to meet the enemy.	Music.
		65: *Autonomous shot (nondiegetic)*	
345	A page of a calendar: "August 8" with planes in animation flying above. The leaves of the calendar fly off. Graphic: "26 major attacks."	In the first ten days of the Battle of Britain, Goering launched 26 major attacks to get command of the air.	Music.

Shot No.	Image	Speech	Noise/ Music

66: *Autonomous shot (nondiegetic)*

346	Animation: design of planes at left, with a swastika above, turns into the number 697. British planes appear at the right (a smaller grouping). British planes are transformed into the number 153.	And lost 697 aircraft. The British lost 153.	Music.

67: *Bracket syntagma*

347	Ship in the water; a parachutist lands nearby (very long shot).	And sixty British pilots bailed out.	Music.
348	Parachute in the air (long shot).		Background noise. Music.
349	A boat speeding through the water (long shot).		Background noise. Music.
350	A man with binoculars (seeing, medium shot).		Background noise. Music.
351	A parachutist in the water (seen, long shot).		Background noise. Music.
352	A rescue plane flying above a rubber raft in the sea (long shot).		Background noise. Music.

195

Shot No.	Image	Speech	Noise/ Music
353	A rubber raft seen from a boat; a line is thrown.		Background noise. Music.
354	A plane with pontoons lands near the rubber raft (long shot).		Background noise. Music.
355	A man being pulled aboard the boat (medium long shot).		Background noise. Music.
356	The survivor shakes hands with another (medium shot).	Valuable trained men were saved and ready to fight again.	Music.

As André Bazin points out, the films of the *Why We Fight* series are above all the skillful product of *montage* and the emphatic intervention of the spoken commentary. The discourse of images and the linguistic discourse function in a shifting relationship of symbiosis so as to construct a quite imaginary space-time of history. For Bazin, the whole text is sleight of hand, illusionism:

> I believe that far from furnishing the historic sciences with an advance toward objectivity, cinema gives, by its very realism, an added power of illusion. The invisible commentary, which the spectator forgets as he watches Capra's admirable editing, is the history of tomorrow's masses, the ventriloquist of this awesome prosopopoeia, resurrecting at will men and events, which is brewing in the film archives of the entire world.[39]

Thus Bazin the realist expresses his sense of scandal at texts that change something "real" (fragments of archival material) into something imaginary (an historical representation constructed by *montage*). And perhaps even more scandalous, such texts expose to view the structuring function of language in cinema: film is an act of writing in which language informs the basic levels of filmic organization. The image, which should serve to reveal the "structural depth" of reality, instead becomes the hollow projection of a

196

human voice. Bazin clearly disapproves of a new kind of deception practiced in this kind of cinema, a modification of the play that the spectator and the cinematic apparatus engage in. The commentary is an excrescent text the spectator works to assimilate through identification with the disembodied voice that appears unanchored in space. The commentary is ventriloquial: its source dissimulated, the voice is displaced and projected onto the position the spectator occupies.

The text of the commentary is a discourse in the historic mode: it contains few marks of enunciation. It considers the events of the film as already past (the triumph of Britain assured in advance), thus taking its distance from the field of reference the film evokes. This objectification also stems from a national difference: it is an American voice that refers to the British struggle. As verbal realization, the voice is nonetheless empty: a certain familiarity of tone together with a passing colloquialism evoke the addressee, the apathetic draftee of popular origin or the middle American whose identification is solicited. The figurative frame of discourse is never specifically constituted: the codes of implication, the discursive exchange of person are lacking. The enunciating voice never assumes his enunciation—never says "I" or uses the collectivized "we"—nor does it acknowledge itself as address by designating its object, the spectator.

The term *prosopopoeia* ("rhetorical figure by which an imaginary or absent person is represented as speaking or acting," according to the Oxford English Dictionary) is evocative. Bazin clearly refers to an economic exchange that takes place between the two discursive agencies: "The principle of this kind of documentary consists essentially in lending the images the logical structure of discourse and to the discourse itself the credibility of photographic evidence."[40] If we examine the image track, we find the syntagmatic units highly elliptical and fragmentary, often quite lacking in the elements of continuity that are essential to the construction of unitary space-time in the classic fiction film. The commentary, on the other hand, constantly combines and arranges, producing the film's continuity with the semantic power of language. It establishes a geometry of space that the image alone does not represent: "Fighters above at high altitudes! Fighters at both sides! Fighters in the front and in the rear!" The commentary relays the image, sutures its gaps, and at the most extreme—when the imaged discourse is gaping—it produces the diegesis from the "fragments" of the image. It establishes the narrative articulations of the text: "Then it came." "Here come the Luftwaffe." It supplies information that is invisible or exterior

197

to the image: "The RAF came, facing odds of six, eight, ten to one."
It generalizes, historicizes, recapitulates: "In the first four days,
the RAF knocked 182 German planes out of the sky." The image, in
return, serves as the alibi of the commentary. It assures the narrative's historical and necessary character by constituting its irre-
futable denotation. The photographic image as document masks
with its prestige the working of the global text, its *montage*.

In *The Battle of Britain,* the extreme segmentation of the text—
the unusually large number of syntagmatic units—is a sign of the
decomposition of the image track. There is, for example, a very
high proportion of autonomous shots (the minimal autonomous
segment): the image is reduced to pure illustration of the commentary for which it serves as the sufficient denotation. The dominant
commentary also accounts for the high frequency of inserts, most
of which are nondiegetic. Here, the linguistic text intervenes directly into the composition of the image, giving us visual mate-
rializations of its discourse: maps, emblems, numerals, animation
of narrative sequences or of rhetorical figures initiated by the
commentary. Shots 345 and 346 are examples of this graphic manipulation whose figures reiterate and compress the historic events the
narrative evokes.

The commentary is full of eloquence; it is fluent, forceful, per-
suasive. It develops its faultless argument in a constant progression.
Never at a loss, the voice adopts a tone of complete mastery: from
an unassailable vantage point, it enunciates the unfaltering propositions that tell the truth of history. In this sample, the linguistic text
that spans segments 58–67 recounts the Luftwaffe's ill-fated attacks
against British port towns and airfields, describes the twists and
turns of German strategy, British courage and cunning, and recapitulates the gains and losses. It moves effortlessly from one
locale to another, from one topic to the next, enlarges the field of
reference, establishes causality and consequence—all with that discursive ease that belongs only to language.

If we look at the image track that moves alongside the unfolding
argument, we have a quite different impression. The image discourse is in fact quite disorderly. We see in the sequence of shots
the signs of an apparently irreconcilable heterogeneity. In the signifying material itself, first of all, there exists a disparity between
the documentary footage and the incursions of animation and
graphic writing, which are all the more distinct in that they imply a
quite different position of enunciation. Second, the succession of
syntagmatic types (autonomous shot / bracket syntagma / insert /

autonomous shot / autonomous shot / ordinary sequence / bracket syntagma / autonomous shot / nondiegetic insert / nondiegetic insert) resembles in no way the orderly progression of narrative sequences in the fiction film, and if we attempt to follow the development of the diegesis, we find that the image track in and of itself remains, at the level of the scenario, quite unarticulated. Third, if we descend to the level of the internal organization of the syntagmas themselves, we find a rather general lack of all those elements of continuity that in the fiction film motivate the change from one shot to the next. We cannot, for example, establish the identity of objects and persons in successive shots, nor do we find the matches of position and movement that are commonplace in the editor's craft. Furthermore, the image does not exploit any of the "figures" of articulation that motivate the shifts in camera set-ups: eye-line matches, reverse-angle shots, cut to the source of an off-screen sound, and so forth. Finally, the noise track, which serves to fill out the space of the fiction film and opposes its constancy to the fragmentation of the image, often gives way completely to the commentary.

Are these units of discourse in fact sequences as we know them in the fiction film? Have they not lost pertinent features that distinguish them from one another in Metz's typology of syntagmas? What is the difference between narrative and nonnarrative syntagmas in a film whose dominant commentary radically alters the position of enunciation essential to the classic narrative film? The difference is in a certain sense quite superficial: it depends precisely on the presence or absence of the textual markers of continuity we have been discussing. In segment 62, for example, it is the pattern of alternation (A B A1 B1) based on the repetition of like motifs (shots of bombers followed by aerial views of the ground target) which allow us to read these doubtless disparate shots as pieces of a coherent space-time. In segment 59, it is the absence of elements of continuity linking shots of the unloading cargo that lead us to identify this as a bracket syntagma. For if we cannot make a unitary space-time of these fragmentary views, we must assume that another sort of resemblance, a "kinship," binds these occurrences together. No one would in fact question this resemblance because the motifs clearly represent similar activities (even if the commentary were not present to specify the meaning of their relationship). But it is the lack of order that characterizes what we have identified as bracket syntagmas in *The Battle of Britain* (and in many classic documentary films). The category as it is manifested

199

in this text is defined purely in its negativity: a unit that is not (at the level of the image track) of the narrative order. The principle of organization is elsewhere.

If we move to the next higher level of textual organization, we immediately see that the distinction between narrative and nonnarrative that gives the syntagmas their principle of order is no longer pertinent. At this level, where the articulation of the major units of the scenario occurs, it is the commentary that holds sway, assuming the function of establishing textual continuity. It is here that narrative as we know it in the fiction film lets go its hold on the text. The bracket syntagma is not a momentary break in the general movement of the plot; like the narrative syntagma, it is an integral part of a discursive progression that is in fact narrative. If we examine the function of the two segments discussed above (59 and 62), it is quite apparent that they both "illustrate" phases of the action that the commentary articulates: the bombings of the ports (59) and air fields (62). Illustration—the word is entirely appropriate, since the commentary, performing its iterative function, is intent on describing a historical "reality" that transcends the capacity of the image (these images) to represent. It is, finally, a question of textual economy. The failure of the image discourse to control the production of meaning on this higher plane explains the weakness of the large syntagmatic code: the units it produces are subjugated by the linguistic text.

But the commentary does intermittently retreat from the scene of enunciation, reinvesting the image with its sound track and its sense of autonomy. I carefully chose this passage to include an ordinary sequence (55) that retains all the qualities of the fiction effect. It is one of the few segments in the film that is the obvious product of *mise en scène:* actors appear in a setting that has the coherence that belongs only to fiction. An establishing shot (295) orients us to the scene: a civilian bus moves across the English countryside. Background noise alerts us to the as yet invisible presence of the approaching enemy. The bus driver's look off-screen followed by the object of his view, a Nazi plane in the air, initiates a brief pattern of alternation in its most classic form (pursuer-pursued). Diegetic noise has completely displaced the commentary; it lends the image its full real effect and brings into play the space beyond the edges of the screen. A bit of real dialogue emerges as the bus driver shouts to his passengers: "It's the Gerries! Take cover!" Ordinary sequence 57 follows quite "naturally": the narrative consequence of this assault against the innocent is the counterattack by the RAF. Another system, another modality, a different position of enunciation have taken hold, but only briefly. The linguistic discourse is ready to profit from its momentary absence.

Transcription 4: *The City*

William Van Dyke and Ralph Stiener's *The City* (1939) is the classic documentary of the urban renewal movement. The film is divided into three parts. The first is a nostalgic view of the American preindustrial urban community in which technology has not yet overwhelmed nature and human relations. The presence of a character, a small boy, briefly lends the text narrative continuity; we follow his trajectory across the represented space of an idealized past. The second part, which is entirely discursive, evokes the trials of modern urban existence: unbridled industrial development, the misery of ghetto life, the alienation and impersonality of the modern city. The third section describes the city of the future, a creation of science and rationality in which citydwellers are restored to their "human" relationship to work, leisure, and nature. Interpolated within this descriptive sequence we find a series of narrative syntagmas whose continuity is assured by the appearance of a young boy, the renascent counterpart of the character in part 1.

The following transcription is taken from the second part of *The City* and is preceded by a long descriptive syntagma in which the fiery images of a steel foundry are accompanied by Aaron Copland's harsh, percussive musical score.

Shot No.	Image	Speech	Noise/ Music
	13: *Bracket syntagma*		
100	Succession of different industrial landscapes (long shot).	Machines, inventions, power! Black out the past!	Woodwinds and brass (mournful tune which contrasts with the pulsating rhythm in the last sequence).

201

Shot No.	Image	Speech	Noise/ Music
101	Industrial landscape (long shot).	Forget the quiet cities. Bring in the steam and steel . . .	Music.
102	Industrial landscape (long shot).	. . . the iron men, the giants!	Music.
103	Industrial landscape (long shot).	Open the throttle! All aboard! The promised land!	Music.
104	Industrial landscape (long shot).	Pillars of smoke by day! Pillars of fire by night! Pillars of . . .	Music.
105	Industrial landscape (long shot).	. . . progress! Machines to make machines. Production to expand production. There's wood and wheat and kitchen sinks and calico—all ready-made in tons and carload lots.	Music.
106	Industrial site, river, urban housing development (discovered in pan shot).	Enough for ten, thousands, millions. Millions! Faster and faster! Better and better!	Music.
107	Housing in an industrial setting (long shot).		Music continues in strings.
108	Housing in smoky industrial setting (long shot).		Music.

202

Shot No.	Image	Speech	Noise/ Music
109	Housing in smoky industrial setting (long shot).		Music.

14: *Bracket syntagma*

Shot No.	Image	Speech	Noise/ Music
110	Pan across buildings discovers a man walking in a ghetto street (long shot).	It doesn't make us any happier to know there are millions more living here on top of it.	Strings fade out.
111	Children walking up a wooden stairway. Industrial background (long shot).	There are prisons where a guy sent up for crime can get a better place to live than we can give our children.	Bassoon and oboe continue the tune.
112	An agglomeration of shacks (long shot).	Smoke makes prosperity, they tell you.	Music.
113	Shacks, wooden sidewalks (very long shot).	Smoke makes prosperity . . .	Music.
114	An urban landscape (very long shot).	. . . no matter if you choke on it.	Music.
115	Factories, smokestacks (very long shot).		Music.
116	A child standing on a wooden sidewalk (medium shot).	We gotta face life in these shacks and alleys.	Music.

Shot No.	Image	Speech	Noise/Music
117	Children playing on wooden sidewalks, one boy descending a banister (long shot).	We gotta let our children take chances here . . .	Music.
118	A child standing, looking blankly (medium shot).	. . . with rickets, t.b., or worse.	Music.
119	A child, partially masked by a sidewalk banister.	They grow up blank, the kids.	Music.
120	A row of shacks; a child walking (long shot).	They have no business here, this is no man's land.	Music.
121	A train passes in upper frame as people below descend a wooden stairway (long shot).	This slag-heap wasn't meant for them. There's poison in the air we breathe. There's poison in the river. The fog and smoke below. . .	Music (ends with the shot).

15: *Scene*

122	A woman looks frame right (seeing, in medium shot).	. . . rise up and choke us.	
123	A group of children running across railroad tracks (seen, in long shot).		Noise of an approaching train (crescendo, off).
124	The train passes (in long shot).		Train noise (on).

Shot No.	Image	Speech	Noise/ Music
125	The train passing (in long shot).		Train noise (on).
126	The train passing (in medium long shot).		Train noise (on).
127	The train passes, discovers a group of children on the track; a boy runs across the track (in long shot).		Train noise (decrescendo, on then off).
128	The woman (as in 122) looks frame right (seeing, in medium shot).		
129	The boy (as in 127) picks up the ball on the tracks (long shot).		Background noise.

16: *Bracket syntagma*

130	An urban dirt street: shacks, laundry hanging (long shot).	Don't tell us that this is the best you can do in building cities.	Music: oboes and bassoons.
131	A ghetto street (long shot).	Who built this place?	Music.
132	A child's face at a window (medium close shot).	What put us here?	Music.
133	Shacks on a hillside; people walk on a path (very long shot).	And how do we get out again? We're asking. Just asking.	Music.

Shot No.	Image	Speech	Noise/ Music
134	An agglomeration of shacks (long shot).	We might just as well stay in the mills and call that home. They're just as fit to live in.	Music.
135	A man with a wooden leg picks up a coat and moves toward the door of a shack (long shot).	We mine the coal, load the furnace, roll the steel, drive the rivets, we lock the bolts on the assembly line. Lucky if we have the chance to keep . . .	Music.
136	A black man enters a shack, closes the door (medium shot).	. . . a job from day to day, from month to month.	Music: strings added.
137	A woman emerges from a shack and tosses the contents of a bowl (medium shot).		Music.
138	Children climb a wooden stairway. Pan discovers a woman on a porch (medium shot).		Music.
139	Two small children play with a puppy (medium close shot).		Music.
140	Two children in a doorway, forlorn (medium close shot).		Music.

Shot No.	Image	Speech	Noise/Music
141	A lone child with a dirty face (close-up).		Music.
142	A single child (close-up).		Music.
143	A woman hanging out laundry at left; a child walks from the right, opens the door of an outhouse (long shot).		Music.
144	An old man pumps water in front of a shack (long shot).		Music.
145	A woman hangs out laundry left; a man enters left; camera pans with him to the door of the shack (long shot).	The dirty work alone don't get us down. We're not ashamed to handle coal and iron all the way from mine shaft to skyscrapers. We turn out cars and tractors we're mighty proud of. Same as you.	Music.
146	An old woman pumps water (medium shot).	But how does that make sense with this?	Music.
147	Another woman pumping water (medium shot).		Music.
148	An old man pumping water (medium shot).		Music.

207

Shot No.	Image	Speech	Noise/ Music
149	The old woman (as in 146) takes the pail of water and goes toward the shack (medium shot).		Music.
150	A man at a table with a basin of water prepares to wash his hands (medium shot).	We never get the gritty dirt out of our nose, our eyes, our guts.	Music.
151	The man (as in 150) washing his face (medium shot).	We never get a chance to see how blue the sky can be, unless the mills are all shut down.	Music.
152	A woman at her stove (medium shot).	Smoke makes prosperity, they say.	
153	A woman's hand shoveling coal into a stove (close-up).	Does this mean there's no way out for us? There must be something better. Why can't we have it? A decent house?	
154	A household chimney, smoke pouring out (medium shot).		Music.

17: *Descriptive syntagma*

155	Smokestack of a locomotive-crane (medium long shot).		Music.
156	Locomotive-crane moves left (very long shot).		Music.

Shot No.	Image	Speech	Noise/ Music
157	Industrial landscape: factories, smoke (very long shot).		Music.
158	Burning smokestacks (very long shot).		Music.
159	A train; smoke emerging from its smokestack whitens the screen (very long shot).		Music ends with shot.

18: *Descriptive syntagma*

160	A skyscraper—no people (very long shot).	Follow the crowd! Get the big money! You make a pile and raise a pile. That makes another pile for you.	
161	A skyscraper (very long shot).	Follow the crowd!	
162	A skyscraper against the sky (very long shot).	We've reached a million!	
163	A skyscraper (very long shot).	Two million! Five million! Watch us grow!	
164	A skyscraper (very long shot).	Going up! It's new. It's automatic. It dictates . . .	

Shot No.	Image	Speech	Noise/ Music
165	Slow pan down a skyscraper (very long shot).	. . . records, seals, sterilizes, stamps and delivers in one operation, without human hands. What am I bid? What am I offered? Sold! Who's next? Follow the crowd to the city, the Windy City, the fashion city! (etc.) The people, yes! The people, perhaps.	Music begins over the end of the shot.

If we use narrative structure as a principle indicator, *The City* would appear to deviate in significant ways from the model of the classic narrative film. The analysis we made of the syntagmatic structure of *The Battle of Britain* applies to this film, but to a more radical degree. Nonnarrative syntagmas—in particular, the bracket syntagma—occupy nearly four-fifths of the filmic chain. Not only are narrative syntagmas infrequent, they are enclosed within a discursive order to which it is their function to bring the emotion of human drama: the warmth of the close-knit community, the maternal anxiety for children of the ghetto, boyhood dreams of adventure. As we found in *The Battle of Britain*, it is the reemergence of elements of continuity that signals a return to the narrative mode. In segment 15 of this sample, classed as a scene, the shots are ordered in a pattern of alternation articulated by the structure of point of view: a ghetto mother looks out of frame (A) at a group of children chasing a ball across railroad tracks (B). The continuity of the scene is established through axis matches, continuity of movement, and the repetition of camera set-ups (shot 128 "repeats" 122, 129 echoes 127). Moreover, the noise track, which has been held in abeyance, reemerges and momentarily displaces both commentary and music. It plays its role in completing the fullness of the represented space and articulating the movement between one shot and the next.

In *The City* narrative syntagmas are infrequent, isolated, and clearly marked off by a shifting of register that, as we saw in *The Battle of Britain*, is precisely a change in the text's position of enunciation. As in *The Battle of Britain,* we also see a considerable disordering of the image discourse. There is, first, a weakening of the distinction between syntagmatic types. The text sees no need for example to distinguish between the purely descriptive and the conceptual—what in the fiction film would constitute the difference between the descriptive and bracket syntagmas. The bracket syntagma groups motifs together according to their likeness, i.e., they belong to the same order of facts. The descriptive syntagma joins motifs on the basis of their contiguity—we presume the referents of the image are related by their spatial proximity. Subordinated to the logic of the linguistic text, the notion of time loses its pertinence. Whether or not a given sequence of images is ordered according to simultaneity of occurrence and unity of space is immaterial; the order of reality the film seeks to evoke is abstracted from any precise relationship to space and time.

A further indication of the decomposition of the image track is the long chains of bracket and descriptive syntagmas that pose considerable problems in segmental analysis. Of the three criteria for demarcation (change of cinematic treatment, punctuation, change in the course of the plot), only one is consistently operable. (1) Changes in cinematic treatment depend on distinctions between syntagmatic types and these distinctions have, as I have indicated, been considerably weakened. (2) Punctuation—dissolves and fades—are infrequently used as syntagmatic markers in *The City.* (3) In the absence of spatio-temporal references, the third criterion must be reformulated if it is to be applied to this text. The autonomous segments of *The City* can be identified not according to significant "gaps" in the signified of temporal denotation, but according to significant permutations of the motifs of the image track. These permutations—shifts between different "orders of reality"— are often more clearly marked on the sound track, by the commentary in an explicit fashion, or by shifts between materials of expression: from music to commentary, from commentary to diegetic speech, and so forth.

Let's look at an example. At the end of bracket syntagma 13 in this sample, a lateral pan in extreme long shot establishes a spatial relationship between the industrial landscape of factories and smokestacks and the maze of ghetto housing (110). The shot gives us a visual bridge between two topics, two series of motifs: the long pan shot, initiated as part of a description of unimpeded industrial development, stops as it reveals a worker returning home in a street of shanties. The relationship of contiguity that moves us across the syntagmatic break also carries the logical relationship of cause and

211

effect: industrialization causes ghetto housing and human misery. It is the commentary however that marks the change: a change in the content of its remarks, after a silence that lasts for three shots. There is also a change in the tone of the voice, the role it assumes, its mode of address. The shrill voice of capitalist opportunism is exchanged for the modulated tone of a voice that identifies with the plight of ghettoized workers. Moreover, a shift in orchestration on the music track supports this demarcation: oboes and bassoons, replacing the strings, become the connoters of the urban wasteland.

The brief "scenes" on the image track—rarely longer than a single shot—succeed each other according to a thematic logic, a general principle of congruity. Images of the faces of the children of the urban poor or of the primitive conditions of domestic labor in the industrial ghetto take their places on the filmic chain in thematic groupings. These sequences are weakly motivated. They lack the sequential determinism that seems to preside over the unfolding of narrative, and one could in fact change the order of the sequence of images without compromising its meaning. No development of action, no specific relation in time or space requires that the figures of ghetto children taken in medium shot (116–19) or the four images of shantytown residents pumping water (146–49) be arranged as they are in the film. Setting aside certain formal considerations, there is a great deal that is arbitrary about sequentiality in these segments and in the *montage*-figures characteristic of many social documentaries of the classic period.

Still the image maintains a certain autonomy from the closed discourse of the commentary. It does not simply illustrate; it is not merely dependent and fragmentary. The commentary does not appear to evoke (in the magical sense) the image, although it continually refers to it, makes of it the world of reference it holds in common with the spectator. The image has a coherence of its own. If we were to subtract the commentary from the film text, the image would continue to produce a meaning; it would continue to create, through the addition and arrangement of its fragments, the synecdochic space of a specific social reality. Thus by its apparent arbitrariness, the image constructs a world apart which, no matter how abstract, continues to obey the referential imperative. This realism of the visual field guarantees the innocence of the linguistic discourse. The particularity of the image supports the generality of the commentary: its concreteness excuses the abstraction.

By their very fragmentation the individual shots invoke the myth of cinematic realism. They have been "cut out" of a reality that hangs at the edges of the frame: off-screen space is the pure con-

212

tinuity of the real (Bazin). Image is discourse insofar as it submits to the order of the text, but it also partakes of the real. What has been filmed implies all that has not been filmed. The return from work, the child's game, the fleeting gestures of domestic labor continue elsewhere in time and space, outside of representation. Here as in narrative cinema, the cinematographic image is, as Pascal Bonitzer suggests, "haunted by what is not there."[41] But it constructs a different scenography. There is no "centered space" in imitation of the Italian theater. The concern of technique is not to assure the orientation of the spectator to the space of the "scene": the scene shifts perpetually, each piece of space-time obliterating the one that preceded it. This incessant displacement of the scene serves to increase the allusive power of the image—the off-screen space it would appear to animate—so that the succession of images signifies not the enclosed space of the diegesis but the mythical space of the real.

The textual dynamic of *The City* is built on the repartition of the materials of expression between two quite distinct agencies: the image and the voice. The image has been divested of sound. Diegetic sound is quite rare in the film and when it does occur, it often works in counterpoint to the image. In one segment, for example, images representing the dangers of life in the street are accompanied by announcements presumably taken from a hospital public address system. Dialogue and the noise track as they are manifested in the fiction film do not exist in *The City*. Thus the image gives up much of its immediacy and its power to unify. It stands apart, representing the reality, the documentation to which the commentary makes reference. The film does not attempt to conceal this textual splitting, which is in fact at the heart of its functioning. There are two positions of enunciation, both of which must exist for there to be a discourse of truth. The image may operate autonomously, as it does quite often, with the support of the music. Copland's brilliant score is the image's constant ally. It fills the gaps of the image's fragmentation and lends the sequence a sense of development and duration. The music's modal shifts and in particular its subtle instrumentation perform the essential work of connotation.

Released from its duty of conjuring the image, the commentary develops what we might call a theatrical structure of dialogue. There are three distinct "actors" and three voices—which are of course all one: a voice that takes the part of industrial expansionism, a second that speaks for the "people," that is, for the victims of industrialization, and a third metadiscursive voice stand-

213

ing above the others, the *deus ex machina* that intervenes in order to overcome the irreconcilable, to bring about the denouement by offering science's solution for city planning. To speak of dialogue is somewhat inaccurate. It is, rather, a question of a debate since the voices never address each other but an absent and shifting interlocutor, who is at times the spectator as individual or as collective force, at others, the unidentified parties of social responsibility.

The voice undergoes a process of impersonation by assuming certain signs of a social personality. The voice of capital is aggressive in its tone and its relation to the addressee. It exhorts to action, its major mood is the imperative: "Forget the quiet cities. Bring in the steam, the iron men, the giants. Open the throttle! All aboard! The promised land!" (101–3) The voice, which has the neutral character of standard American English, is nonetheless marked with irony and affectation. The text's rhetoric and its emphatic delivery show the voice to be a mask. Most importantly, there is the textual irony. The voice avoids reference to the field of the image—a series of ominous industrial landscapes. The image track tells the truth and gives the lie to the linguistic message. On the other hand, the second voice possesses many more signs of its enunciation. In contrast to the voice of capital, it makes constant reference to the field of the image, using gesture in its speech—the ostensive indicators: "We gotta face life in these shacks and alleys. We gotta let our children take chances here with rickets, t.b., or worse" (116–18) The voice takes its place in the image—it is a discourse of truth. Its tone is angry, but submissive. When it addresses its interlocutor, it is in the interrogative mood: "Who built this place? What put us here? And how do we get out again? We're asking. Just asking." (131–33). The identificatory "we," the colloquialisms, the plain accent of class (although clearly affected) situate the voice's social origin.

Four transcriptions, four ambivalent texts containing quite different discursive tendencies. The frame of enunciation shifts between the discourse of fiction and the fiction of a real discourse. Each text sets up its major and minor keys and its strategy of resolution. The discursive partner, who is sometimes acknowledged, sometimes not, is caught up in this textual play. The spectator-subject positions and repositions himself, vacillating between identification and distanciation. It is time to turn our attention to this ambivalent figure of the spectator.

214

5

The Nonfiction Film and Its Spectator

What occurs when the documentary text is placed within the cinematic apparatus—the system that establishes the conditions of reception for all films? The darkened theater; the configuration of the seating that assures passivity and isolates us as spectators maintaining at the same moment our distance from the screen; the cone of light that projects from behind us and as if out of our consciousness; and the image itself, immense, dazzling, hypnotic. What becomes of documentary realism under such conditions of reception? Is there a nonfiction effect, that is, does the documentary text, attached, as we presume it is, to real occurrences and verifiable historic moments, engage the spectator in a specific kind of affective participation in the film?

Film theory has most often spoken of the spectator's experience in terms of the "realism" of the cinematographic image. Taking on the appearance of real forms and endowed with real movement, the motion picture is a highly iconic and indexical system of signs that seems to close the gap between objects in the world and their representation. It is this sense of immediacy, theoreticians argue, which engenders in the spectator an intense feeling of participation in the film. Until recently, there has been little consideration given to the moment of reception and to the conditions in which the spectator consumes the image. As Jean-Louis Baudry points out, this failure to examine the cinematographic apparatus in the totality of its functioning is part of a general resistance to considering the place of the subject within cinema:

Actually, cinema is a simulation apparatus. This much was immediately recognized, but, from the positivist viewpoint of scientific rationality which was predominant at the time of its invention, the interest was directed towards the simulation of reality inherent to the moving image [and] to the unexpected effects which could be derived from it without finding it necessary to examine the implications of the cinematographic

215

apparatus being initially directed towards the subject and simulation's possible application to states or subjects-effects before being directed toward the reproduction of the real.[1]

In order to discuss documentary's particular situation within the cinematographic apparatus, it is first necessary to describe the subject-effect which that apparatus produces.

Baudry's analysis suggests that the motivating desire of cinema is not to replicate reality but rather to produce within the spectator-subject a specific condition of consciousness, which Christian Metz calls the filmic state. Cinema is a simulation apparatus—a perfected configuration whose partial realizations can be found in other historical devices. But what it represents (repeats) for the spectator is not the real as such, but the "ghosts" that have not been laid to rest and that still occupy the scene of the unconscious: "In order to explain the cinema-effect, it is necessary to consider it from the viewpoint of the apparatus that it constitutes, apparatus which in its totality includes the subject. And first of all, the subject of the unconscious."[2]

In order to describe the subject-effect that cinema produces, Baudry, and Metz in his essay entitled "The Fiction Film and Its Spectator,"[3] draw on the psychoanalytic theory of certain psychic states—the special economic situations that Freud called the "hallucinatory psychoses of desire." In particular, Baudry draws parallels between the dream state and the filmic state, underscoring the material conditions of the cinematic spectacle—the darkness of the place and the passive immobility of the spectator—which recall the somatic conditions of sleep. Sleep, Freud tells us, is a "reviviscence of one's stay in the body of the mother." It permits a developmental regression to the stage of primitive narcissism in which the subject's libido withdraws the cathectic energy it deployed into objects in the subject's waking state in order to reinvest it in the ego itself. As Freud argues, the human psychic organism always retains its capacity to retrace its steps, to return to earlier forms of object relations: "The primitive stages can always be reestablished; the primitive mind is, in the fullest meaning of the word, imperishable."[4] In the *Interpretation of Dreams,* Freud notes that temporal regression in the dreamer is accompanied by topographical regression. Excitation, instead of moving from the sensory extremity to the motor extremity of the psychic apparatus, is allowed through deactivation of the conscious, preconscious, and unconscious systems to flow in a backward direction until it produces the "hallucinatory revival of the *perceptual* images."[5]

216

As Metz's analysis in "The Fiction Film and Its Spectator" demonstrates, the filmic and oneiric states are related by a complex set of partial similarities and differences. In dreams, mental images, as products of the regressive movement of libidinal energy and the cathexis of the perceptual apparatus, are taken to be perceptions of reality, i.e., they are hallucinated. Cinematic images on the other hand belong in essence to the order of reality and are recognized as originating in the outside world, in a play of projected light on a screen. And yet the experience of the spectator demonstrates that it is not the "moving visual and sonic impressions"—the cinematic signifier—which are taken as real, but the characters and actions represented. The initial impression of reality that the filmic image produces in us indicates in itself at least the beginning of a regressive movement and the desire to confuse what is real with what is imagined. Furthermore, the spectator is subject to fleeting moments of intense belief, which Metz accounts for in economic terms. The psychic conditions of the filmic state are the result of a very specific organization of the perceptual and somatic situation. On the one hand, the flow of libidinal energy that is normally dissipated in the waking state is blocked by the absence of motor discharge because of the passive, immobile position of the spectator. It tends to turn back in the direction of the perceptual agency, which it hypercathects. Simultaneously, on the other hand, the film presents the spectator with an unusually intense sensual experience, that nourishes his perception from without:

> What defines this equilibrium is a *double reinforcement* of the perceptual function, simultaneously from without and within: apart from the filmic state, there are few situations in which a subject receives particularly dense and organized impressions from without at the same moment that his immobility predisposes him to "hyper-receive" ["*sur-recevoir*"] them from within. The classical film plays on this pincer action, the two branches of which it has itself set up. It is the double reinforcement which renders possible the impression of reality.[6]

Both Baudry and Metz point to the resemblance between the filmic and oneiric flux that is a resemblance of their signifiers. The topographical regression of the dream produces a transformation of the word-representation of dream-thought into the image-representation of the manifested dream. Indeed Freud considers the question of representability—the displacement of expressions toward pictorial substitutes—as the third factor in addition to condensation and displacement responsible for the transformation of dream-thoughts.[7] Hence the cinematic signifier—images in movement accompanied by sound—has a certain kinship with the figuration of dream. It is of course necessary to distinguish the secondary, bound character of cinematic discourse from the freely flowing psychical energy that is characteristic of the primary process. However, the cinematographic image is never completely consumed by discourse; it never completely submits to the chain of logical sequence in which it is caught: "The unconscious neither thinks nor discourses; it figures itself forth in images; conversely, every image remains vulnerable to the attraction, varying in strength according to the case, of the primary process and its characteristic modalities of concatenation."[8]

Regression in dream is topographical in that it describes the redirection of excitation; it is temporal in that it implies a return to past phases of development; it is formal in that its modes of expression involve a reversion to primary process. Through this complex psychical experience, the dreamer reinstitutes an archaic mode of identification. He or she rediscovers an immediate relationship to the object in which there is no distinction between interior and exterior, between self and other; the dreamer occupies the entire field of the dream:

One might even add that we are dealing with a more-than-real in order to differentiate it from the impression of the real which reality produces in the normal waking situation. The more-than-real translating the cohesion of the subject with his perceived representations, the submersion of the subject in his representations, the near-impossibility for him to escape their influence and which is dissimilar if not incompatible with the impression resulting from any direct relation to reality.[9]

Cinema belongs to the order of reality and what the spectator experiences in the movie theater is regression in a partial and incipient form. Yet, if we agree with Baudry's compelling argument, it is precisely this archaic mode of being that the subject seeks to repeat by assuming the position already marked out for the spectator within the cinematographic machine. It is obvious that the delusion coefficient is less in cinema than in dreams, and cinema's capacity for wish fulfillment is less certain. The film is not a production internal to the spectator. Yet, as Metz asserts, cinema derives much of its power from the fact that its illusion is produced within a spectator who is awake. Within the darkened walls of the movie theater we as spectators permit ourselves to lower, just slightly, our defenses, to mitigate the authority of the reality principle and secondary process in order to mimic within this apparatus our own

218

archaic subjectivity in this scene of instinctual representation, which has been denied and excluded:

> In other words, without his always suspecting it, the subject is induced to produce machines which would not only complement or supplement the workings of the secondary process, but which could represent his own overall functioning to him: he is led to produce mechanisms mimicking, simulating the apparatus which is no other than himself. The presence of the unconscious also makes itself felt through the pressure it exerts in seeking to get itself represented by a subject who is still unaware of the fact the he is representing to himself the very scene of the unconscious where he is.[10]

Baudry and Metz, among others, have advanced our understanding of the metapsychology of the spectator of the fiction film. They have analyzed the state of the subject—the effect produced by the conjoining of the psychic and cinematic apparatuses. My analysis of documentary has thus far centered on the text and its modalities of enunciation and this study has necessarily included the spectator. However I would like to shift attention to spectatorship itself and attempt to describe in economic and topographical terms how documentary modifies the filmic state. For in order to produce something other than the fiction-effect, documentary must modify the classic arrangement of parts of the cinematographic apparatus; it must have another manner of articulating the imaginary, the symbolic, and the real. As I will attempt to demonstrate, documentary institutes a rather specific inflection-deflection of the desire for cinema which it both acknowledges and denies.

Metz has demonstrated in his analysis of the scopic regime in cinema that the cinematographic image partakes of the imaginary by its very system of representation. The cinematic signifier combines in its production a certain presence and a certain absence. In films the actors, their actions, and the settings within which they act are present only as moving traces of light on the screen; their models, really present only at the moment of the shooting, are elsewhere; everything is recorded:

> The cinema only gives [its object] in effigy, inaccessible from the outset, in a primordial *elsewhere*, infinitely desirable (= never possessible), on another scene which is that of absence and which nonetheless represents the absent in detail, thus making it very present, but by a different itinerary. Not only am I at a distance from the object, as in the theatre, but what remains in that distance is now no longer the object itself, it is

a delegate it has sent me while itself withdrawing. A double withdrawal.[11]

By this double withdrawal of the signifier, as Metz asserts, every film is a fiction film.

The documentary image as signifier is no more a part of the real it represents than is the image in the fiction film. It has been cut off from its model, deferred, transformed. And yet the documentary image, or rather the sequence of images that constitute the film, shares at least one feature with the image (perception) of the real: it does not produce or produces intermittently or perhaps produces only in its marginal (aberrant) productions the specific kind of pleasure that is the whole aim of the fiction film as institution. We find ourselves faced with the question that Daniel Sibony poses in opening his analysis of the effect produced on the German public by the televising of the American serial melodrama, *Holocaust:* "Let's start with this simple question: why is it the fictive image which works on the spectator and overwhelms him, while the real image (indeed the event itself) leaves him indifferent, or at least completely in control of himself, 'master of the game' for which he is the permanent mise en scène."[12]

Why do the images of horror—perceptions of the real—remain bearable, while images of fiction evoke profound and cathartic excitation? If we accept, following Sibony's analysis, that society attains a certain recognition (repetition) of itself through the agency of an orchestrated play of "fictional" images, why does it appear that documentary film has been excluded from this symbolic function? Why does the documentary representation of the holocaust leave the spectator unshaken, whereas fictional images are capable of provoking a sacrificial burning in effigy? What better effigy than the documentary film, which would appear to bear the marks of the real? What closer conjunction of reality and representation, what more prodigious repetition can be imagined?

I can begin to respond by stating what appears to be a tautology: documentary films often fail to engage the spectator's affective participation because they often produce filmic displeasure. But the spectator's displeasure must be understood here in terms of psychical processes. As Baudry and Metz demonstrate in their analyses of the cinematographic apparatus, the spectator goes to the movies in search of a certain pleasure, the satisfaction of specific drives. He or she entertains with the film an object relationship: the images and the stories they tell may either gratify or frustrate according to whether those images and stories satisfy or fail to satisfy the

220

demands of instinctual fantasies. The individual spectator invests him or herself more or less completely in a given film in an infinite gradation between pleasure and displeasure. As Metz points out, distinct filmic displeasure can be described in topographical terms as either the lack of instinctual gratification, i.e., displeasure of the id, or as a threatening excess of excitation that occasions the intervention of the superego,[13] and it is certainly documentary's failure to nurture the spectator's fantasy that is at issue here. Any film may displease by the very fact that its images and sounds are external to the spectator-subject, who does not produce them according to his or her desire:

> The diegetic film, on the other hand, which in certain respects is still of the order of phantasy, also belongs to the *order of reality*. It exhibits one of reality's major characteristics: in relation to the wish (and to the fear which is the other face of the wish), it can "turn out" more or less well; it is not in total collusion with them; it can become so only after the fact, through an encounter or adjustment whose success is never guaranteed: it can please or displease, like the real, and because it is part of the real.[14]

Both fiction and nonfiction films belong to the order of reality, but what remains to be explained is why nonfiction "disappoints" so consistently. It is not because of the greater reality of the signifier in documentary, since the signifier in cinema always evokes that play of presence and absence that links it to the imaginary. It is not the specific content of the images that accounts for their being apprehended in a general way as "good" or "bad" objects: there is no absolute distinction to be made between fiction and nonfiction on the basis of the "semantic fabric." Nor is a clear-cut distinction to be made on the basis of differing forms of content: as we have seen, documentaries tell stories and to do so they often borrow the formal structures of the classic narrative film. If documentary creates special conditions of reception for the spectator, we must look for them not simply in the object, the film, but in the interrelationship of subject and object by which both subject and object are shaped. This relationship is conditioned first from without. We will consider documentary as a social institution whose mythology acts to model the spectator's responses and shape the attitude he or she adopts with regard to the film. Second, we will reexamine documentary from within, from the perspective of the text, in order to weigh the effect of documentary's modes of enunciation on spectatorial consciousness.

If there is one feature that characterizes documentary as institution, it is a basic dependency. Documentary film production takes place within other institutional contexts; it is financed by governmental or industrial public relations agencies or educational and scientific organizations: Sovkino (USSR); the fascist *Statts-auftragsfilme;* the U.S. Information Services, the Farm Security Administration; UNESCO; the Centre National de la Recherche Scientifique (France); the Empire Marketing Board, the General Post Office, the Shell (Oil) Film Unit (Britain), to mention but a few of the most significant "parent" institutions in the history of documentary production. Unlike the commercial film industry, documentary filmmaking is not generally self-sustaining or self-perpetuating; it stands outside the circuit of finance, production, and consumption that defines cinema as institution. Spectators do not normally pay to see documentary films; they do not participate in an exchange of money for pleasure. Consequently, a "bad" film in documentary, one that fails to please on the level of the instinctual fantasies of the spectator, is not necessarily a failure of the institution (although documentarists often feel constrained to make consessions to filmic pleasure).

The spectator who goes to see a documentary film is quite aware that the film is not designed to provide the same experience as the fiction film. Normally, he or she has not chosen the film as a leisure time activity whose goal is to activate the pleasures of the imaginary. The spectator is, rather, conscious of an overriding seriousness of purpose, defined at least in part by special conditions of consumption. If the film is projected within an institutional framework, it is that institution—film society, labor union, university, civic forum—which sets the social context of reception. When it was projected as part of a commercial film program as frequently occurred in movie theaters between 1935 and 1955, the documentary, always a preliminary event, was not to be consumed, as every spectator knew, in the same manner or for the same purpose as the feature film. Always the spectator recognizes a distinct contractual situation in which he or she agrees to maintain a level of wakefulness and a certain activity of secondary process appropriate to this object, just as such an arrangement is established between the spectator and the fiction film: "Thus a sort of compromise is created, a middle level of wakefulness, itself institutionalised in the classical cinema, where film and spectator succeed in being regulated one by the other and both by an identical or similar degree of secondarization."[15]

Documentary requires a higher degree of vigilance from the spectator than does the fiction film. Through its apparent relation to the reality of social existence, it invokes the defense mechanisms of the ego and calls on the operations of waking thought, controled reasoning, and judgment characteristic of the bound energy of the secondary processes. Thus documentary films bring into play within the spectator a resistance to the material conditions of the movie theater which as Baudry and Metz assert, were set in place precisely to permit a certain lowering of defenses. The cinematic apparatus by its very configuration tenders a promise of libidinal pleasure that the spectator here is led to refuse: the documentary film is an object inappropriate to desire. We can then describe in economic terms the unpleasure that documentary films seem to produce so often in the spectator: boredom is the condition of frustration *(Versagung)* in which the subject who is denied consequently denies himself.

The attitude that the spectator adopts toward the documentary film is further nourished by the popular belief in documentary realism. Documentary film succeeds in producing in the spectator a specific sense of the real, which we must distinguish from the impression of reality experienced by the spectator of the fiction film. Metz's work has demonstrated that the impression of reality cannot be explained only by reference to the cinematic signifier: the intensity of belief evoked is not simply a function of the great resemblance between perception of the image and perception of the real:

> The impression of reality is founded, then, on certain objective resemblances between what is perceived in the film and what is perceived in daily life, resemblances still imperfect but less so than they are in most of the other arts. However, I remarked also that the similarity of the stimuli does not explain everything, since what characterises and even defines, the impression of reality is that it works to the benefit of the imaginary and not of the material which represents it (that is, precisely, the stimulus).[16]

The documentary, like the fiction film, is composed of photographic images in movement that produce an impression of depth and provide great perceptual richness. Like the classic narrative film, the documentary hides the traces of its work in order to "open immediately on to the transparency of a signified."[17] It also produces the previous existence effect, but with an authority the fiction film cannot claim: more than the fiction film, documentary creates the impression of merely transmitting to the spectator events that have already taken place. It produces the referential illusion and in fact derives its prestige from that production.

As Metz suggests, it is the absence of actors and objects in the fiction film—more precisely, their presence in the mode of absence—which serves to induce the spectator's imaginary relationship with his or her counterpart in the images. Thus the cinematic signifier is characterized by its perceptual wealth combined with a profound unreality: a most convincing simulation that acknowledges its lack of real being. It is this unreality that is the precondition for the production of another (psychic) reality—the illusion of being-there of the thing.

Documentary shares with the fiction film the character of its signifier. It also produces a pseudo real since the reality it evokes with those same powers of imitation is elsewhere, in another time. However, documentary does not possess the same powers of illusion as the fiction film; it does not lead the spectator to imagine the phantasmic presence of actions, objects, and persons. The sense of the real is strong in documentary, but its effect is achieved through a modification of the spectator's consciousness of the relationship between presence and absence. The signified in documentary has status as document; its signifier conserves the traces in the present of events that have already taken place. The projection of a documentary film is always a retelling. The act of signification is presented as already complete, as redemption (to use the word of realist theory): the signified derives its prestige from its anteriority. Hence the documentary appears invested with certain characteristics that Roland Barthes ascribes to the photograph.[18] Like the photograph, the documentary film is not experienced as illusion: it does not evoke in the spectator the consciousness of the being-there of the thing. Its signified does not belong to the here-now but rather to the having-been-there. It participates in the illogical conjunction of spatial immediacy (the presence of the signifier) and temporal anteriority (the assumed preexistence of the signified). This primordial signified stands in temporal opposition to the realization of the desire of cinema: the assumption by the spectator of the film's images as his or her own present enunciation. As Freud tells us, the present tense is the tense in which wishes are represented as fulfilled. For Benveniste it is the time of enunciation. The impression of reality, then, in documentary film can be described as a belief in the reality of the signified as the having-been-there of the thing.

This sense of reality suggests a distinct spectatorial attitude in which the character of the spectacle itself is modified, in particular the mode in which the spectator engages the object, the images. As Metz has shown in *The Imaginary Signifier,* the major socially

224

accepted arts are based on the senses at a distance, i.e., on sight and on hearing, which suppose a separation between the generative organ and the object of the drive (in cinema, the separation between the eye and the screen institutionalized in the configuration of the seating). All visual spectacle is based on the rejection of fusion and can therefore be characterized as voyeuristic. According to Metz's analysis, the specifically cinematic scopic regime depends on a double withdrawal of the object. Not only is a distance maintained between the eye and the screen, but the object itself is offered only in effigy: it is imaginary, inaccessible *ab origine*. Cinema is distinct in that the two protagonists of the perverse couple (both present in the theater, for example, as audience and actor) are never present at the same time. Technically speaking, it is the chronological separation of the shooting and the projection that acts to create the segregation of spaces in the movie theater: the space of the auditorium, which is real, and the space of the film, which is perspective. The voyeur and the exhibitionist fail to meet and hence voyeurism in cinema dispenses with the consent of its object. Yet just as the domestic voyeur presumes the consent of the passive actors, the spectator in cinema presumes the exhibitionism of the film: "Yet still a voyeur, since there is something to see, called the film, but something in whose definition there is a great deal of 'flight': not precisely something that hides, rather something that *lets* itself be seen without *presenting* itself to be seen, which has gone out of the room before leaving only its trace visible there."[19]

It is, of course, not possible to determine the quality of consent given by the "actors" in documentary film. In one sense, documentary appears to bring cinema closer to the representation of the conditions of the primal scene by adding the element of uncertainty to the consciousness of the spectator-voyeur: to what extent has this exhibitionism been consented to? to what extent is it unauthorized? Paradoxically, as we shall see, it is precisely this uncertainty that arrests the movement of fantasy. The question of consent has always been at the center of theoretical discussions of documentary practice. Theories of ethnographic film or direct cinema, for example, are preoccupied with the notion of consent, and allegations of heresy among documentarists are always grounded in such a notion.

As Jean-Louis Comolli has pointed out however in his article, "Le Passé filmé,"[20] such theoretical discussions are always enclosed within the myth of cinematic realism, as if the central question of cinema were to find the strategies to escape from the *mise en scène* imposed on it by theatrical or literary models. For Comolli, everything in cinema partakes of *mise en scène:*

> There is no "visible" except caught in a *dispositif* of the look and, so to speak, always-already framed; on the other hand, it is naive to situate *mise en scène* only on the side of the camera: it is just as present, and even before the camera intervenes, everywhere social prescriptions order the place, the conduct, and I would add almost the 'form' of subjects in the diverse configurations where they are caught.[21]

Let us assert with Comolli that there is no difference of nature between fiction and nonfiction, nothing in the cinematographic operation that proves the "reality" of any image, the real existence of any referent. Cinema produces effects (I attempted to show in the preceding chapter how at the level of the text documentary produces the nonfiction-effect); that is, it is always a question of the consciousness of the spectator, a question of belief. If the documentary shares with the classic narrative film many of the re-duplications that serve to "articulate together the imaginary, the symbolic and the real,"[22] it is also a special regime of credence. I emphasized from the outset the unsteadiness of this regime: the specific splittings of belief that determine its character operate unevenly, for reasons I will now try to make clear.

The belief—the sense of reality—that the documentary evokes depends in the first instance on a perceived demand that such films make on the spectator: "We ask you to believe that . . ." Belief in cinema is not a question of delusion; it is the result of a highly organized contractual situation in which belief of a certain order is given in exchange for certain institutionalized defenses. As Octave Mannoni's analysis of theatrical illusion suggests,[23] the spectator in theater as in cinema is always aware that a deception is being practiced. The act of going to the theater or to the movies is in fact an act of collusion that assumes that the spectator is well versed in the conventions without which spectacle could not exist. As knowing spectators we identify with the *magister ludi* who orchestrates the unfolding of the imaginary world where we will take our pleasure. But it is also the case that we go to the theater or to the movies in order to be deceived. Some part of ourselves takes the imaginary for the real, and without such deception theater and cinema would be without interest for us: we could not obtain that pleasure that cinema and theater exist to produce. The spectator is then divided: he or she embodies two spectators—one disabused, the other naive.

In his essay, "Je sais bien, mais quand même . . ."[24] Mannoni

226

describes this splitting of belief (Freud's *Verleugnung*) as a fetishistic process. In the Freudian account, the fetishist perpetuates an infantile mode of defense. The child who becomes aware of the feminine anatomy and discovers the absence of the penis repudiates this discovery, which reality imposes, in order to retain an irrational belief in the maternal phallus. Disavowal corresponds to a splitting of the ego: it supposes an agency that recognizes reality and another that repudiates it. For Mannoni, the disavowal of the child with regard to the maternal lack is the prototype of all subsequent splittings of belief: "But like everyone else, by a kind of displacement, [the neurotic] utilizes the mechanism of *Verleugnung* with reference to other beliefs as if the *Verleugnung* of the maternal phallus outlined the first model of all repudiations of reality and constituted the origin of all beliefs which survive even when refuted by experience."[25] We as spectators, secure in our knowledge of the real—secure in our defenses—permit the emergence within ourselves of our own desire to believe, which belongs to the child we know we no longer are. Theater and cinema are sites within which a permissiveness, which is socially highly organized, allows the release of the imaginary powers of the ego:

> When the curtain rises, it is the imaginary powers of the Ego which are at once liberated and organized—dominated by the spectacle. How to say it, for by metaphor, the word *scene* has become the term by which one designates the psychic site where the images display themselves. We can say that the theatrical stage [scène] becomes the extension of the Ego with all its possibilities.[26]

As I already noted, disavowal in cinema functions first of all at the level of the signifier, whose reality yields in order to produce the impression of reality. The exchange between a real instance (the reality of the signifier) and an imaginary instance (the represented: the diegesis) is characteristic of all fiction: "In the cinema as in the theater, the represented is by definition imaginary; that is what characterises fiction as such, independently of the signifiers in charge of it."[27] This exchange is always dialectical, and theater and cinema for example are distinguished not only by their signifiers but by the difference of economy that the different signifiers install. However, with documentary film the spectator cannot make this exchange in quite the same manner. Our knowledge of the spectacle is marked by fissures, areas of uncertainty, which tend to undermine the system of defenses that cinema has set in place. Of course we recognize the objects—what is being represented by the image. However in cinema recognition is only a first step, a setting into motion of the mechanism of the apparatus, the "chain of mirrors" within which we as spectators take our place. This chain by its very configuration positions us so that we may admire ourselves in the mirror of the screen. But the release of those powers of the ego supposes that an exchange takes place within the spectator between the real and the imaginary in which reality is partially repudiated in the interest of a certain belief in the world of the fiction. In documentary film, however, the spectator remains uncertain as to where the real in fact lies. The real is the signifier, but it is also the signified—that historical field of reference to which the signifier gives us immediate access. At least this is what the idea of documentary realism leads us to believe.

As Mannoni asserts, the imaginary always rests on a doubling: "As long as the stage presents itself as a place other than the one it really is, as long as the actor presents himself as another, a perspective of the imaginary will be created."[28] The spectator knows that the stage is not the place of the "action," that the screen is incommensurate with the space of the diegesis. It is precisely in this gap, in this negation of one term by the other, that the theatrical and cinematic "illusion" is generated: "At this moment the theater would play a properly symbolic role. It would be entirely like the great negation, the symbol of negation, which makes possible the return of the repressed in its denied form."[29]

The fictionality of the signifier in cinema is not, however, a sufficient defense for the spectator. Representation is not taking place (as it does in theater) entirely before our eyes, within the perimeters (the safety zone) of the movie theater. We must know that what is absent, whose trace is the object of our desire, is also seized by the imaginary and subject to an initial doubling. The actors present themselves as characters, the real acts in the interest of the production of a pseudo real (the diegesis): "A *place* consisting of actions, objects, persons, a time and a space (a place similar in this respect to the real), but which presents itself of its own accord as a vast simulation, a non-real real; a 'milieu' with all the structures of the real and lacking (in a permanent, explicit fashion) only the specific exponent of real being."[30] This is what Daniel Sibony refers to as the "third degree" of the image: not the image of the real (perception in daily life), nor the deferred image of real events (the "document"), but the image that is "played," which is itself *imaged,* a recognizable counterfeit.[31] What the spectator is seeking then is repetition of a certain order. Cinema is the site of an obsessional ritual within which the spectator-subject can stage the neverending return of the repressed. But the stage of this representation must be carefully delineated, marked off, distanced from reality—a reflection of that distancing that sets the repressed apart from consciousness. As Baudry suggests, the cinematic apparatus is a machine that is fashioned for this particular sort of *mise en scène*.

Thus, in order for the spectator to experience the functional pleasure of the nonrecognized return of the repressed, it is necessary that everything come to nothing, that the forces that have been placed in movement be brought to rest, that the "reality" of this other scene be contained within the ritual of cinema. This is precisely how Mannoni describes the economic situation instituted by theater: "Besides, Hamlet had already said it: 'Players cannot keep counsel.' Actors cannot keep a secret; they will tell all. This suggests that the anxiety and tension provoked by the solicitation of the unconscious will, in the end, be brought back to zero."[32] The pleasure that the cinematic apparatus provides for the spectator is, first of all, a functional pleasure, before the special pleasures that certain images reserve for certain spectators are considered. The unprecedented conjunction of an incipient delusional state and a relative wakefulness (compared to dream) places the spectator in an unusual (and illusory) position of power. Through the symbolic, which is the cinematic apparatus, the spectator achieves a simulation of infantile omnipotence. Our insertion into the apparatus and the regressive movement that we thus undergo enable us, but only partially, i.e., only symbolically, to rediscover by the analogy that this simulation provides something like our primordial subjectivity. A conditional glimpse of our power before the word murdered the thing, before the symbol installed the distance between self and things, between self and others, before the self conceded to the social "I," before the *Spaltung*. Cinema is a way of (conditionally and temporarily) weakening the subject's submission to the signifier, to the powerful mass of symbolism through the fleeting and unrecognized rediscovery of the "underside of the mask," the repressed. It is the (impotent) staging of a revolt against the impossible coincidence between the *I* of subjectivity and the *I* of discourse.

It is, therefore, the dual relationship whose representation cinema stages even before it stages its imitation of the real. The subject, both deluding and deluded, who has been excluded from the production of cinematic discourse, reasserts an illusory power over the text, whose images he or she assumes as the products of subjective desire. Classical representation has led to this substitution that is essential to the subject-effect: the image producer evacuates the ideal point of vision in order that it may be occupied collectively and without contradiction by the many eyes of the spectators. Bertrand Augst observes, "The ultimate achievement of cinematographic discourse is not only to have refined, condensed and disseminated all the rules of discursive exclusion, but also to have created a pseudo-subject who by inserting himself in the place of the spectator-subject, deprives the spectator of the right to speak while deluding him into thinking the other's discourse is really his own."[33]

As we saw in the preceding chapter, the cinematographic apparatus and the film text produce the homogenization of what is actually heterogeneous: the subject-producer / the subject-spectator; the space of the auditorium / the space of the screen; the heterogeneous signifier / the homogeneous signified. Homogenization—psychical, spatial, and discursive—acts so as to produce the impression of immediacy. The darkness and configuration of the movie theater diminish the attachment of the spectator to the real. The cinematic signifier effaces its reality and its multiplicity in the interest of the diegesis. Hence the spectator is able to play at abandoning the "phantoms," the signs of his or her social integration by means of the signifier in favor of phantasm: the illusion of filling in the primordial lack, the breach that the symbolic imposes.

If then this functional pleasure is the goal of the cinematographic apparatus, what can be said of the intrusion of documentary with its uncertain sense of the real and its ambivalent forms of enunciation? To the extent that it asserts its difference from dominant cinema, the documentary film disrupts the functioning of the apparatus, which has achieved a state of economic equilibrium. To the extent it is in fact constituted, its modality of enunciation contradicts the historically imposed classical structure of representation in which the artist is inscribed only as an absence, an ideal point of vision. In documentary, an "enunciator" is already present—represented by the voice of the commentary—and this doubling of the position of subject (subject-producer / subject-spectator) undermines the "rationality" of "pure" representation. It is significant that this already-constituted enunciator can do no better than attempt to hide the irrationality of his presence, to seek his own effacement, to encourage an identification that the spectator can no more than partially accept. It is understandable that the spectator should experience this duplication as duplicity, as an obstruction of desire, for it enjoins the subject to share the power that he or she is used to exercising exclusively.

If the cinematographic apparatus is arranged so as to produce an artifical psychosis without danger to the organism, a return to the duality of narcissistic identification, the documentary text brings about a partial denial of this regressive movement. As we have seen, documentary tends to reassert the heterogeneity that the apparatus functions to deny. It distinguishes the spectator from the enunciator of the images; it reestablishes at least intermittently the heterogeneity of certain elements of the signifier; and consequently it calls attention to the segregation of the two spaces of the movie theater by replacing the spectator in a more knowledgeable relation to his or her perception. In sum, the documentary text reinstalls mediation. This mediation has an expressed form, the voice, which contrasts with the dark muteness of the theater. The documentary text exposes itself as a system of representation and returns the spectator to his or her seat, to a fuller exercise of reality testing. What it restages, then, is the ultimate triumph of the symbolic order over the normal subject with all the sacrifice that the subject's submission entails.

NOTES

Chapter 1. Documentary Film Theory and the Tradition of Historic Discourse

1. Hayden White, *Tropic of Discourse* (Baltimore: Johns Hopkins University Press, 1978), 121–34.

2. Roland Barthes, "Historical Discourse," in *Structuralism, a Reader,* ed. Michael Lane (London: Jonathan Cape, 1970), 153.

3. Andre Bazin, *What Is Cinema,* trans. Hugh Gray, 2 vols., (Berkeley and Los Angeles: University of California Press, 1967), 1:13.

4. Adolphe Thiers, quoted in Barthes, "Historical Discourse," 443.

5. Claude Levi-Strauss, *The Savage Mind,* (Chicago: University of Chicago Press, 1966), 257.

6. Levi-Strauss, *The Savage Mind,* 257.

7. White, *Tropics of Discourse,* 83.

8. Ibid., 60–61.

9. Ibid., 86.

10. Barthes, "Historical Discourse," 155.

11. It is not possible in this context to assess the many personalities of the British movement or to describe the internal ideological and theoretical tendencies that split the movement at various moments of its history. Hence I have not evaluated the importance of such a figure as Alberto Cavalcanti, one of the recognized "aesthetes" of the movement, its link with continental avant-gardism. For an account of the complexity of this history, see Elizabeth Sussex, *The Rise and Fall of British Documentary* (Berkeley and Los Angeles: University of California Press, 1975).

12. Ibid., 3.

13. Ibid., 80.

14. Ibid.

15. Paul Rotha, *Documentary Film* (London: Faber and Faber, 1935), 78.

16. John Grierson, *Grierson on Documentary,* ed. Forsyth Hardy (Berkeley and Los Angeles: University of California Press, 1966), 199.

17. Grierson, *Grierson on Documentary,* 147.

18. Ibid., 148.

19. Ibid., 148.

20. Ibid., 146.

21. Quoted in Georges Sadoul, *Dziga Vertov* (Paris: Editions Champ Libre, 1971), 60.

22. Quoted in Georges Sadoul, *Dziga Vertov,* 71.

23. Quoted in Vlada Petric, "Dziga Vertov as Theorist," *Cinema Journal* 18, 1 (1978): 38.

24. Petric, "Dziga Vertov as Theorist," 29.

25. Quoted in Seth R. Feldman, *Evolution of Style in the Early Work of Dziga Vertov* (New York: Arno Press, 1977), 134.

26. Feldman, *Evolution of Style*, 135.

27. Quoted in Sadoul, *Dziga Vertov*, 74.

28. Quoted in Feldman, *Evolution of Style*, 20.

29. Quoted in Sadoul, *Dziga Vertov*, 61.

30. This choice is, of course, an exclusion. I will not attempt to treat the history of the theory of cinematographic realism, nor will I discuss the often divergent positions of the aestheticians of realism, notably Siegfried Kracauer. Nor is it possible to take account here of the thories and methodologies of documentary realism that were formulated within the practices of various tendencies of *cinéma vérité*, direct cinema, new documentary, and so forth in European and American manifestations. I am interested in evoking in Bazin's theoretical writings those elements essential to the notion of realist representation.

31. Bazin, *What Is Cinema?* 17–22.

32. Ibid. 1:15

33. Bazin, *Qu'est-ce que le cinéma?*, (Paris: Editions du Cerf, 1958) 1:33. Bazin plays on the French word *pellicule* that refers both to a thin layer of skin (in the case of the slough) and to film stock (in the case of cinema).

34. Bazin, *What Is Cinema?* 1:16.

35. Roland Barthes, *Image-Music-Text*, trans. Stephen Heath (New York: Hill and Wang, 1977), 70.

36. Bazin, *What Is Cinema?* 1:13.

37. Serge Daney, "Sur Salador," *Cahiers du cinéma* 222 (1970): 38.

38. Bazin, *What Is Cinema?* 1:35.

39. Ibid. 28.

40. Ibid. 26–27.

41. Ibid. 50.

42. Ibid. 27.

43. Ibid. 27.

44. Roland Barthes, "The Realistic Effect," *Film Reader* 3 (1978): 133.

45. Barthes, "The Realistic Effect," 134.

46. Bazin, *What Is Cinema?* 1:27.

47. Bazin, *Qu'est-ce que le cinéma?* 1:52.

48. Bazin, *What Is Cinema?* 2:26.

49. Jean Rouch, "The Camera and Man," *Principles of Visual Anthropology*, ed. Paul Hockings (The Hague: Mouton Publishers, 1975), 88.

50. Emilie de Brigand, "The History of the Ethnographic Film, *Principles of Visual Anthropology*, ed. Paul Hockings (La Hague: Mouton Publishers, 1975), 14.

51. Gregory Bateson and Margaret Mead, *Balinese Character* (New York: Academy of Sciences, 1942 [reissued 1962]), 49.

52. Margaret Mead, "Anthropology and the Camera," *Encyclopedia of Photography*, ed. W. D. Morgan (New York: National Education Alliance, 1963), 174.

53. Bazin, *What Is Cinema?* 1:15.

54. John Collier, *Visual Anthropology: Photography as a Research Method*, (New York: Holt, Rinehart and Winston, 1967), 2.

55. Collier, *Visual Anthropology*, 2.

56. Margaret Mead, "Visual Anthropology in a Discipline of Words," *Principles*

of Visual Anthropology, ed. Paul Hockings (The Hague: Mouton Publishers, 1975), 10.

57. K. G. Heider, *Ethnographic Film* (Austin: University of Texas Press, 1976), 97–117.

58. Collier, *Visual Anthropology,* 7.

59. Jean-Dominique Lajoux, "Ethnographic Film and History," *Principles of Visual Anthropology,* ed. Paul Hockings (The Hague: Mouton Publishers, 1975), 170.

60. Claudine de France, *Cinéma et anthropologie* (Paris: Editions de la Maison des Sciences de l'Homme, 1982).

61. Claudine de France, *Cinéma et anthropologie,* 268.

62. Luc de Heusch, *The Cinema and Social Science,* Reports and Papers in the Social Sciences, no. 16 (Paris: UNESCO, 1962), 3–5.

63. Jean Rouch, "Mettre en circulation des objets inquiétants," *Nouvelle Critique,* No. 8a (63), nouvelle série (1975): 74.

64. White, *Tropics of Discourse,* 126.

Chapter 2. Order and Sequence in Documentary Film

1. Christian Metz, *Film Language: A Semiotics of Cinema,* trans. Michael Taylor (New York: Oxford University Press, 1974), 93.

2. Metz, *Film Language,* 95.

3. Christian Metz, "The Fiction Film and Its Spectator: A Metapsychological Study," trans. Alfred Guzzetti, *The Imaginary Signifier,* (Bloomington: Indiana University Press, 1982), 139.

4. John L. Fell, *Film and the Narrative Tradition* (Norman, Oklahoma: University of Oklahoma Press, 1974), 12–36.

5. Noel Burch, "Film's Institutional Mode of Representation and the Soviet Response," *October* 11 (1979): 77–96.

6. Metz, *Film Language,* 94.

7. Christian Metz, " 'Montage' et discours dans le film: un problème de sémiologie diachronique du cinéma," *Word* 23, 1–3 (1967): 391.

8. Metz, *Film Language,* 108–46.

9. Raymond Bellour, "To Analyze, To Segment," trans. Maureen Turim, *Quarterly Review of Film Studies* 1, 3 (1976): 332.

10. See Metz's General Table of the Large Syntagmatic Category of the Image-Track in *Film Language,* 146.

11. Christian Metz, *Language and Cinema,* trans. Jean Umiker-Sebeok (The Hague: Mouton, 1974), 126.

12. Gérard Genette, "Boundaries of Narrative," *New Literary History* 8, 1 (1976): 6.

13. Genette, "Boundaries of Narrative," 7.

14. Emile Benveniste, *Problems in General Linguistics,* trans. Mary Elizabeth Meek (Coral Gables, Florida: University of Miami Press, 1971), 208.

15. Andre Bazin, *What Is Cinema?,* trans. Hugh Gray, 2 vols., (Berkeley and Los Angeles: University of California Press, 1967), 1:27.

16. Andre Bazin, *Qu'est-ce que le cinéma?* 4 vols., (Paris: Editions du Cerf, 1958), 1:31–36.

17. Genette, "Boundaries of Narrative," 8–12.

18. Ibid. 11.

19. Christian Metz, "Ponctuation et démarcation dans le film de diégèse," *Cahiers du cinéma,* 234–35 (1971–1972): 72.

20. Metz, *Film Language,* 126.

Chapter 3. A Figurative Strategy: *Listen to Britain*

1. Gérard Genette, "Boundaries of Narrative," *New Literary History* 8, 1 (1976): 8.

2. Genette, "Boundaries of Narrative," 11.

3. Christian Metz, *Language and Cinema,* trans. Jean Umiker-Sebeok (The Hague: Mouton, 1974), 100.

4. Metz, *Language and Cinema,* 103.

5. Christian Metz, "Metaphor and Metonymy," *The Imaginary Signifier,* trans. Celia Britton and Annwyl Williams (Bloomington: Indiana University Press, 1982), 266.

6. Gérard Genette, *Figures II* (Paris: Editions du Seuil, 1969), 94.

7. *The Compact Edition of the Oxford English Dictionary* (New York: Oxford University Press, 1971).

8. Roland Barthes, *Image-Music-Text* (New York: Hill and Wang, 1977), 40.

9. Quoted in Elizabeth Sussex, *The Rise and Fall of British Documentary* (Berkeley and Los Angeles: University of California Press, 1975), 144.

10. Roland Barthes, *S/Z,* trans. Richard Miller (New York: Hill and Wang, 1974), 27.

11. Metz, *The Imaginary Signifier,* 212–28.

12. Metz, *The Imaginary Signifier,* 218.

13. Group μ, "La Chafetière est sur la table," 36–49.

14. Metz, *The Imaginary Signifier,* 292.

15. Group μ, "La Chafetière est sur la table," 45.

16. Christian Metz, "Aural Objects," *Yale French Studies* 60 (1981): 26–28.

17. John Grierson, *Grierson on Documentary,* ed. Forsyth Hardy (Berkeley and Los Angeles: University of California Press, 1966), 162.

18. Daniel Percheron, "Sound in Cinema and Its Relationship to Image and Diegesis," *Yale French Studies* 60 (1981): 16–23.

19. Barthes, *Image-Music-Text,* 101.

20. Christian Metz, "Ponctuation et démarcation dans le film de diégèse," *Cahiers du cinéma* 234–35 (1971–1972): 72.

21. Barthes, *S/Z,* 75.

22. Christian Metz, *Film Language: A Semiotics of Cinema,* trans. Michael Taylor (New York: Oxford University Press, 1974), 129–30.

23. Metz, *Film Language,* 126.

24. Raymond Bellour, "To Analyze, to Segment," *Quarterly Review of Film Studies* 1, 3 (1976): 338.

25. Bellour, "To Analyze, to Segment," 339.

26. Ibid.

27. Ibid. 344.

28. Barthes, *S/Z,* 67.

29. Ibid. 68.

30. Ibid. 95.

31. Ibid. 206.

32. Stephen Heath, "Film and System: Terms of Analysis," *Screen* 16, 1 (1975): 15.

33. Metz, *The Imaginary Signifier*, 274–80.

34. Tzvetlan Todorov, *The Poetics of Prose*, trans. Richard Howard, (Ithaca: Cornell University Press, 1977), 83.

35. Barthes, *S/Z*, 20.

36. Metz, *Film Language*, 129–30.

37. Roland Barthes, "Historical Discourse," in *Structuralism*, 155.

38. Hayden White, "The Value of Narrativity in the Representation of Reality" in *The Content of the Form* (Baltimore: The Johns Hopkins University Press, 1987), 24.

39. Metz, *Film Language*, 235.

Chapter 4. Documentary Film: History of Discourse?

1. See Marcelin Pleynet and Jean Thibaudeau, "Economique, idéologique, formel," *Cinéthique* (1969) 3, 7–14.

Jean-Louis Comolli, "Technique et idéologie," *Cahiers du cinéma* 229:4–21, 230:51–57, 231:42–49, 233:39–45, 234–235:94–100, 241:20–24 (1971–72).

Jean-Louis Baudry, "Ideological Effects of the Basic Cinematographic Apparatus," trans. Alan Williams, Film Quarterly 27, 2 (Winter 1974–75): 39–47. Originally appeared as "Cinéma: effets idéologiques produits par l'appareil de base," in *Cinéthique* 7–8 (1970): 1–8.

2. Jean-Louis Comolli, "Machines of the Visible," in *The Cinematic Apparatus*, ed. Teresa de Lauretis and Stephen Heath (New York: St. Martin's Press, 1980), 126.

3. Baudry, "Ideological Effects," 40.

4. Emile Benveniste, *Problems of General Linguistics* (Coral Gables, Florida: University of Miami Press, 1971), 195–230.

5. Benveniste, *Problems in General Linguistics*, 206–07.

6. Emile Benveniste, "L'Appareil formel de l'énonciation," *Langages* 17 (1969): 16.

7. Benveniste, "L'Appareil formel de l'énonciation," 12–18.

8. Ibid. 15.

9. Christian Metz, *The Imaginary Signifier* (Bloomington: Indiana University Press, 1982), 91.

10. Benveniste, *Problems in General Linguistics*, 208.

11. Metz, *The Imaginary Signifier*, 97.

12. Ibid. 93.

13. Christian Metz, "'Montage' et discours dans le film: un problème de sémiologie diachronique du cinéma," *Word* 23, 1–3 (1967): 388–95.

14. Noel Burch, "Film's Institutional Mode of Representation and the Soviet Response," *October* 11 (1980): 82.

15. Christian Metz, *Film Language: A Semiotics of Cinema*, trans. Michael Taylor (New York: Oxford University Press, 1974), 45.

16. Metz, *The Imaginary Signifier*, 139.

17. Roland Barthes, "Upon Leaving the Movie Theater," in *Apparatus*, ed. Theresa Hak Kyung Cha, trans. Bertrand Augst and Susan White (New York: Tanam Press, 1980), 2. Originally published as "En sortant du cinéma," *Communications* 23 (1975): 104–07.

18. Edgar Morin, *Le Cinéma ou l'homme imaginaire* (Paris: Les Editions de Minuit, 1956), 215.

19. Metz, *The Imaginary Signifier*, 40.

20. Claude Bailblé, "Programmation de l'écoute, 2," *Cahiers du cinéma* 293 (1978): 6.

21. Ibid. 7.

22. Ibid. 9.

23. Claudia Gorbman, "Narrative Film music," *Yale French Studies* 60 (1981): 183.

24. Benveniste, "L'Appareil formel de l'énonciation," 12.

25. Ibid. 13.

26. Ibid. 14.

27. Roland Barthes, *Image-Music-Text* (New York: Hill and Wang, 1977), 142.

28. Metz, *The Imaginary Signifier*, 55.

29. Ibid. 94.

30. Ibid. 48.

31. Ibid. 93.

32. Baudry, "Ideological Effects," 44.

33. Gérard Genette, *Figures III* (Paris: Editions du Seuil, 1972), 147–53.

34. Genette, *Figures III*, 211.

35. Christian Metz, "Ponctuations et démarcations dans le film de diégèse," *Cahiers du cinéma* 234–35 (1971–72): 72.

36. Michel Marie, "Le Film, la parole et la langue," *Cahiers du 20e Siècle* 9 (1978): 70.

37. Barthes, *Image-Music-Text*, 15–31.

38. Christian Metz, "Le Perçu et le nommé," *Vers une esthétique sans entrave* (Paris: Union Générale d'Edition, 10/18, 1975), 357–58.

39. André Bazin, *Qu'est-ce que le cinéma?*, 4 vols., (Paris: Editions du Cerf, 1958), 1:36.

40. Bazin, *Qu'est-ce que le cinéma?*, 35.

41. Pascal Bonitzer, "Hors-champ (un espace en défaut)," *Cahiers du cinéma* 234–35 (1971–72): 16.

Chapter 5. The Nonfiction Film and Its Spectator

1. Jean-Louis Baudry, "The Apparatus," trans. Jean Andrews and Bertrand Augst, *Camera Obscura* 1 (1976): 118. Originally appeared as "Le Dispositif," *Communications* 23 (1975): 56–72.

2. Baudry, "Apparatus," 119.

3. Christian Metz, *The Imaginary Signifier* (Bloomington: Indiana University Press, 1982), 99–147.

4. Sigmund Freud, "Thoughts for the Times on War and Death," *Standard Edition of the Complete Psychological Works of Sigmund Freud*, 24 vols., (London: Hogarth Press,. 1953–73), 14:286.

5. Sigmund Freud, *The Interpretation of Dreams*, trans. James Strachey (New York: Basic Books, 1960), 543.

6. Metz, *The Imaginary Signifier*, 118.

7. Freud, *The Interpretation of Dreams*, 339–49.

8. Metz, *The Imaginary Signifier*, 124.

9. Baudry, "The Apparatus," 116.

10. Ibid. 123.

11. Metz, *The Imaginary Signifier*, 61.

12. Daniel Sibony, "L'Image brûle," *Analytiques* 3 (1979): 3.

13. Metz, *The Imaginary Signifier*, 111.

14. Ibid. 113.

15. Ibid. 127.

16. Ibid. 140.

17. Ibid. 40.

18. Roland Barthes, *Image-Music-Text,* trans. Stephen Heath (New York: Hill and Wang, 1977), 32–51.

19. Metz, *The Imaginary Signifier,* 63.

20. Jean-Louis Comolli, "Le Passé filmé," *Cahiers du cinéma* 277 (1977): 5–14.

21. Comolli, "Le Passé filmé," 14.

22. Metz, *The Imaginary Signifier,* 71.

23. Octave Mannoni, *Clefs pour l'imaginaire ou l'autre scène* (Paris: Editions du Seuil, 1969), 161–183.

24. Mannoni, *Clefs pour l'imaginaire,* 9–33.

25. Ibid. 12.

26. Ibid. 181.

27. Metz, *The Imaginary Signifier,* 67.

28. Mannoni, *Clefs pour l'imaginaire,* 161.

29. Ibid. 166.

30. Metz, *The Imaginary Signifier,* 141.

31. Sibony, "L'Image brûle," 4.

32. Mannoni, *Clefs pour l'imaginaire,* 182.

33. Bertrand Augst, "The Order of [Cinematographic] Discourse," *Discourse* 1 (1979): 54.

Bibliography

Augst, Bertrand. "The Order of [Cinematographic] Discourse." *Discourse: Berkeley Journal for Theoretical Studies in Media and Culture* 1 (1979): 39–57.

Bailblé, Claude. "Programmation de l'écoute." *Cahiers du cinéma* 292:53–9, 293:5–12, 297:45–54, 299:18–27 (September 1978–April 1979).

Barsam, Richard Meran, ed. *Nonfiction Film: Theory and Criticism*. New York: E. P. Dutton, 1976.

Barthes, Roland. "Historical Discourse." In *Structuralism, a Reader*. Edited by Michael Lane, 145–155. London: Jonathan Cape, 1970.

————. *Image-Music-Text*. Translated by Stephen Heath. New York: Hill and Wang, 1972.

————. *Mythologies*. Translated by Annette Lavers. New York: Hill and Wang, 1972.

————. *S/Z*. Translated by Richard Miller. New York: Hill and Wang, 1974.

————. "The Realistic Effect." *Film Reader* 3 (1978): 131–35. Originally appeared as "L'Effet de reel." *Communications* 11 (1968): 84–89.

————. "Upon Leaving the Movie Theater." In *Apparatus*. Edited by Theresa Hak Kyung Cha. Translated by Bertrand Augst and Susan White. New York: Tanam Press, 1980. Originally appeared as "En sortant du cinéma." *Communications* 23 (1975): 104–07.

Bateson, Gregory, and Margaret Mead. *Balinese Character*. New York: New York Academy of Sciences, 1942 (reissued 1962).

Baudry, Jean-Louis. "Ideological Effects of the Basic Cinematographic Apparatus." Translated by Alan Williams. *Film Quarterly* 27, 2 (Winter 1974–75): 39–47. Originally appeared as "Cinéma: Effets idéologiques produits par l'appareil de base." *Cinéthique* 7–8 (1970): 1–8.

————. "The Apparatus." Translated by Jean Andrews and Bertrand Augst. *Camera Obscura, a Journal of Feminism and Film Theory* no. 1 (1976): 104–26. Originally appeared as "Le Dispositif." *Communications* 23 (1975): 56–72.

Bazin, André. *Qu'est-ce que le cinéma?*, 4 volumes. Paris: Editions du Cerf, 1958–1962.

————. *What Is Cinema?*, volume 1. Translated by Hugh Gray. Berkeley and Los Angeles: University of California Press, 1967.

————. *What is Cinema?*, volume 2. Translated by Hugh Gray. Berkeley and Los Angeles: University of California Press, 1971.

Bellour, Raymond. "To Analyze, To Segment." Translated by Maureen Turim. *Quarterly Review of Film Studies* 1, 3 (1976): 331–53.

Benveniste, Emile. *Problems in General Linguistics.* Coral Gables, Florida: University of Miami Press, 1971.

———. "L'Appareil formel de l'énonciation." *Langages* 17 (1969): 12–18.

Bergala, Alain. *Initiation à la sémiologie du récit en images.* Paris: Cahiers de l'audio-visuel, 1978.

Bonitzer, Pascal. "Hors-champ (un espace en défaut)." *Cahiers du cinéma* 234–35 (December 1971–January/February 1972): 15–26.

de Brigand, Emilie. "The History of the Ethnographic Film." *Principles of Visual Anthropology,* ed. Paul Hockings. The Hague: Mouton Publishers, 1975.

Burch, Noel. "Film's Institutional Mode of Representation and the Soviet Response." *October* 11 (1979): 77–96.

Collier, John. *Visual Anthropology: Photography as a Research Method.* New York: Holt, Rinehart and Winston, 1967.

Comolli, Jean-Louis. "Technique et idéologie." *Cahiers du cinéma* 229:4–21, 230:51–57, 231:42–49, 233:39–45, 234–35:94–100, 241:20–24 (1971–72). Partial translation in *Film Reader* 2 (1977): 128–48.

———. "Le Passé filmé." *Cahiers du cinéma* 277 (1977): 5–14.

———. "Machines of the Visible." In *The Cinematic Apparatus.* Edited by Teresa de Lauretis and Stephen Heath. New York: St. Martin's Press, 1980, 121–42.

Crofts, Stephen, and Olivia Rose. "An Essay Toward *Man with the Movie Camera.*" *Screen* 18, 1 (1977): 9–58.

Daney, Serge. "Sur Salador." *Cahiers du cinéma* 222 (1970): 38–43.

Feldman, Seth R. *Evolution of Style in the Early Works of Dziga Vertov.* New York: Arno Press, 1977.

Fell, John L. *Film and the Narrative Tradition.* Norman, Oklahoma: University of Oklahoma, 1974.

de France, Claudine. *Cinéma et anthropologie.* Paris: Editions de la Maison des Sciences de l'Homme, 1982.

Freud, Sigmund. *The Interpretation of Dreams.* Translated by James Strachey. New York: Basic Books, Inc. 1960.

———. "Thoughts for the Times on War and Death." In *Standard Edition of the Complete Psychological Works of Sigmund Freud.* vol. 14. London: Hogarth Press and the Institute of Psychoanalysis, 1953–73.

Genette, Gérard. *Figures II.* Paris: Editions du Seuil, 1969.

———. *Figures III.* Paris: Editions du Seuil, 1972.

———. "Boundaries of Narrative." *New Literary History* 8, 1 (1976): 1–13. Originally appeared as "Frontières du récit." In *Figures II,* 49–69. Paris: Editions du Seuil, 1969.

Gorbman, Claudia. "Narrative Film Music." *Yale French Studies,* no. 60 (1981): 183–203.

Griaule, Marcel. *Méthode de l'ethnographie.* Paris: Presses Universitaires de France, 1957.

Grierson, John. *Grierson on Documentary.* Edited by Forsyth Hardy. Berkeley and Los Angeles: University of California Press, 1966.

Group μ (Dubois, Edeline et al.). "La Chafetière est sur la table." *Communication et langages* 29 (1976): 36–49.

————. *A General Rhetoric*. Baltimore: The Johns Hopkins University Press, 1981.

Heath, Stephen. "Film and System: Terms of Analysis." *Screen,* 16, 1 (1975): 7–77 and 16, 2: (1975): 91–113.

Heider, Karl G. *Ethnographic Film*. Austin: University of Texas Press, 1976.

de Heusch, Luc. *The Cinema of Social Sciences*. Preface by Edgar Morin. Reports and Papers in the Social Sciences, no. 16. Paris: UNESCO, 1962.

Hockings, Paul, ed. *Principles of Visual Anthropology*. The Hague: Mouton Publishers, 1975.

Lajoux, Jean-Dominique, "Ethnographic Film and History." *Principles of Visual Anthropology,* ed. Paul Hockings. The Hague: Mouton Publishers, 1975.

Leroi-Gourhan, André. "Le Film ethnologique existe-t-il?" *Revue de géographie humaine et d'ethnologie* 3 (1948): 42–51.

Lévi-Strauss, Claude. *The Savage Mind*. Chicago: University of Chicago Press, 1966.

Mannoni, Octave. *Clefs pour l'imaginaire ou l'autre scène*. Paris: Editions du Seuil, 1969.

Marie, Michel. "Le Film, la parole et la langue." *Cahiers du 20e Siècle* 9 (1978): 67–75.

Mead, Margaret and Gregory Bateson. *Balinese Character*. New York: New York Academy of Sciences, 1942. Reissued 1962.

————. "Anthropology and the Camera." In *Encyclopedia of Photography*. Edited by W. D. Morgan. New York: National Educational Alliance, 1963.

————. "Visual Anthropology in a Discipline of Words." *Principles of Visual Anthropology,* ed. Paul Hockings. The Hague: Mouton Publishers, 1975.

Metz, Christian. " 'Montage' et discours dans le film: un problème de sémiologie diachronique du cinéma." *Word* 23, 1–3 (1967): 388–95.

————. "Ponctuation and démarcation dans le film de diégèse." *Cahiers du cinéma* 234–35 (1971–72): 63–78.

————. *Film Language: A Semiotics of Cinema*. Translated by Michael Taylor. New York: Oxford University Press, 1974.

————. *Language and Cinema*. Translated by Jean Umiker-Sebeok. The Hague: Mouton Publishers, 1974.

————. *The Imaginary Signifier*. Translated by Celia Britton, Annwyl Williams, Ben Brewster, and Alfred Guzzetti. Bloomington: Indiana University Press, 1982.

————. "Le Perçu et le nommé." In *Vers une esthétique sans entrave*. Edited by Mikel Dufrenne. Paris: Union Générale d'Edition, 10/18, 1975. Partially translated as "Aural Objects" in *Yale French Studies* 60 (1981):24–32.

Morin, Edgar. *Le Cinéma ou l'homme imaginaire*. Paris: Les Editions de Minuit, 1956.

Percheron, Daniel. "Sound in Cinema and Its Relationship to Image and Diegesis." *Yale French Studies* 60 (1981): 16–23.

Petric, Vlada. "Dziga Vertov as Theorist." *Cinema Journal* 18, 1 (1978): 29–44.

Pleynet, Marcelin, and Jean Thibaudeau. "Economique, idéologique, formel." *Cinéthique* 3 (1969): 7–14.

Rotha, Paul. *Documentary Film*. London: Faber and Faber, 1935.

Rouch, Jean. "Mettre en circulation des objets inquiétants." *Nouvelle Critique* 8a (63), nouvelle série (1975): 74–79.

———. "The Camera and Man." *Principles of Visual Anthropology,* ed. Paul Hockings. The Hague: Mouton Publishers, 1975.

Sadoul, Georges. *Dziga Vertov.* Paris: Editions Champ Libre, 1971.

Sibony, Daniel. "L'Image brûle." *Analytiques* 3 (1979): 3–7.

Sussex, Elizabeth. *The Rise and Fall of British Documentary.* Berkeley and Los Angeles: University of California Press, 1975.

Todorov, Tzvetlan. *The Poetics of Prose.* Translated by Richard Howard. Ithaca, New York: Cornell University Press, 1977.

White, Hayden. *Metahistory: The Historical Imagination in Nineteenth-Century Europe.* Baltimore: Johns Hopkins University Press, 1973.

———. *Tropics of Discourse.* Baltimore: Johns Hopkins University Press, 1978.

———. *The Content of the Form.* Baltimore: The Johns Hopkins University Press, 1987.

Filmography

Buñuel, Luis, producer and director. *Land Without Bread (Las Hurdas)*. 1932. Spain. 28 minutes.

Capra, Frank, producer. *The Battle of Britain (Why We Fight* series). 1943. U.S.A. 54 minutes. Capt. Anthony Veiller, direction and script.

Cavalcanti, Alberto, director. *Rien que les heures.* 1926. France. 45 minutes. Prod., Neofilm.

Flaherty, Robert, director. *Nanook of the North.* 1922. U.S.A. 60 minutes. Prod., Revillon Frères.

Franju, Georges, director. *Le Sang des bêtes (Blood of the Beasts).* 1949. France. 20 minutes. Jean Painlevé, commentary. Prod., Force et Voix de France.

Jennings, Humphrey, and Stewart McAllister, directors. *Listen to Britain.* 1942. Great Britain. 21 minutes. Prod., Crown Film Unit.

Lorentz, Pare, director and script writer. *The River.* 1937. U.S.A. 32 minutes. Prod., Farm Security Administration.

Rouch, Jean, director. *Les Maîtres fous.* 1953. France. 30 minutes.

Shub, Ester, director. *Fall of the Romanov Dynasty (PADENIYE DINASTI RO-MANOVIKH).* 1927. USSR. 75 minutes. Prod., Sovkino.

Van Dyke, William, and Ralph Stiener, directors. *The City.* 1939. U.S.A. 43 minutes. Henwar Rodakiewicz and Lewis Mumford, script. Aaron Copland, music. Prod., American Documentary Film.

Wright, Basil, and Henry Watt, directors. *Night Mail.* 1936. Great Britain. 24 minutes. Alberto Cavalcanti, sound. W. H. Auden, verse. Benjamin Britten, music. Prod., G.P.O. Film Unit.

Index

245

Franju, Georges, 59; *Le Sang des bêtes,* 49, 51, 52, 53–55, 58–59, 66, 161

Freud, Sigmund: on collective figures, 121; on disavowal *(Verleugnung),* 227; on displacement, 74; on dream, 216, 217; on wish fulfillment, 224

Functional pleasure in cinema, 229

General Post Office Film Unit, 19–20, 92, 222

Genette, Gérard: on changes in focalization, 176; on description, 52; on iterative functions, 175; on motivation and sequence, 76, 122; on narrative and discourse, 60, 71; on narrative and dramatic poetry, 72

Genre: documentary as, 47–48, 49

Gorbman, Claudia, 157

Grass, 44

Griaule, Marcel, 34

Grierson, John, 19–24, 92–93

Griffith, D. W., 43, 46, 152

Group μ: on metaphor and iconic metaphor, 89–91

Heath, Stephen, 119

Heider, K. G., 38

Hermeneutic codes, 104–5, 138

Hess, Myra, 124, 141

Heterogeneity: of cinematic apparatus, 230–31; of documentary text, 69–70, 71, 73, 76–77, 157–59, 213–14; of filmic signifier, 103, 155–57

Historian and documentarist, 17

Historical discourse, 30–31, 32–33

Historical narrative, 187–88, 196–201

Historical reference and the sign, 14

Historiography: Claude Lévi-Strauss on, 15; and documentary film, 13–19, 132–33; Hayden White on, 13, 16–17, 133; Louis Adolphe Thiers on, 14; and realism, 31; relation to fiction, 13–18; Roland Barthes on, 14, 16–17, 18

History and discourse: definition of, 150–51; in film, 151–52; in literature and film, 13–18

Holocaust, The, 220

Iconic metaphors: compared with linguistic metaphors, 90–91; definition of, 89–91; in *Listen to Britain,* 91–92, 94–95

Identification: with character, 160–61; with perceiving instance, 150, 152, 162

Illusionism: in cinema, compared with theater, 228; in documentary cinema, 224

Image representation in film and dream, 217–18

Imaginary: and the cinematic signifier, 219–20, 224, 228; as doubling, 228

Impression of reality, 227; in documentary film, 223, 224

Inserts (autonomous shots), 58. *See also* Large Syntagmatic

Jakobson, Roman, 151

Jennings, Humphrey, 59, 79; *Listen to Britain,* 48, 51, 52, 55, 56, 59, 77–148, 154

Kon-Tiki, 33–34

Land Without Bread, 48, 51, 52, 55, 60–61, 66, 161

Langue: in enunciation, 150–51, 157–58; and speech *(parole)* in film, 185

Large Syntagmatic, in analysis of documentary films: ambiguity of functions of types, 65–68; ambiguity of types, 62–65; bracket syntagma, 46, 55–56, 105–6, 211–12; descriptive syntagma, 52–55, 86–87, 105, 211; disruption of narrative, 198–200, 210–12; dominance of narrative, 52, 154, 172; frequency of occurrence, 50–51; the scene, 46, 105, 126, 138–41

Large Syntagmatic Code: in analysis of documentary films, 48–68; definition of types, 45–47

Legg, Stewart, 19

Lévi-Strauss, Claude, 15

Listen to Britain, 48, 51, 52, 55, 56, 59, 77–148, 154

Lumière, Louis, 21–22, 47

Maîtres fous, Les, 49, 50, 51, 57, 60, 176–87

Malraux, André, 45

Mannoni, Octave, 226–29

246

Marey, Etienne-Jules, 21, 35, 38
Marie, Michel, 185
Mead, Margaret, 34–37
Méliès, Georges, 21, 43
Metaphor: definition, 89–90; iconic, 89–92, 94–95; *in praesentia,* 90
Metonymy, 88; and synecdoche, 141
Metz, Christian: on the aural object, 92–93; on cinema and narrativity, 153–54; on demarcation, 62–63, 102, 119, 184, 211; on the dissolve, 121; on filmic pleasure, 220–21; on the filmic state, 216–19, 223; on film's primitive period, 34–35, 43; on the group of films, 48; on history and discourse in film, 151; on the iconic metaphor, 89, 90, 91; on identification with character, 160–61; on identification with the perceiving instance, 152, 162; on the imaginary and the cinematic signifier, 219–20, 224–25; on the impression of reality, 223; on the Large Syntagmatic Code, 45, 62, 66, 86–87, 172, 199; on marginality of nonnarrative film, 45; on the moment of the code, 75, 148; on perception and nomenclature, 186–87; on referential illusion, 156; on the scopic drive, 219–20, 224–25; on textual system as displacement, 73–75
Mise en scène: and ethnographic film, 35–36, 40–41,; in fiction and documentary, 75; "natural," in documentary film, 22–23; psychic, 229; realist in documentary film, 29, 31–34; theatrical and documentary film, 18–19, 21, 25–26, 27, 225–26
Mise en scène documentaire, 15, 26
Mitry, Jean, 45
Moana, 47
Moment of the code, 75, 148
Mondo Cane, 15
Monocular perspective, 149–50
Montage: Bazin on, 32; in ethnographic film, 35–36, 37–38; figurative, 94–95; historical development of, 45, 152–53; and language, 185; and metaphor, 86–95; and metonymy, 88; and representation of space-time in documentary film, 59, 212–13; Vertov on, 27–29
Morin, Edgar, 40, 45, 155

Mumford, Lewis, 61
Murnau, F. W., 32, 33
Music in film, 157, 212, 213

Nanook of the North, 26, 32, 34, 44, 48, 50, 51, 57–58, 109
Narrative and discursive order in documentary film, 56–62, 210–11
Narrative codes: hermeneutic and proairetic codes, 104; weaving the text, 76
Narrative modes: mimetic and discursive, 71–72; narration and description, 52–55; narrative and dramatic poetry, 72
Narrativity: in documentary film, 154; in film's primitive period, 152–54
Newsreel and documentary, 30
Nightmail, 48, 50, 51, 57, 163–76
Nonfiction-effect, 157, 163, 215

Object relationship in cinema, 220–21, 224–25
Order of reality in film, 221
Ordinary sequence: definition, 47. *See also* Large Syntagmatic
O'Reilly, Patrick, 34

Painlevé, Jean, 59
Paradoxism, 88–89
Parallel syntagma: definition, 46. *See also* Large Syntagmatic
Perception and identification: role of language in, 186–87
Percheron, Daniel, 93–94
Photographic image: and linguistic message, 79, 186–87; and the real, 14, 29–31, 224
Plato, 72
Porter, Edwin S., 43, 152, 153
Primal scene, 225
Primitive period of film, 34–35, 43–44, 152–54
Proairetic codes, 104
Projection: conditions of, in documentary film, 222
Prosopopoeia, 197
Psychic apparatus (Freud), 216
Punctuation of segments, 121–22

Quattrocento, 149

Realism and film technology: Bazin on, 14, 29–30, 31; in British documentary film, 21–23; Vertov on, 25–26

Realist discourse, 33, 79

Realist theory and documentary film, 29–34

Récit, the: and historic discourse, 18

Referential illusion, 156, 223

Regnault, Félix-Louis, 35

Regression: denial of, in documentary film, 231; in dream, 217, 218

Repetition and resolution: in the classic text, 106–7; in the documentary text, 107–8

Repressed: return of the, in cinema, 228–29

Rhetoric: antithesis, 87–89, 91, 141–42; the emblematic and the real, 78–79, 107; montage and metaphor, 86–95; narrative and symbolic structures in documentary, 87–88, 133–48; use of sound, 92–95, 105

Rien que les heures, 47, 48, 51, 56, 66

River, The, 48, 50, 51, 56, 61–62, 63–65, 66

Rodakiewicz, Henwar, 61

Rotha, Paul, 20, 21

Rouch, Jean, 34, 40–41, 50, 176; *Les Maîtres fous,* 49, 50, 51, 57, 60, 176–87

Sadoul, Georges, 25, 26

Sang des bêtes, Le, 49, 51, 52, 53–55, 58–59, 66, 161

Scenario in documentary film, 56–62, 200

Scene: analysis of, 105, 126, 138–41; definition of, 46. *See also* Large Syntagmatic

Schoedsack, Ernest B., 44

Scopic drive, the, 219–20, 224–25

Secondary process in cinema, 74, 218–19; in documentary cinema, 222–23

Segmentation: codes of sequence in documentary film, 102–10, 119–48, 184–85

Sequence, notion of, 102

Shell Film Unit, 222

Shot, the (visual and acoustic segments), 102–3

Shub, Ester, 46; *Fall of the Romanov*

Dynasty, 46, 48, 51, 56, 57, 59, 60, 66–68

Sibony, Daniel, 220, 228

Simulation apparatus in cinema, 224

Smith, G. A., 43, 152

Soundtrack: acoustic matches, 119–21, 147; the aural object, 92–93; dialogue, 108, 158, 173, 175–76, 185, 213–14; and the fiction-effect, 200–201; heterogeneity of, in documentary film, 69, 92–93, 213–14; music, 157, 212, 213; as real-effect, 78–79; rhetorical function of, in documentary, 92–95, 105; structuring function of speech, 185; as suture, 126; visual and acoustic space in the classic cinema, 155–57. *See also* Commentary; Voice

Soundtrack, analytic categories of the: diegetic and extradiegetic, 94; off- and on-screen, 93–94; synchronous and asynchronous, 94, 127–32

Sovkino, 222

Spectator, the: ambivalent position in documentary cinema, 158–63, 230–31; belief and disavowal, 226–31; belief in documentary cinema, 226, 227–31; in documentary cinema, 219; of ethnographic film, 187; expectations in documentary cinema, 222–23; and the filmic state, 216–19; identification with the voice of the commentary, 159, 160–61, 161–63, 197; and the impression of reality, 215; position of, in cinema, 149–63; role in finance and distribution, 20–21; the subject-effect, 152, 229–30

Stattsauftragsfilme, 222

Stiener, Ralph, 46, 201; *The City,* 46, 48, 50, 51, 56, 61–62, 66, 201–14

Stroheim, Erich von, 32

Suprasegment, the: in documentary film, 106–8, 123, 138–41

Tableau, notion of the, 30

Textual articulations in documentary film, 122–24. *See also* Continuity

Textual system as displacement, 73–75

Textual system in documentary film: compared with literature, 71–73; a mixed discursive form, 69–77;

249